149 N

The Kings Depart

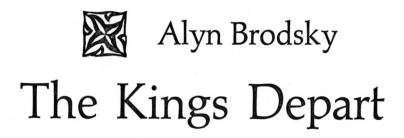 Alyn Brodsky

The Kings Depart

HARPER & ROW, PUBLISHERS

New York

Evanston

San Francisco

London

FIRST EDITION

Designed by Dorothy Schmiderer

Library of Congress Cataloging in Publication Data

Brodsky, Alyn.
  The kings depart.
  Bibliography: p.
  1. Maccabees. I. Title.
DS121.7.B73   933   74–1794
ISBN 0–06–010486–4

For my parents, Tillie and Joe—

a belated Golden Wedding anniversary simcha

Contents

Foreword

When Alexander the Great died unexpectedly in 323 B.C. at the age of thirty-three, the awesome empire he had forged was bitterly and bloodily contested for by his closest lieutenants. While history has only tantalizingly suggested the path civilization might have taken had Alexander lived a while longer, it has fully documented the course civilization followed as a result of his unanticipated demise. This course was sometimes incomprehensible, occasionally farcical, often tragic, always incredible, and, given the circumstances and the various personalities involved, probably inevitable.

Out of a generation of chaos that shook the world from the Balkans east to India, three major dynasties emerged: the Macedonian in Europe, and, in the East, the Ptolemaic and Seleucid. With the first we need only be concerned tangentially. Rather, our concern is with the Seleucids and Ptolemies—the Jukes and Kallikaks of ancient history. Born to rule as mighty monarchs, they reigned as tatterdemalion buffoons. To the Ptolemies went Egypt, with natural resources that made it the most economically viable nation in the eastern Mediterranean. To the Seleucids went the entire Asiatic portion of Alexander's realm, with the imperial seat at Syria.

Politically, both dynasties were disastrous. Hereditarily, both were Macedonian Greek. On rare occasions the Seleucids allowed their Syrian subjects to enter into the family, but through the back door via concubinage and bastardy. The Ptolemies were more exclusive. They practiced dynastic incest, and thus, save for one or two lapses, managed to keep the strain pure. The first Ptolemaic monarch to marry outside the Greek faith was also the last Ptolemaic monarch: Cleopatra VII Thea Philopator ("having a glorious father, father-loving goddess")—*the* Cleopatra. Further testimony to Ptolemaic exclusivity is the historical suspicion, rooted in Plutarch, that Cleopatra VII was probably the first dynast to learn the language of the people over whom her family had by then ruled haphazardly for three hundred years.

The Ptolemies and Seleucids intermarried, ostensibly for dynastic purposes, but instead of propping each other up they only succeeded in knocking each other down. For more than a century they fought in the buffer state of Palestine for control of Asia Minor—as well as of one another—while from the west Rome was slowly metastasizing the entire area. Caught up in the middle of this battleground, strictly through an accident of geography, was the Hebrew nation of Judaea.

Prior to the coming of Alexander, Judaism had been an obscure Semitic cult scornful of, if not oblivious to, the many and varied religions and philosophies amid which it had flourished on a restricted scale. Greek culture—Hellenism—which arrived in the East with Alexander's conquering armies, served to rescue Judaism from its obscure status and to bring it into the mainstream of international civilization—thus enabling its moral and ethical precepts to exert their enduring influence on Western thought and tradition.

Following the sixth-century B.C. Babylonian Exile, the Jews of Palestine were content with their status as a province of the Persian Empire. The Persians, having conquered the Neo-Babylonians who had exiled the Israelites originally, permitted them to return to their ancestral homeland. Contentment derived in large measure from the fact that the Israelite "nation"—territorially confined to Jerusalem and a number of suburban settlements—was permitted to function as a provincial theocracy, a temple-state, within the context of Persian imperialism. Although their political independence had long since been lost—they had begun to lose it in the eighth century B.C.—these Jews still enjoyed religious independence. Inured to being someone else's subjects, so long as they were able to pursue their extraordinary religion they could live without their national integrity. Perhaps they were pragmatic enough to realize they had little choice in the matter.

The Palestinian Jews had no difficulty in living under the Ptolemies, who, having established suzerainty over them following Alexander's death, did little more than exact tribute while permitting their Israelite subjects to practice unmolested their unique contribution to the human condition: monotheism and its concomitant, the moral law. And when the Seleucids evicted the Ptolemies at the beginning of the second century B.C., the Israelites had little difficulty in accepting their status as a tributary of Syria. This attitude was highly appreciated by the early Seleucids, who were vitally concerned with executing a twofold program: trying to hold together their sprawling and already fragmented empire, all the while attempting to gain control of the eastern Mediterranean world by crossing swords with the ever-increasing might and avarice of Rome. (They failed magnificently on both counts.)

Far from merely accepting the imposition of Hellenism, the Jews of Palestine openly embraced it. Rather, the elitist priesthood and power brokers embraced it. And in a nation constituted as was Judaea, sacerdotal acceptance was tantamount to national acceptance. But the Hellenism that the Judaeans helped impose upon themselves was of the baser, political variety, as opposed to the cultural Hellenism prevalent outside Palestine. This was not unfortunate so far as religion went; the Judaism practiced in Palestine during the third century B.C. had become out-moded as well as somewhat debased, whereas the Jews living outside the ancestral homeland in the Diaspora, influenced by cultural Hellenism, evolved a religion that allowed for flexibility and was more consonant with the changing times—the *rational* Judaism that has survived to this day.

But from a nationalistic point of view, Hellenism proved to be most unfortunate. National suicide had become endemic among the successors (the *Diadoch*) of Alexander through the wars precipitated by his failure to name his own heirs. By the Hasmonaean period (142 B.C.) the Seleucids and Ptolemies were doing a yeoman's job of destroying themselves as well as each other. Had the Palestinian Jews of this period directed toward their common enemies a fair modicum of the venom they directed toward each other, or, better, if they had in effect elected to play the waiting game, they would have been in a most tenable position to arrive at a modus vivendi with—and perhaps even survive the seemingly preordained downfall of—the Roman Empire. But, due less to the actions of their various overlords than to the venality and hypocrisy of their leaders, they helped bring about the destruction of their nation and in the process precipitated the birth of Christianity, in whose name world Jewry was condemned to two millennia of persecution.

The Maccabee revolt of 167–166 B.C. was justified. Faced with the extirpation of their religion by the infamous Antiochus IV Epiphanes, they had no alternative but to fight back. And having gained religious independence, they were probably justified in fighting for political independence from their Syrian suzerains. The often incredible blunders perpetrated by the Seleucids (and their in-laws, the Ptolemies) had unwittingly created a climate in which only political nonrealists and certifiable idiots would not attempt to regain their national integrity. Too, one could probably justify the coming into being of the Hasmonaean Dynasty (regnal name of the Maccabees) *if only as an alternative*—and a bleak alternative at that—to the status quo ante of a thoroughly unrealistic autocratic theocracy.

But what is difficult to justify is the manner in which the Palestinian Jews of the Hasmonaean period, having finally established themselves as the most powerful nation in Asia Minor, contributed so unequivocally to the destruction of that nation.

The Hasmonaeans were a protean family. They practiced homicide, suicide, matricide, fraticide, regicide; sibling rivalry was a way of life among this dismal crew—as well as in the nation as a whole.

The last books of the Old Testament that deal with biblical history, those of Ezra and Nehemiah, record the return of the Jews following the Babylonian Exile and the first seven or eight decades of the postexilic period. The opening books of the New Testament, the so-called synoptic Gospels (Mark, Matthew, Luke), record the birth and ministry of Joshua ben Joseph (Jesus Christ) four centuries later. Thus the lacuna, biblically speaking, between the two epochs is known as the Intertestamental period. Historically, it was the Hellenistic period. It is this era which forms the background for the events covered in *The Kings Depart*. Some of these events are dealt with in the First and Second Books of the Maccabees, concluding books in the canonical Apocrypha, and a few words about these curious and fascinating literary endeavors might be in order here.

"The rest of the story of John [Hyrcanus], his wars and the deeds of valour he performed, the walls he built, and his exploits, are written in the annals of his high-priesthood from the time when he succeeded his father [Simon]."* With this literary cop-out, and a cop-out it is, the canonical record of the Maccabees/Hasmonaeans comes to an end. No "annals of his high-priesthood" have ever come to light. Historians and scholars, as well as archaeologists, have long since abandoned the search.

Written during the reign of John Hyrcanus's miserable son Alexander Jannaeus, I Maccabees opens with the career of Hyrcanus's uncle, Judah Maccabee, and closes with the murder of the last of Judah's brothers, Hyrcanus's father Simon—the last of the Hasmonaeans possessed of any pretense, however attenuated, to morality and integrity. At the time of the book's composi-

* All biblical quotations are from the New English Bible, unless otherwise indicated.

tion, the beginning of the first century B.C., the fight against Syrian suzerainty begun by old Mattathias, progenitor of the Hasmonaeans, had, thanks to his lineal descendants, become as perverted as the very polity against which the revolt had been initially undertaken. The unknown author was a member of the Sadducees who, during Alexander Jannaeus's reign, formed the party of hierarchs comprising the religious and financial support of the morally bankrupt dynasty. Though the author was, on balance, a fairly reliable historian, he was also a self-serving one. His theme is that Hellenism was the root of all the nation's evil. In fact, long before the Sadducees had gained their stranglehold on the nation, the root of its evil had become a class struggle: Sadducees versus Pharisees, the aristocrats and priests versus the masses. To have continued the story down to his own time, the chronicler would have found himself in a rather tenuous position: trying to justify the actions of the Jewish monarchs through whose miserable machinations the Sadducees had managed their rapid rise to eminence.

The author of II Maccabees, on the other hand, chose to end his version before the death of Judah Maccabee. It is the work of a Pharisee-oriented Alexandrian Jew who, having read the Sadducee account, appears to have set out to write not a sequel to that work but a parallel account—to set the record straight, as it were, by retelling the story of the Maccabee wars in Pharisaic terms. But whereas I Maccabees is an historical (and at times hysterical) work, its successor in the canon is an ecclesiastical (and at times fantastical) one. The author of I Maccabees maintained a rather high standard of historical veracity—as far as he cared to carry his story. The writer of II Maccabees, on the other hand, chose to infuse his chronicle with accounts of religious rituals, miracles, martyrdom, angelic visitations, moral pontificating. The Pharisaic bias is also evident in the scope of II Maccabees: its author concerns himself almost entirely with Judah Maccabee's attempt to restore religious worship, thus ignoring his presumed political ambitions. Also ignored in totality are the careers of Judah's sibling successors Jonathan and Simon, who brought to fruition Judah's vision of political independence—a vision that the Pharisees did not initially share.

Thus if so many Jewish commentators down to our own day, out of some misplaced sense of chauvinism or perhaps atavistic embarrassment, seem eager to pretend that the hair-raising antics of the Hasmonaeans never occurred, they could well be following a precedent that was established, and canonized, two thousand years ago. Chauvinistic historians will, to be sure, chronicle ancient traumas, but they tend to gloss over those traumas that were self-induced.

Perhaps as testimony to the arcane procedures through which the Bible became fixed and immutable ("canonized"), I and II Macabees are considered Holy Scripture by the Roman Catholic and Protestant churches, but not by the Jewish people. Yet the Jews revere the books' protagonist, Judah Maccabee, as one of their all-time liberators—though in many respects it is rather questionable as to what he liberated them from.

What is not questionable is that countless other once powerful dynasties long since gone to dry rot managed to prove Lord Acton's thesis on the corruptibility of power two millennia before he defined the tyrannical tendencies of nations. But with the Maccabees/Hasmonaeans, it was something quite extraordinary. Starting with the most altruistic and uncomplicated intentions, they evolved (actually, degenerated) into the very paradigm of the venal, decadent, and despotic monarchy from which they had determined to free themselves. Like Othello, the Hasmonaeans—and the entire Palestinian Jewish nation they ruled—sowed the seeds of their own destruction.

While the Hellenistic period cannot be termed the period during which Western Civilization was born, it was decidedly the period during which Western Civilization reached pubescence. For the purposes of argument, that civilization can be analogized to a three-legged man, the three legs—all of equal importance for total stability—being Judaism (and itṡ stepchild, Christianity), Hellenism, and Romanism.

Judaism, the singular concept of ethical morality bound up with the belief in one supreme deity, had thrived—despite, or perhaps because of, its countless detractors and adversaries—for more than a thousand years. Hellenism, the Greek concepts of philosophy, culture, and ideals, was being exported out of the Balkans by Alexander and his successors. Romanism, with its extraordinary ideas of governmental organization and civil law, embellished with many of the nobler aspects of Hellenism, was about to be imposed upon the then known civilized world by a small city-state which was emerging with ferocious rapidity as the mightiest empire the world was ever to know. In essence, the period during which the Hasmonaeans rose, flourished, and immolated themselves was the period during which the three "legs" of Western Civilization were learning to trot in unison.

Between the years 167 B.C., when the Maccabees began their fight, first for religious and then for political independence from the Syrians, and 29 B.C., by which time Herod the Great had killed off the last legitimate pretenders to the by then defunct Hasmonaean throne, the forces of Judaism, Hellenism, and Romanism met on a collision course. This course not only led to the birth of Christianity (which managed to embrace the very best of the three cultures, as well as the very worst), it also resulted in the coalescence of civilization as we know it today. It was a bloody coalescence. And the Hasmonaean-led Jewish nation gave as well as took their share of the blood—especially their own.

A.B.

 # The Rise...

1   The Desecration

On the fifteenth day of Kislev (December) in the year 167 B.C., the Second Temple at Jerusalem was entered by Antiochus IV Epiphanes, king of Syria, thus precipitating a pogrom which traumatized the Jews as they had not been traumatized since the fall of the First Temple 420 years earlier to Nebuchadnezzar, king of Babylon. Unlike Nebuchadnezzar, Antiochus did not raze the holy edifice to the ground. Worse, he desecrated it. The Temple was the all-pervasive font of Hebrew worship. The concept of the synagogue, which gave Judaism the portability that enabled it to survive the ultimate loss of the Jewish homeland, had not yet taken root among Palestinian Jewry. They felt that only with the Temple—the House of the Lord—as the cynosure of their collective being could they maintain their identity as a people. Thus Antiochus Epiphanes's actions were to them not so much a material loss as a spiritual tragedy of inestimable magnitude: in desecrating the Temple, he had desecrated their faith.

The so-called Abomination of Desolation was set up on the High Altar: a gigantic statue of the pagan deity Zeus Olympios which bore an amazing likeness to Antiochus Epiphanes masquerading behind a beard. While this abomination was being set in place, Antiochus looted the Temple of its sacred appurtenances: the golden altar itself, the lamp-stand, the table for the Bread of Presence (also known as the Showbread or Shewbread), and the Veil, in addition to various sacred cups and bowls, golden censers, and crowns. He also carted away "the silver, gold, and precious vessels, and whatever secret treasures he found," in addition to having "stripped off all the gold plating from the temple front." (Those "secret treasures" were probably the private fortunes that shared vault space with the numerous cultic objects and furnishings. Banking was an unheard of institution; the wealth to be found within the Temple at all times bordered on the near-legendary.) By the time Epiphanes was finished, all that remained were the bare walls.

But the booty carted off was as nothing when compared to the proscriptions imposed: all Temple sacrifices and offerings were forbidden on pain of death, as was the rite of circumcision (the special sign of the Covenant the Jews shared with their One God), the observance of all Sabbaths and festival days, and the reading of the Law (the Torah, the first five books of the Bible, ascribed by tradition to Moses but actually written centuries after he is alleged to have flourished). If the Jews felt that no further calamity could befall them, they were in for a rude awakening.

Ten days later came the crowning insult: the Jews were compelled to offer sacrifices to the pagan deity—sacrifices in the form of swine "and other unclean beasts." Not only were they to offer these abominable sacrifices, they were "driven by brute force to eat the entrails of the sacrificial animals"—this in celebration of the king's birthday. And to compound the horror, it was decreed that the king's birthday was to be celebrated once a month! Also during the course of these festivities, the Jews were compelled to stand by numbly as Syrian soldiers partook of drunken revelries and obscene sex orgies within the sacred precincts. This was hardly the first time such antics had taken place in the Temple: many of the preexilic kings of Judah had done much worse, most notably Manasseh, who even practiced the rather quaint pagan custom of child-sacrifice. But these kings had come and gone, their departures heralded with repurification rites; also, they had not carried away the sacred cultic treasures. Furthermore, they had never gone to the extreme of compelling their own people to submit to such indignities as sacrificing pigs to a living Gentile and eating the sacrifices (though it is quite possible they might have, had the idea occurred to them).

Thus the account of the Temple's desecration, as set down in I and II Maccabees—for those who would have them as such, the only acceptable source of Jewish history during the Maccabee period. But to consider these books as the only acceptable source of Maccabee history would be akin to accepting as the sole source of American Civil War history the diary of Scarlett O'Hara.

The biblical text informs us that at the time of Epiphanes's accession to the Syrian throne in 175 B.C., "there appeared in Israel a group of renegade Jews, who incited the people . . . and some of them in their enthusiasm went to the king and received the authority to introduce non-Jewish laws and customs. They built a sports-stadium in the gentile style in Jerusalem. They removed their marks of circumcision and repudiated the holy covenant. They intermarried with Gentiles, and abandoned themselves to evil ways."

Here the chroniclers have conveniently overlooked two points: the renegades "appeared in Israel" long before Antiochus Epiphanes came to the throne—indeed, long before he was born; and the "group of renegade Jews" were led by the self-serving priests who had, in the name of that holy covenant they were now repudiating, bled their nation dry and made a mockery of their holy office. We also read that "disaster upon disaster had overtaken" the Jewish nation. In fact, the Jews had not been "overtaken" by disaster; they had undertaken it.

At this point the chroniclers would have us believe that after "he was firmly established on his throne, Antiochus made up his mind to become king of Egypt and so to rule over both kingdoms [Egypt and Syria]. . . . On his return from the conquest of Egypt . . . Antiochus marched with a strong force against Israel and Jerusalem." Here one must enter two historically supportable demurrers. Antiochus never "made up his mind to become king of Egypt" (though he probably would have welcomed the chance, had he been able to get away with it). Antiochus knew that Rome, which had a vested interest in Egypt, would never tolerate such a unification. Also, while it is true that he returned from Egypt and "marched with a strong force against Israel and Jerusalem," this return did not come on the heels of any "conquest" but rather on the heels of his enforced expulsion from Egypt by an overfed and undersized legate speaking in the name of the Roman Senate.

It is, of course, only human nature for a people to view history in terms of their own experience, to give to their particular stitch an exaggerated importance out of all context to the rest of the broad tapestry. The Poles of the eighteenth century, for example, assumed that Catherine the Great of Russia divided her waking hours between seducing her courtiers and raping Poland's national integrity. There is no denying that of all that was happening in the Seleucid Syrian kingdom the events in Judaea were to be the most consequential over the long haul of history: were it not for Epiphanes and the events he set in motion as a result of his proscriptions, the Jews would have been spared the Hasmonaeans; but for that chain of events, the Jews might never have been evicted from their ancestral homeland; indeed, Christianity might never have evolved, and countless Jews through the ages would have been spared the sanguinolent horrors inflicted on them "in the name of Christ."

To equate Antiochus Epiphanes with Hitler—as do so many whose knowledge of history is limited to what they (or their "Sunday school" teachers) have read in the Bible—is to insult the former and compliment the latter. Hitler saw *all* Jews as his enemies; he was concerned less with exterminating their religion than with exterminating them. Epiphanes's attempt to extirpate Judaism *was confined only to Judaea;* the Jews living in the rest of Palestine, as well as throughout his far-flung realm, were free to practice their religion and traditions unmolested.

Like his predecessors, Epiphanes followed the Hellenistic policy toward Eastern religions in general: noninterference—in return for the loyalty and support of the priests. Such a policy included recognition of priestly prerogatives and such material assistance as construction (or, in the case of the Jews, reconstruction) of magnificent temples. The hold which religion enjoyed over the masses of the ancient world cannot be overemphasized—a factor which the various priesthoods, including the one at Jerusalem, were palpably aware of and eager to exploit.

Also like his predecessors, especially his father Antiochus the Great, Antiochus Epiphanes was less concerned with furthering the spread of Hellenism than with strengthening Seleucid holdings in western Asia and reconquering the runaway provinces and satrapies. By the time of Epiphanes's accession, the once isolated and politically obscure Palestinian Jews had acquired a new importance. Being close to the Egyptian-Syrian frontier, Judaea was the main line of communication between the two countries. For Epiphanes, it was an important link in his southern defenses—as well as a potentially weak point, should Jerusalem be drawn to side with Ptolemaic Egypt either by old memories or Alexandria-inspired intrigues. Doubtless, Epiphanes had more important things on his mind than Judaism—a religion of which he was in all probability quite ignorant.

The activities of Antiochus Epiphanes regarding Palestinian Jewry have been magnified out of all proportion. As extra-biblical and more objective history have shown, Antiochus Epiphanes did not initiate the Hellenizing of Judaea. Rather, he simply carried through a process that had already been set in motion, largely through the actions and attitudes of Judaea's own hierarchs, long before Epiphanes came to power. And though his attempts to extirpate Judaism *in Judaea* were ill-advised—as well as heinous and, for the Seleucids ultimately, a total disaster—his program was based essentially on *political* considerations.

It was out of "the many in Israel [who] found strength to resist" the Epiphanean proscriptions that the Hasmonaean Dynasty evolved—a dynasty of which an amazing number of Jewish people are ignorant and others "in the know" would prefer to believe never even existed. The Hasmonaean Dynasty was less an innovative experience than a tragic exercise in *déjà vu*. The concept of monarchy had been tried in the preexilic First Commonwealth (or First Temple) period. But, whereas the Hasmonaeans had been subtly (almost surreptitiously) imposed upon the Palestinian Jews by their own self-serving leaders within as well as without the priesthood, the earlier Davidic monarchy had been created through popular demand. . . .

2   The Exile

According to the Bible, the Twelve Tribes of Israel, having fled under the leadership of Moses from Egyptian servitude, invaded the land of Canaan (that is, western Palestine) under Moses's successor Joshua, thus beginning the fulfillment of the vow made by the Lord to Abraham that this "Promised Land" was to belong to his heirs in perpetuity (Genesis 12:7).

So much for the traditional view.

According to the more historically supportable account, some of the Israelite tribes—quite probably including the all-powerful tribe of Judah—were already resident in Canaan at the time Moses was leading their Semitic brethren on that forty-year trek through the Sinai Desert, sometime around the middle of the thirteenth century B.C.

Views notwithstanding, by the opening of the twelfth century B.C., the Chosen People were a rather loosely knit confederation, with its sacred totems and cultish paraphernalia situated at Shiloh, east of Jerusalem. (It is probable that the Hebrew people were "chosen" not out of some divine exclusivity but as the mortal agency through which the concept of morality was to be transmitted to the human condition.)

The Israelite foothold on the Promised Land was tenuous in the extreme: not only were they hemmed in on all sides by enemies, they were often unable to expel the foes who dwelt within their midst. Most notable of these, in addition to the indigenous Canaanites, were the Philistines, preexilic Israel's only major non-Semitic adversary, who had invaded Asia Minor from

9

the Mediterranean at the time the Hebrews came in from the east
(and from whom the place name Palestine is derived). The
tribes lacked any semblance of unity. Political cohesion had died
with Joshua, and the tribes had slid into two centuries of modi-
fied anarchy. From time to time, some man (or, as in the case of
Deborah, some woman) would arise to "judge" the people.
Thanks to these Judges (paramilitary figures, as opposed to
magistrates), numerous Semitic and Philistine incursions would
be beaten back.

Temporarily.

Spread out from Phoenicia in the north to the Sinai Desert and
the Egyptian frontier in the south, the Israelites were continuously at the mercy of, in addition to the Philistines and Canaanites, numerous incursive legions of Arabs from the Transjordan,
ranging in groups from petty though powerful "kingdoms" to
roving squads of *condottieri*. And as if it were not enough to be
continuously at the mercy of their by then traditional enemies,
the Israelites were often at the mercy of each other—as witness
the instance (Judges 19–21) when the southern tribe of Benjamin was almost destroyed to a man by some of its sister-tribes
following a rather silly misunderstanding over a minor priest and
an equally insignificant concubine.

And then came Samuel—the first and last powerful figure in
Old Testament history since Moses (assuming Moses actually
lived) to wield enormous influence in both the political and the
spiritual life of his people. Samuel had been raised from infancy
as a priest at Shiloh, this in fulfillment of a vow made by his
mother Hannah to dedicate her first son to the Lord—provided the
Lord gave this barren woman a son thus to dedicate. He did and
she did.

Sometime around 1020 B.C., while in residence at Ramah, a
village northwest of the Dead Sea from which he made yearly
rounds of his fractious and religiously recidivistic people in the
manner of some ecclesiastical circuit judge, the aged gentleman

was handed an extraordinary request by a deputation of popularly chosen elders:

"Appoint us a king to govern us, like other nations" (I Samuel 8:5).

Israel's enemies all had been led by kings. Reasoned the elders, with rather tenuous logic: if the Israelites had a king, they would be able to meet their enemies on equal terms.

The idea of a temporal sovereign was anathema to Samuel, who held that all men are equal before the Highest King of Them All—a cogent philosophical insight that was but one of the ennobling contributions of the Hebrew nation to the human intellect. Samuel tried to reason with the elders. When they would not be put off, he decided to discuss the matter with the Lord—with whom he appears to have been on speaking terms. The Lord was enraged, taking the request as a rejection of His leadership. He had "delivered" the Israelites from Pharaoh's bondage, and now they were showing themselves to be ingrates.

After expressing His anger, the Lord told Samuel to go ahead and give them their monarchy—adding, in high dudgeon, "give them a solemn warning and tell them what sort of king will govern them." "Sort of king" was, to be sure, intended in a pejorative sense; as history was to demonstrate, most of Israel's monarchs proved to be that "sort of king." The picture of monarchy as painted by Samuel was a horrendous one:

> He will take your sons and make them serve in his . . . cavalry, and will make them run before his chariot. . . . Others will plough his fields and reap his harvest. . . . He will take your daughters . . . and will seize the best of your cornfields, vineyards, and oliveyards, and give them to his lackeys. Your slaves, both men and women, and the best of your cattle . . . he will seize and put to his own use. He will take a tenth of your flocks, and you yourselves will become his slaves.

And then came the clincher:

> When that day comes, you will cry out against the king whom you
> have chosen; but it will be too late.

But the elders were not to be dissuaded:

> We will have a king over us; then we shall be like other nations,
> with a king to govern us, to lead us out to make war and fight our
> battles (I Samuel 8:9–20).

Samuel checked back with the Lord, and was told to give the
ingrates what they desired. A monarchy they wanted, a monarchy they would get! Whether the dire words of Samuel were
not in fact a hindsight account—the final recension of the text
was undertaken around 550 B.C., by which time Israel had
suffered a staggering number of royal wretches—there is no
denying that the Cassandra-like prophecy hit the mark.

The first Hebrew monarch, handpicked by Samuel & Friend,
was Saul, whose realm was not over all of Israel, as the elders
had requested, but extended little beyond his own southern tribe
of Benjamin. Saul was very successful in repelling various incursions by Arabs from east of the Jordan, and only temporarily
successful in beating back the numerous Philistine forays from
the coastal area. Unfortunately, the northern tribes were left to
fend for themselves. Unfortunately also, success bred paranoia
on Saul's part. Samuel decided to try again. After further con-
sultations with the Lord, he came up with David—a young
shepherd as well as, it would seem, a self-trained musician of no
mean talent. The lad began his march along the road to kingship
by tossing boulders at Philistines and soothing Saul's jangled
nerves with nightly serenades on the lyre.

David was of the powerful tribe of Judah, whose eclipse by
Saul's tribe of Benjamin the Judahites tolerated with ever-
mounting antagonism: since Israel was to have a king, why
should not that king come from Judah, the most powerful of the
tribes? (Lest Samuel be accused here of having practiced tribal
favoritism, let it be noted that he was of the northern tribe of

Ephraim. As for the Lord, He was above tribal affiliations.) A rationalist could not but suspect that David was put forth as an active candidate by his tribe, and that his selection by the Lord in collusion with Samuel is but another of the many instances of retrojection of past events by the unknown biblical chroniclers to conform with the Teleological Argument (which postulates that the existence of God is rooted in the assumption that order in the universe was ordained by the Deity and not arrived at through natural selection).

Saul showed his esteem for David by giving him a daughter in marriage. He subsequently took her back, resentful of the extent to which David's slaying of the Philistine giant Goliath had made him a darling of the people. The monarch's "melancholia" (probably a clinical disorder undiagnosable by the court physicians) soon became transmogrified into pathological jealousy, and David was forced to head south. He then embarked upon a period of outlawry, being compelled at times to take refuge from the pursuing Saul among, of all people, the Philistines. It is, of course, quite probable that the biblical account of these events was the chroniclers' way of "explaining" the contest between Judah and Benjamin for leadership of the Israelite confederation. However, to their credit, Chapter 25 of I Samuel admits that David, in order to give sustenance to his growing band of followers, carried on a rather lucrative "protection racket" among the prosperous ranchers and sheepherders who peppered the provinces.

The climax came when Saul was killed in battle with the Philistines atop Mount Gilboa, along with his son Jonathan who had been David's companion and champion at court (and not, as is often believed, David's catamite). Saul's only surviving son, the inept Ishbaal, became the figurehead behind whom Saul's cousin and military chieftain, Abner, hoped to continue the dynasty. Now it was Abner against David. Before long, the Israelites were on the verge of being destroyed by the Philistines. David and his outlaw band managed to seize the vital city of

Hebron, there to challenge Abner's authority in the north. Bowing to the inevitable, Abner abandoned his own dynastic ambitions and threw in his lot with David. The northern tribes quickly followed suit. Thus it came about that by the beginning of the first millennium B.C., the Twelve Tribes of Israel were at long last united under one monarch.

It was the last time in their history they were to be so united.

After disposing of the Philistine threat, the astute David exploited the temporary weakness of his Egyptian neighbors to the south and the Syrians to the north; he also managed to establish hegemony over the powerful Edomites (who were to emerge so prominently and painfully as the Idumaeans during the Hasmonaean period). Through clever diplomacy and military panache, David succeeded in establishing a powerful border kingdom that stretched from the Sinai Desert to the banks of the Euphrates; though unable to conquer the Philistines along the Mediterranean coast, he managed to establish a suzerainty of sorts that was to obtain throughout the five centuries of his ill-fated dynasty.

The young king then established the national capital at Jerusalem, thereby bringing the seat of government into closer propinquity with the northern tribes; organized a strong civil service; and established the policy that the priests should share national leadership instead of, as they were to do in the postexilic period, preempting it. He also won the recognition and respect of his neighbors and quondam adversaries, both for himself and for his people. And he entered into a series of marriages with, it would seem, the choicest maidens from each of the many factions within his realm, thereby further consolidating unity: what faction could but fail to swear fealty to a darling of the people who had chosen one of *their* own to be one of *his* own? In his spare time he wrote many Psalms (certainly nowhere near the number ascribed to him, but enough to establish his literary credentials) and sired many children—a brace of whom, most notably Absalom, undertook insurrections that almost resulted in the aging monarch's dethronement and more civil war. The Children of Abraham were rapidly learning the grislier concomitants of the monarchical way of life.

And then at long last arriving at the point where he could glance back over an era of dynastic and literary accomplishments—as well as a good deal of personal tragedy, much of it self-induced—David bequeathed to his son Solomon, through the machinations of Bathsheba and the court prophet Nathan, the most powerful nation the Hebrew people were to enjoy in their long, tortured history until the establishment of the Republic of Israel three millennia later.

There are a number of interesting parallels in the careers of Solomon, the last king of a united Israel, and John Hyrcanus, the first Hasmonaean king in deed if not in name. Of these, probably the most pertinent—certainly the saddest—is that each polarized the nation he had carried to heights of grandeur and viability, thus, however unintentionally, laying the groundwork for the eventual collapse that followed his demise. With John Hyrcanus, his particular mistake was to favor one sect, the aristocratic Sadducees, over another, the more popularly supported Pharisees. Solomon's great error was to favor his own southern tribe of Judah over the northern tribes, individually ineffectual but collectively a force with which to be reckoned. And being succeeded by dreadfully simple, and simply dreadful, sons, far from alleviating situations the respective fathers had brought about, served only to exacerbate them.

Solomon undertook an expansive trade-relations program that saw highly prized silks and spices flowing into Jerusalem—while most of his subjects struggled to make do with what was left of their crops and herds after sending along to the royal coffers the enormous solicitations their monarch demanded and his deputies forcibly collected. He cemented international relations by entering into a dazzling series of dynastic alliances that included marriage to a pagan Egyptian princess for whom he forced his already overtaxed subjects to build a gaudy palace—in the precincts of the Temple, no less!—the extravagance of which bordered on the obscene. (For the record, Solomon was not the first prominent Hebrew to marry outside the faith: both the patriarch Joseph and Moses himself had espoused *shiksas*.) He built the Temple as the national seat of Israelite monotheism—and openly tolerated henotheism throughout the realm. He led his people in adhering to the precepts laid down by Moses—while establishing a royal whorehouse of egregious magnitude and meretriciousness, and, into the bargain, outdoing even his highly potent father by siring a veritable battalion of royal bastards the total number of which has yet to be satisfactorily ascertained. Also, he undertook a monumental building program in Jerusalem—all with impressed labor from the northern tribes; and he further strengthened the civil service by dividing the country into twelve commissariat districts—and proceeded to give the choicest positions to men of his own tribe of Judah (including a stray son-in-law or two).

Disaffection in the north against Solomon's economic, political, and religious outrages crystallized around Jeroboam, a leader of the most powerful of the northern tribes, that of Ephraim. Jeroboam had risen to prominence in the Solomonic kingdom as overseer of a corvée of northerners on one of the potentate's model-cities programs in Jerusalem. This position he exploited to assume the role of spokesman for the northern malcontents, who abominated a myopic southerner who took their taxes and impressed their men into labor battalions all the while disdaining to bring them into the mainstream of the nation's sociopolitical life. I Kings informs us (11:40) that Solomon "sought to kill Jeroboam, but he fled to King Shishak in Egypt and remained there till Solomon's death."

If we are to believe the biblical text—and I Kings is, on balance, fairly credible history, its often seemingly fanciful emendations notwithstanding—when Solomon died, the northern tribes were willing to arrive at an accommodation. Jeroboam rushed back from Egypt to represent them as Solomon's dismal heir Rehoboam journeyed north to receive their fealty and thus be confirmed in his accession. In the ensuing encounter, Jeroboam said: "Your father laid a cruel yoke upon us; but if you will now lighten the cruel slavery . . . and the heavy yoke he laid on us, we will serve you." Rehoboam requested three days to consider what was in fact a fair and mutually beneficial proposition, and then gave his answer: "My father made your yoke heavy; I will make it heavier. My father used the whip on you; but I will use the lash" (12:4–14).

So much for the unification of the Twelve Tribes of Israel.

The ten secessionist northern tribes constituted themselves as the Kingdom of Israel; the Davidic monarchy continued in the south, taking the dynastic name Judah from its major component tribe. Allowing his subjects to continue worshipping the presumably irritated Lord at the Temple in Jerusalem would have implied tacit recognition of Rehoboam as the only legitimate Hebrew king. Therefore, Jeroboam's first act was to establish sanctuaries in the north. Next, he invited his former host, Pharaoh Shishak, to invade the southern kingdom. Shishak accepted the invitation—and then went on to invade the northern kingdom as well. The dual Hebrew monarchy was off to an ominous start.

Unlike Judah, whose kings were descended lineally from David, Israel went through nine dynasties in its grisly two-century existence. The eight that succeeded Jeroboam's were established by military upstarts, much in the manner of what makes Latin American countries so amusing to people who do not have to live therein. Israel's longest dynasty, that of Jehu, lasted one century; its shortest, that of Zimri, lasted one *week*. The tragedy of the northern kingdom was played out against periodic incursions from the powerful Arab kingdom of Damascus, and, in due time, against the rise of the Assyrian Empire (whose tactics were not to be equalled until the coming of Nazi

Germany). Israel met its ultimate grief in 721 B.C., when the Assyrians razed the capital of Samaria and deported its leading citizens—who disappeared into history as the legendary "Ten Lost Tribes of Israel." By then the secessionist kingdom had gone through nineteen dynasts, only one of whom, a religious deviant and homicidal wretch, had achieved the dubious distinction of dying in his own bed from (presumably) natural causes.

Israel's estranged kin to the south fared little better, though they did manage to maintain their independence for more than a century after the Assyrian conquest of the north. Of the twenty dynasts, most ran the gamut from the dreadful to the incredible. After conquering Israel, the Assyrians set their sights on Judah, whose problems were compounded when Egypt, which had gone into one of its periodic declines after Shishak's double cross of Jeroboam, had become temporarily revivified and had reentered the lists. Just when it appeared that Judah must succumb to either or both of her powerful adversaries, a new specter loomed on the horizon. Within less than a generation, a coalition of Chaldeans and Medes had evolved out of the by then disintegrating Assyrian Empire. The great prophet Jeremiah, the most pragmatic and magnetic personality during these, Judah's twilight years, urged his countrymen to accept the might of this new power, known to history as the Neo-Babylonian Empire. But the corrupt monarchy at Jerusalem preferred to cast its lot with what it foolhardily believed to be an invincible coalition of anti-Chaldean nations led by the Egyptians and Edomites—whose "power" was little more than a chimerical nostrum compounded, in equal parts, of ill-founded bravado and outrageous public relations gimmickry.

In 597 B.C. Nebuchadnezzar, the first (and last) of the truly great Neo-Babylonian kings, invaded Jerusalem.[1*] Evidence indicates that he had come to conquer, not to destroy. He installed a pro-Chaldean King (of the Davidic line), established a timetable of tribute payments, and decreed that if the Hebrews accepted

* Notes to chapters begin on p. 271.

his hegemony their nation would remain inviolate under his benign protection. Nebuchadnezzar had little difficulty in perceiving the obvious: Judah's importance as a buffer state between Egypt and Syria was solely geographical. He then set out to conquer those states which posed a threat to his ambitions. While he was away campaigning, a powerful pro-Egyptian court faction deposed the pro-Chaldean government, praying frantically that the Lord would cause Nebuchadnezzar to fall in battle.

The Lord refused to cooperate. In 586 B.C. the still highly ambulatory Nebuchadnezzar, by now master of the Fertile Crescent, returned to Jerusalem and in a fury delivered the *coup de grace*. The Temple was sacked, the city's walls were leveled, and the leading citizens were deported to Babylonia. The Hebrew monarchy created, albeit unwillingly, by Samuel half a millennium before, was ended. The fifty-year Babylonian Exile had begun.

Deporting the leaders and influential citizenry of conquered lands was a common practice in the ancient Near East; it served as a means of reducing the likelihood of local resistance to the central authority of the suzerain power. The practice, which may have originated with the Assyrians (like the Nazis, the Assyrians were highly innovative), also included resettlement in the conquered areas of loyal subjects from other portions of the suzerain's realm. In the case of Jerusalem, however, there was no resettlement; the city was such a mess, colonists were probably unwilling to undertake a reconstruction of its ruins.

Many of the more penitent Judahites accepted the inevitability of exile as a manifestation of the Lord's anger at their having turned away from a spiritual monarch to the more earthly, and earthy, breed. In that acceptance, they found consolation. They vowed to return to their Promised Land and to "turn back to the ways of the Lord," who would deliver them out of their affliction and back to Holy Jerusalem (they assumed). And when that glorious day came, they vowed, there would be no more requesting some father-figure to "appoint us a king to govern us, like other nations."

Whether it was indeed the Lord who delivered them is a theological question as well as an academic one. As for having had their fill of monarchy, the shackled Hebrews shuffling across Mesopotamia were true to their word. They would not request a monarchy when they did in fact return to Jerusalem fifty years later.

Worse, they would tolerate a theocracy.

3   The Return

The Lord had promised His recalcitrant children that the Neo-Babylonian Empire would not endure. He was right. As it went though its agonizing death throes under a rapid succession of ineffectual monarchs, the empire's many vassal and tributary states proclaimed their independence, much in the manner of what befell the Ottomans as their once mighty empire stumbled across the nineteenth century like a mortally wounded mastodon before finally dropping dead on the eve of World War I. But the independence of the component states was as short-lived as the empire itself. Out of the Neo-Babylonian shambles, a new power —the Persian Empire—was born. A dividend of its birth for the Jewish exiles was their release from Babylonian captivity.

When the leading citizens of Judah (the Bible quaintly euphemizes them as "princes") were marched off to Babylonia, they had assumed they were being marched off to an unknown fate of horrific proportions. They were pleasantly surprised. Though forced to live in an alien land, they were permitted to enter into business life, to intermarry, and—most consequentially—to pursue their religion unimpeded. The Exile taught the Hebrews how to survive in dispersion from their homeland—a lesson that was to stand them in good stead through all their subsequent history and which was to guarantee the perpetuity of the "Jewish nation." Indeed, but for the Exile, Judaism might never have survived.

Prior to the Exile, the cultus of Judaism had devolved upon the

Temple at Jerusalem. How, cried the deportees, could they continue to worship God if they were more than four hundred miles from His House? The prophet Jeremiah sent along an epistle to the effect that God was with them wherever they were (provided, of course, they recognized His presence), that one need not go to a central shrine in order to seek divine grace, and that, in effect, it was quite possible to be a better Jew from a distance of four hundred miles than had been (and were again to be) for those who never left the Temple precincts and worshipped Him under a penumbra of fraudulent piety.[1]

Attesting to the manner in which the exiles were permitted to flourish in Babylonia is our knowledge that when the Persian monarch Cyrus the Great decreed that those Jews who wished to could return to Jerusalem, there to rebuild the city and practice their religion free of any imperial interference, many chose to remain behind. These had already laid the foundation for what became the most prosperous, intellectual, and forward thinking Jewish community in the Diaspora until the founding of the great Egyptian Jewish community at Alexandria in the third century B.C. The Babylonian Jews did not forget their returning coreligionists. Much in the manner of the support, both financial and moral, given by American Jewry to the Republic of Israel, those who remained behind in Babylonia were exemplary in their assistance to those kin who returned to rebuild—and ultimately to relose—the ancestral homeland.

The new empire, a vast and polyglot one, was ruled by monarchs known to their subjects as the Great King (Shah). The Great Kings were pragmatic kings: so long as their subjects paid their annual tribute (via the pockets of the local satraps, or governors, who administered the imperial system), they were permitted to manage their own internal affairs. Equally pragmatic was the latitudinarianism practiced by the Great Kings. Since the countless component states practiced countless variations of paganism and idolatry, any attempt to establish a single, official theology would have been both impractical and unenforceable.

Sometime around 538 B.C. the first caravans began the homeward trek across Mesopotamia (the total number of those who chose to return has been estimated at about 40,000). The first wave was led by Zerubbabel, an acknowledged scion of the Davidic line, who bore the imperial authority of *tirshatha* (governor) of Jerusalem—a subprovince of Palestine, which was in turn but one of the twenty satrapies of the Persian Empire, with its overall administrative center at Damascus. Contemporary with Zerubbabel was Joshua, a member of the hereditary Levitical priesthood, who assumed the role of High Priest. But although the nation seemed destined to see a religious chief ruling in tandem with a descendant of the old royal family, any attempt to rivive the monarchy, even within the context of the overall Persian imperial system, ended with Zerubbabel. Henceforth, until the rise three centuries later of the Hasmonaeans—who were to combine their own peculiar brand of religious leadership with their Oriental brand of kingship—the Jewish nation of Judaea was an out-and-out theocracy. (It was during this period that the Hebrew people began to be known as *Yehudim,* "men of Judah," the only tribe other than the priestly tribe of Levi that had survived with its identity intact; hence Jew, Judaism, Jewish.)

When the Assyrians had conquered Israel in 721 B.C. and deported its leaders, they had imported colonists, all of whom brought with them their variant forms of idol-worship. This commingling of Hebrews and pagans, the Samaritans (from Samaria, the former northern capital), were soon practicing a religious syncretism: monotheism and polytheism. By the time the southerners returned to Jerusalem from Babylonia, the progeny of the original Israelites to the north had done away with many of the syncretist tendencies, but a variant form of Judaism had evolved. Through a sense of kinship, the Samaritans looked with sympathy on their returning brethren; they even expressed a willingness to collaborate in rebuilding the Temple as well as the Holy City itself. But these overtures were firmly rejected. The returnees were unwilling to jeopardize their newly purified religion by allying themselves with those whose pagan history made them suspect. The Samaritans, in their turn, undertook a campaign of attrition which was to reach its zenith during the governorship of Nehemiah, at which time the schism between the two branches of Judaism became irrevocable. Any hopes of reunifying the Twelve Tribes of Israel were laid to rest for all time.[2]

Nehemiah, whose memoirs form the core of the biblical book which bears his name, was an orthdox Babylonian Jew (and quite possibly a eunuch) who around 445 B.C. sought permission of the Great King to go to Jerusalem in the role of *tirshatha*. The Second Temple, completed seventy years previously, stood in all its majesty and dignity. As much could not be said for the rest of the city, whose inhabitants were "facing great trouble and reproach" (and belligerent Samaritans) and whose walls were still "broken down" (Nehemiah 1:3). The scars from Nebuchadnezzar's campaigns had not healed; the Holy City was an unholy slum. Nehemiah, who had risen to the eminence of Cupbearer to King Artaxerxes Longimanus, was anxious to do what he could to clean up the city and get its citizens back on the holy path. Nehemiah had never seen Jerusalem, but he *had* seen a vision of his beloved ancestral homeland returning to the ways of the Lord. (In addition to enjoying the high honor of serving the monarch his wine—and the low honor of tasting it first, lest some contentious courtier attempt an assassination—the Cupbearer, a post indigenous to practically all the Near Eastern courts of the period, was usually a close confidant of the king, often in a position to wield political influence and exact political favors. The fact that an orthodox Jew had arrived at this high estate p̄robably speaks less for the acclimatization of the exiles than for the tolerance of their Persian overlords.)

With his monarch's blessing as well as material and financial assistance, Nehemiah journeyed to Jerusalem and immediately undertook a program of national and religious reorganization; his textbook was the Torah. The Torah had already been "fixed" and made accessible to all the people by Ezra the Scribe—who had flourished before Nehemiah and was not, as traditionalists claim, a contemporary. Nehemiah continued the religious reforms begun by his predecessor (who, on the basis of the biblical text, seems to have worked himself into knots in his determination that all those who had taken "foreign wives" during the Exile must summarily divorce them—"put them away"). He brought the entire nation together in a new Covenant with God (actually, a reaffirmation of the original Covenant which tradition dates back to Abraham). He excommunicated the Samaritans. And he oversaw the reconstruction of the city walls, in addition to the complete reorganization of the Temple worship and the tithes-collection program. Nehemiah's zeal seems to have been exceeded only by his faculty for getting things done in a hurry: the biblical text insinuates that all of his accomplishments were carried out within two months!

Assisted financially by the Diaspora Jews—who moved forward, learning to harmonize their religion with rapidly evolving intellectual and social concepts without abandoning their identity—Palestinian Jewry now took a great leap backward, unable, or perhaps unwilling, to realize that much of the Mosaic legislation that had gone into the corpus of their Law was by now out of step with the times, if not with reality itself. As is the case with Karl Marx, whose philosophy was predicated on a set of conditions which no longer obtain, much of the Law ascribed to Moses (but actually written by the Israelite priests centuries after he is alleged to have flourished) was hopelessly outdated and without intellectual or social justification.

Having tried monarchy, the Jews of Palestine now went to the other extreme, constituting their nation less as a religion-oriented temporal state than a closed church. The High Priest, who was the nation's acknowledged leader, discharged the functions and enjoyed the perquisites of president, prime minister, and pope all embodied in one sancrosanct person. Unlike their Christian successors, these priests did not practice celibacy; the law of primogeniture obtained in the line, which descended from Moses's brother Aaron, ancient Israel's first High Priest. Assisting the High Priest in both temporal and religious leadership were the men of the hereditary Levitical priesthood, all of whom were successful in tracing their genealogies, of which the Old Testament has more than a tolerable share, from some elder of Moses's tribe of Levi. The inability of the Hasmonaeans to trace their descent from Aaron—not that they wasted any time trying—was one of the many factors that led to the divisiveness which contributed so much to the collapse of the Jewish nation. Aaron had allegedly flourished more than a *thousand* years before the Return. The Hasmonaeans could barely trace their lineage back a *hundred* years.

No one (certainly not the priests) objected to the ecclesiastical nature of Judaea: the "constitution" was the Torah, the Law, from which the priesthood derived its authority. It was also from the Law that the priests derived their authority to bleed the nation dry. Priestly perquisites were carefully defined in the Mosaic books of Leviticus, Numbers, and Deuteronomy, a casual perusal of which by a rationalist might well induce a reaction wavering somewhere between outrage and nausea.[3]

Every offering brought to the Temple went to the priests, who also received the choicest cuts of every animal sacrificed, in addition to the first fruits of every peasant's crop (and most of the citizenry were mere peasants). And then there was the tithe, called the *t'rumah* (which English Bibles translate rather indelicately as "heave-offering"): a tenth of each man's crops had to be turned over to the *lower* order of Temple servants (porters, attendants, musicians, and the like), who in their turn had to give a tenth of *this* tenth to the *senior* priests. Among other requirements were the surrender of the firstborn of all domestic cattle (or, if circumstances warranted, a cash indemnity) and the "redemption" of all firstborn sons at the age of one month, by a payment of cash into the sacerdotal coffers. Still another windfall came the priests' way should a citizen in a moment of personal crisis extort Divine Aid by "devoting" either himself or some possession (an animal of burden or perhaps a slave) to His temporal deputies. And yet another license enjoyed by the theocrats was the instance, far from occasional, when a citizen might become conscience-stricken after having stolen someone else's property: were the rightful owner not found, the priests were only too happy (and legally qualified) to deputize themselves as the victim's surrogate and accept the forthcoming compensation.

The priests did not assert their claims by force. They did not have to. Satisfaction of all claims was left to the conscience of the people, and the people were quite conscientious. Logic would dictate that there must have been some instances when even a sincerely religious citizen might balk. But from what little evidence we have of life in Judaea during the years between Nehemiah and the rise of the Maccabees, it can be assumed that the Judaeans—infused as they were with zeal for the Mosaic Law—heeded the admonition of Jesus ben Sirach whose apocryphal book of Ecclesiasticus was composed during this period: "Fear the Lord and honour the priest and give him his dues, as you have been commanded." (Ben Sirach goes on to enjoin his people to be "open-handed with the poor"—but considering all the average citizen had to surrender to the priests, one suspects that the only open hand the poor could expect was an empty one.)

Testimony to the insignificance of the Hebrew nation prior to the coming of the Ptolemies is our knowledge that that ubiquitous fifth-century B.C. Greek historian Herodotus, who traveled extensively along the seacoast of Palestine, does not even mention the Jews. The "nation" consisted of little more than Jerusalem and a smattering of villages and settlements within an approximately seventeen-mile radius. To the north lived the Samaritans, who chose to ignore them out of cordial detestation. To the south lay the Edomites, who had pushed up from their original territories during the immediate preexilic period and had occupied the southern regions of what had once been the mighty Davidic domain. (The Edomites had even urged Nebuchadnezzar to annihilate the Hebrew nation completely, so that they might occupy Jerusalem—something the Maccabees were to remember with a vengeance.) But the Edomites, or as they had now become, the Idumaeans, posed no threat, having been pushed back by their Arab brethren, the Nabataeans. These Arabs, who were to play a major, painful role during the Hasmonaean period, also ignored the Judaeans. They were more concerned with exploiting the lucrative caravan trade that passed through their land (present-day Jordan) between the Persian Gulf and the major southwestern Palestinian trading cities of Gaza, Ascalon, and Ashdod. The three were Philistine cities which had survived Israelite suzerainty and become revivified during the captivity period; they were too preoccupied with being major links in the traffic of the eastern Mediterranean to pay any heed to their erstwhile foes. Northwest, along the Mediterranean, lay the Phoenicians, a great seapower as far back as the pre-Solomonic period and still enjoying that status. These busy seafaring people were all but oblivious to the Judaeans, who certainly posed no threat to their position.

The Palestinian Jews did not object to leading so thoroughly isolated and insular an existence. They entertained no territorial ambitions and they were economically self-sustaining: they lacked any interest in, or pressing need for, the spices and gums and precious materials which flowed about them in all directions. Contact with the outside world was all but limited to the far-flung Diaspora communities, all of which were faithful in transmitting their yearly tithes to the Temple's upkeep. The Judaeans had no ambitions of a proselytizing nature; they simply ignored their pagan neighbors. They were satisfied with tilling their lands, making their *t'rumahs,* scanning their Torahs. As for the elitist priests, we need barely remark upon their absolute and collective satisfaction.

Thus, for a period of two hundred years, the Judaeans were content with "doing their own thing." Meanwhile, outside their constricted world, a succession of convulsive upheavals were precipitating drastic changes in their lives as well as the lives of all peoples of the then known civilized world.

Alexander the Great was about to march, under the banner of Hellenism.

4 The Hellenizers

Alexander (the name means "defender of men") was, militarily and politically, the most influential man of antiquity. The empire he forged was the largest the world had known prior to that of the Romans three centuries later. Ironically, his empire fell apart when Alexander died. And his incredible career lasted little more than a decade.

Alexander was barely eighteen when he succeeded his father Philip II as King of Macedon in 336 B.C.; before he was nineteen, he was master of all Greece; before he was twenty-one, he had crossed the Hellespont and conquered western Asia. Within a year he had moved south to take Egypt, and then backtracked northward to complete the conquest of the area geographically referred to as Coele-Syria or "Hollow Syria"—Palestine, Phoenicia, and Syria itself.[1] In October of 331 B.C., he routed the remaining Persian forces at Gaugamela, thus marking the end of their once mighty empire. In what seemed less a sweeping conquest than a royal progress, he moved from Babylonia to Parthia (today Iran) to Bactria (Afghanistan) and then on to the Punjab Region of northern India where, at the Indus River, he was finally stopped—by his own men. Those of his soldiers who had not settled in the conquered lands wanted to go home; also, they had become disillusioned with Alexander's demands that he be paid physical obeisance and that his deification be recognized.

After replacing disloyal satraps of the various conquered states with his own hand-picked lieutenants and disbanding the private armies that posed a threat to his authority and ambitions, Alexander encamped at Susa, the former Persian imperial capital, where he established himself as the Great King, and where, amidst a splendiferous court, he gathered his resources, indulged his penchant for bisexuality, and planned still further exploits. A year later he fell victim to a fatal fever.

Alexander's was a lofty dream: that all peoples should look upon each other as equal partners in a common culture; to unite the then known civilized world under the umbrella of what was tantamount to a "new enlightenment." Being pragmatic, he realized that success would be best achieved were he to harmonize Hellenism with local traditions and diverse cultures instead of imposing it. And while it may not have been his original intent, Alexander's breaking down of barriers between East and West led to a reciprocity of ideas, all of which worked to Western Civilization's ultimate advantage. As some of the noblest ideals of the new enlightenment, such as the concept of popular participation in local government, were being carried from West to East, the sciences of astrology and cosmology were traveling in the opposite direction. From Persia alone came such novel ideas as determination of history, eschatology, and the Final Judgment concept, all of which, together with the by then ancient Babylonian concepts of demonology and angelology, were to be of paramount importance in the evolution of Christianity (itself the offspring of the mating of Hellenism and Judaism).

To introduce and foster the spread of Greek culture, Alexander practiced a policy—pursued by his successors in Asia—of founding and fusion. He would organize large Greek-style cities —twenty-five at latest count, including Alexandria in Egypt— and encourage his men to marry local women and settle therein. (In one mass ceremony, eighty officers and 10,000 enlisted men took Persian brides.) These cities served not only as a means of building up international mercantile and intellectual commerce, but as the loci for the Hellenistic pattern of life. Here were to be found, encased in architectural marvels, such institutions as the *gerousia,* or council, elected by the citizenry; the sports-stadiums; and the *gymnasia,* educational institutions where youth could gain an appreciation of literature, music, and the arts, as well as physical culture—this last considered by some to be the true essence of Greek civilization.* It was largely through these gymnasia that the teachings and creations of the great philosophers, artists, and belletrists of Greece's Classical Age served to influence and thus mold society. (The awareness that the youth of today are the leaders of tomorrow was about the only concept Alexander was not obliged to foster.)

The Diaspora Jews could not help but be influenced by Hellenistic culture. Rapidly becoming exposed to a philosophy that stood in healthy opposition to their own tradition of exclusivity, as well as to the veritable myriad of new sciences and liberal arts, many began to question much within the Mosaic Law that was by then intellectually constricting as well as hopelessly socially outdated. In so many respects, the traumas of Sophocles made better reading than the *t'rumahs* of Moses; admiring a statue by Praxiteles or mulling over the dialogues of Plato in no way threatened the special relationship the Jews enjoyed with the One God.

For the Palestinian Jews, initial contact with Hellenism came when the Ptolemies established suzerainty over the area at the beginning of the third century B.C. However, the Ptolemies did not impose, or even encourage the spread of, Hellenism beyond their own borders. But when the Seleucids ousted the Ptolemies from Palestine a century later, the impact of Hellenism on the Jews became more pronounced. Under the Seleucids, Hellenism quickly degenerated to the point where, as the early first century

---

* Only young men were enrolled in these institutions and allowed to partake of the games and festivals patterned after Greek ways. Young women were held to have been created for purpose of procreation—or, in the case of the *haeteirae,* recreation. Thus, in addition to gaining an appreciation of the finest ideals of Hellenism, many of the young men presumably gained an appreciation of each other.

B.C. Stoic philosopher Posidonius informs us: "Life [had become] a continuous series of social festivities."

It would seem that the theocrats who ruled Judaea would have been in the vanguard of anti-Hellenism. They had gotten rich off the people, a situation the people had accepted wholeheartedly and most conscientiously. Obviously, much of political Hellenism, that is, the concept of participation by the laity in the democratic process, was something the priests found a threat to their position. Too, the new religions and traditions permeating the Near East should have spelled anathema to a class whose only presumed justification for existence—the worship of a singular, ineffable deity—was so antithetical to the myriad manifestations of idol worship, anthropomorphism, and even emperor worship surrounding them. But when political Hellenism finally did take root in Palestine, it was, perhaps not so ironically, the aristocratic priests who led the nation in "going Greek." They appear to have been less concerned with religious and traditional principles than with accommodating their Hellenistic overlords—especially as it involved, as will be seen, so much self-aggrandizement.

To reduce the history of the decades between the death of Alexander and the Hellenizing of Judaea to less than fifteen hundred words is like reducing the Old Testament to a two-hour Hollywood spectacle: it is an unsupportable literary conceit. But since our primary concern is with the Jewish nation (our secondary concern being the limitations of space), the present writer—in establishing the rise of the Ptolemies and Seleucids—will knowingly commit that conceit.

Because Alexander's blood heirs were limited to a half brother who was a congenital idiot and a posthumously born son who was a Bactrian half-breed, his chief lieutenants immediately set to the task of disposing of the empire (as well as of each other).

Ptolemy Lagus, one of Alexander's most distinguished chief-

tains, was at the time satrap of Egypt. He simply declared Egypt
his; thus was founded the first, and longest-lasting, of the Hellenistic dynasties, the Greek-Macedonian Ptolemaic. Ptolemy's decision was a shrewd one: the Sinai Desert, the Nile River Delta,
and a rough, inhospitable Mediterranean coastline rendered this
rich and resourceful land invulnerable to attack. Casting an eye
on Coele-Syria in hopes of spreading his suzerainty northward
into Asia Minor, Ptolemy invaded the contiguous land of Palestine. Taking Jerusalem—by then the most socially cohesive and
militarily vital city in Coele-Syria south of Damascus—posed no
problem. He simply marched into the Holy City on the Sabbath
day, when Mosaic Law precluded the pursuit of any extrareligious endeavors—including self-protection.*

In the meantime, Seleucus, a former cavalry officer under
Alexander, had claimed Babylonia as his independent fiefdom,
and was rapidly conquering all of the eastern portions of Alexander's realm. Thus was founded the Seleucid Dynasty of Syria.
By 305 B.C. all the successors had assumed the title "king" in their
respective spheres of influence. Ptolemy, who already had an
heir, added the Roman numeral I, to which was subsequently
appended the cognomen Soter ("savior"); Seleucus, also a father,
had appended to his Roman numeral the cognomen Nicator
("conqueror").

As a result of the Battle of Ipsus (301 B.C.), which marked the
end of any central authority over what had been Alexander's
empire, and which "fixed" the successor empires, Seleucus was
allotted all of Coele-Syria. Ptolemy refused to surrender the area.
Out of friendship and loyalty to an erstwhile comrade-in-arms,
Seleucus did not force the issue—but he did maintain a claim to

* In so doing, he established a pattern: succesive conquerors would wait
until Saturday, that is, to take Jerusalem with a minimum of fuss and bother
—until the advent of Mattathias, progenitor of the Maccabees. It is interesting to note that as recently as 1948, when the Republic of Israel was
fighting against incredible odds to be born, many Orthodox rabbis tried to
prevent their beleaguered people from fighting on the Sabbath. Apparently
old traditions die hard among the often irrational faithful.

the area, a claim that was to become the major contention between the successors of these two particular *diadochoi*.

While Seleucus spent the opening decades of the third century
B.C. in building up the great empire his descendants were to
throw away, Ptolemy prudently remained in his capital at Alexandria where, under his aegis, Egypt became the leading mercantile and maritime nation in the entire eastern Mediterranean
basin. Contact with his seven million aboriginal subjects was
minimal—and this only through the half-million Macedonian
bureaucrats working in conjunction with the self-serving native
priests. Ptolemy was nominally a Pharaoh, but in actuality—as
were his heirs—he was the active and unapproachable board
chairman of a powerful maritime corporation.

Meanwhile, Seleucus spent the remaining years of his reign in
furthering the spread of political Hellenism. This was limited to
the founding of a number of Greek-style cities throughout a
realm that was rapidly shrinking by degrees as various vassal
states, client-kingdoms, and disloyal satrapies broke away from
the sprawling and quite unmanageable empire.

Ptolemy Soter was succeeded by his youngest son, Ptolemy II
Philadelphus ("brother-lover"), who murdered his first wife,
married his sister, and acquiesced in his own divinity, thus firmly
fixing three family traditions—uxoricide, incest, and deification—
that were to obtain until the end of Ptolemaic misrule over
Egypt. Still another tradition, intermarriage with the Seleucids—
to the eternal detriment of both royal houses—soon followed
with the accession of Seleucus's grandson, Antiochus II, cog-
nominally Theos ("divine" or simply "god"). Theos was a de-
bauched and inept young man whose reign saw the Parthians—
who were to play a major role in Hasmonaean history—gain their
independence.

The two royal houses began to squabble over Coele-Syria, with
the mutual buffer state of Palestine serving as the battleground.
In the hope of arriving at some sort of peace, Antiochus Theos
married Ptolemy Philadelphus's daughter Berenice, on the under-

standing that any son of this union would inherit the Seleucid throne—this despite the fact that Theos had already sired two heirs by his wife Laodice. The marriage proved to be a disaster for all parties concerned. When Theos died, Berenice—backed by her brother Ptolemy III Euergetes ("benefactor")—attempted to take the Syrian throne on behalf of her infant son by the Seleucid king. She and the infant were murdered by forces loyal to Laodice, whose eldest son, Seleucus II Callinicus ("gloriously victorious"), succeeded in ousting the "Egyptians," though he failed to win back Phoenicia, and the eastern satrapies beyond Babylonia were now beyond his grasp. The Benefactor returned to Alexandria, where he spent the remainder of his reign in peace. Callinicus spent the remainder of *his* reign gloriously and victoriously losing even more of the family holdings.

Callinicus was succeeded by his eldest son, Seleucus III Ceraunos, a pitiful young man whose three-year reign (226–223 B.C.) led many to suspect that his cognomen ("thunderbolt") was surely some anonymous courtier's idea of a grotesque joke. It was the Thunderbolt's younger brother and successor, Antiochus III ("the Great"), who was to regain all the dominions lost by his immediate predecessors. His reign was to mark the apogee of Seleucid sovereignty in Asia. It was Antiochus III who was to be one of the greatest friends the Jews ever had among the Syrians —a fact which has somehow been overlooked in the less objective histories of the times.

But before we record how Antiochus III won—and lost—so much of the ancestral property, it might behoove us to take note of how the Children of Abraham were faring amid all this Ptolemaic-Seleucid turmoil.

Of the three great Jewish communities of the time—Babylonia, Jerusalem, and Alexandria—it was in the last that the effects of cultural Hellenism were most directly felt. Josephus claims that the first Jews to settle in Alexandria were the descendants of those who had fled to Egypt following Nebuchadnezzar's destruction of the First Temple. Though there is no way either to prove or challenge this, it is more probable that the basis of this progressive community were the approximately 100,000 Jews who migrated to Egypt during Ptolemy Soter's reign—a good number of whom may have been taken there as slaves with the guarantee that their release would be granted after one generation. (Upward of 30,000 are said to have been impressed into Soter's armies, and of these, many are believed to have served willingly as hired mercenaries.)

Membership in the Jerusalem priesthood was still limited to those whose Levitical descent was provable, but a class of nonsacerdotal aristocrats—landowners, merchants, and just plain peculating opportunists—was rapidly establishing its influence with the priests. Also, Judaea was by then surrounded by numerous Greek cities, many of which were planted by the various *diadochoi* while contesting Ptolemy Soter for control of Palestine. Thus it is safe to assume that for many of the more sophisticated Judaeans, disenchantment with the rigid and corrupt theocracy, along with a growing awareness of the new enlightenment, were undoubtedly contributory factors in this migration.

Except for the Macedonian Greeks, the Jews at Alexandria soon became the largest and most prosperous non-Egyptian element in this grandest of Hellenistic cities. Though not reckoned as citizens, they were assured a status equal to that of the Macedonian population. Permitted to form their own community, they were granted considerable autonomy and privileges; relations between the Jews and their suzerains were, on the whole, amicable. Removed from the Jerusalem Temple, and in dire need of centers of worship, the Egyptian Jews began to build synagogues. For all Diaspora Jews, the Temple remained a tropismatic symbol, toward the upkeep of which they contributed regularly and generously. But whereas the Temple was the splendid symbol of the Lord's House, the synagogue was the place where scattered Jewish communities could be assured communication with Him personally. Thanks to Jeremiah and

Ezekiel, and the exigencies of history, the Babylonian Exile had taught the Jews that their Heavenly Friend was peripatetic.

The Alexandrian Jews, like their brethren in Palestine and Babylonia, were allowed to live according to their Mosaic tradition—though it is to be assumed they were sophisticated enough to accept that some tenets of the Divine Legislation were no longer consonant with conditions. The majority, especially those of a high intellectual and rationalistic bent, became influenced by the noble philosophical and cultural ingredients of Hellenism; in time, there arose a type of Judaism marked by the fusion of Mosaic and Greek ideals and ideas. Indeed, it was the Alexandrian community that gave the world Philo Judaeus ("Philo of Alexandria"), the first great Jewish philosopher and theologian, whose biblical expositions and secular writings helped to make Judaism relevant to both the Hellenized Hebrews and the Gentiles (non-Jews) in the earliest stages of Christianity, and whose thought was subsequently of inestimable influence in the development of Christian theology.[2]

As for the Jews of Palestine, with their land divided into small administrative units in the charge of officials appointed by the Alexandrian bureaucracy, they were left in comparative peace during the Ptolemaic period. No attempt was made to introduce even political Hellenism, such as reorganizing Jerusalem as a Greek-style city. (That was something the Judaeans would do by themselves.) The Ptolemies wanted Palestine as a buffer state against Syria. So long as Judaea was firmly under the control of the aristocratic priesthood, whose members led the nation in accommodating their overlords, and so long as they paid their taxes regularly and surrendered the prescribed number of conscripts, the Judaeans were left to pursue their monotheism undisturbed. Indeed—and this must be stressed—it was *never* the policy of the Ptolemies *or* the Seleucids to impose Greek-style worship and traditions, especially in the temple-states over which they ruled. Antiochus Epiphanes's blundering miscalculation was the exception that proved this rule. *Koine,* vernacular Greek, emerged as the lingua franca throughout the Hellenistic world, of which Palestine was now a vital part, and the more aesthetic (and probably more comfortable) Greek mode of dress was popular—but this was less through imposition by the suzerains than adoption by their subjects.

As much can be said for political Hellenism. As the Diaspora Jews harmonized Greek culture with Mosaic tradition without losing their religious integrity, the Palestinian Jews wedded Greek polity to Mosaic tradition and lost theirs. Two major factions were evolving in Jerusalem—the Oniads and the Tobiads —whose rivalry was to polarize the nation, thus paving the way for its destruction during the Seleucid period. The Ptolemies registered no objections.

The Oniads, who were to monopolize the High Priesthood until the rise of the Maccabees a century later, were lineally descended from Onias I, the High Priest during the reign of Ptolemy Soter. ("Onias" was the Hellenized form of his given name, Ananiah; the Hellenistic influence is indicated in the fact that even the conservative priests took Greek names.) The Tobiads, the nonpriestly aristocrats who emerged as the earliest champions of Hellenism in Judaea, were descended from Tobias, a man of considerable cunning who had laid the basis of the family fortune by bribing the Ptolemaic bureaucrats—as well as the royalties themselves—in exchange for a number of lucrative rewards, such as being named tax collector for the provinces of Palestine and Phoenicia. The Tobiads' pro-Ptolemaic sympathies were understandable. The Oniads, on the other hand, were pro-Seleucid less out of sheer arbitrariness than sheer practicality. The Jews at Antioch were in closer proximity to the Temple than those at Alexandria. Also, since the Seleucids did not practice cultural Hellenism, the Antioch Jews, being less sophisticated than their coreligionists in Egypt, felt a stronger tie to the Jerusalem priesthood. There was also another major factor to account for the division of loyalties between the two factions: the Oniads, not completely divorced from political reality, could see that it was but a matter of time before the Seleucids would oust the Ptolemies from Palestine altogether.

Matters became slightly complicated, and party lines crossed, when Tobias married the sister of the High Priest, Onias II. Some time after his inheritance of that august office in 245 B.C., Onias II refused to pay the annual Jerusalem taxes to Ptolemy Euergetes. When punitive action was threatened, Tobias's son and heir, Joseph, kindly undertook to negotiate directly with the king on his uncle's behalf. As a result of the wily Joseph's "negotiations," Onias was forced to relinquish to his nephew the secular leadership of Jerusalem. The battle lines were drawn.

Joseph began his tenure of office as civil head of Jerusalem by persuading a good number of the elders to abandon their support of Onias and reaffirm their loyalty to the Ptolemies. Then, with money borrowed from friends in Samaria (who were enjoying the schism in the Jerusalem hierarchy) he returned to Alexandria where through lavish bribes he managed to win even more highly placed friends at the thoroughly decadent Ptolemaic court. When Joseph died, his wealth passed to his eight sons, of whom the favorite and chief beneficiary was Hyrcanus, the only issue of Joseph's second marriage. Hyrcanus's success in winning the position of tax collector, so long held by his father, roused the jealousy of his seven half brothers. In addition to being pitted against the Oniads, the Tobiads were now pitted against each other.

In the meantime Ptolemy IV Philopator ("father-lover") began an eighteen-year reign that was to carry Egypt from the heights of power and international influence to the depths of political weakness from which it was never to recover. This decadent voluptuary managed to hold on to Palestine—thanks in no small measure to well-placed friends in the Jerusalem hierarchy—but the hold was a transitory one. Antiochus III, after assuming the Syrian throne (223 B.C.), swiftly occupied areas of the Ptolemaic realm before a number of revolts in the eastern satrapies forced his withdrawal. Returning to Egypt in 216 B.C., he was defeated by Ptolemy's armies at Raphia. But far from determining who was to control Palestine, Antiochus's defeat at Raphia merely postponed his conquest, which was to come a decade and a half later.

For Ptolemy, victory at Raphia became disaster at home. Native Egyptian levies had been used for the first time; these troops, on returning victoriously (and well armed), decided to expel their Macedonian overlords. A period of civil strife ensued that was to consume the nation for the remainder of Philopator's reign and into that of his son, Ptolemy V Epiphanes, before the natives were persuaded—by hired mercenaries—to return to their farms and allow the Macedonians to rule their economically healthy though politically diseased nation.

From the time of Philopator's accession (221 B.C.) until the conquest of Palestine by Antiochus III two decades later, Jerusalem was caught up in the crosscurrents of war, especially during the crucial years 202–198 B.C., when the fate of all Palestine was in the balance. Jewish loyalties were divided. The majority, laity as well as priests, supported the pro-Seleucid Oniads, whose leader was Simon the Just. Hyrcanus the Tobiad led the elitist Jerusalem merchants in favoring Egypt, though his half brothers—whether out of political pragmatism or sibling rivalry—joined the Oniads in support of the Seleucids. To settle the issue, a Greek-style *gerousia* was called, at which time the decision was taken by Judaea's elders—priests as well as aristocrats—to support the Seleucid cause. In 201 B.C. Antiochus arrived at Jerusalem and was duly welcomed by Simon the Just and a deputation of elders—including those pro-Ptolemaic aristocrats who did a fast shuffle to the Seleucid side.

Unfortunately, the welcoming ceremonies were brief. Ptolemaic-purchased mercenaries arrived, and Antiochus—whose armies were scattered throughout western Asia—was forced to withdraw. Temporarily. When he was at last able to establish his ancestral claim to all of Coele-Syria two years later, and entered

Jerusalem in triumph, Antiochus was to remember the loyalty shown him by the Oniad-led majority.

Antiochus III succeeded his inept elder brother (the Thunder-bolt) at the age of eighteen and spent all of his thirty-six-year reign in a concerted effort—initially successful, eventually disastrous—at reextending the Seleucid domains to their traditional limits. Following his setback at Raphia, he embarked upon the campaign to the east that was to win him the cognomen "Great." By 204 B.C. he had reached as far as India, having regained much of the eastern portions of the empire. The moment had come to avenge his defeat at Raphia and to secure his grip on Coele-Syria. The timing could not have been more propitious: the situation at Alexandria was catastrophic; the reigning Ptolemy—Epiphanes—was but a child and the native Egyptians were still threatening to expel the dynasty.

Antiochus had little difficulty in defeating the Egyptian army at Panion (or Panium), and as the third century B.C. ended, so did Ptolemaic rule over Palestine. Antiochus was well received in Jerusalem. The Judaeans were able to relax after the deprivations caused by more than a generation of constant warfare; they had bet on the right king.

The Seleucid victor expressed his appreciation for the loyalty shown him by the Judaeans. In addition to retaining the state subsidy of their religion and tax-exempt status for all Temple personnel, he remitted all taxes for three years, released all Jewish captives taken during previous wars, and ordered the return of all Jewish refugees scattered throughout Coele-Syria who wished to live in Judaea proper (a gesture which many were subsequently to regret having accepted). Following the standard Seleucid policy of accommodating local religions instead of interfering with them, Antiochus reasserted the right of the Jews to live according to their own traditions; he even went so far as to subsidize repairs to the Temple and to provide wood tax-free for the ritual fires that were, by Law, to be continuously stoked for the roasting of sacrifices.* For the Jews throughout the rest of his realm, he offered land grants, allowing them to form colonies should they so choose. These colonies, the nuclei of which were Jewish mercenaries who served in the Great One's armies, formed the basis of numerous communities which began to spring up throughout the Seleucid areas of the Diaspora in addition to the already flourishing community at Antioch. Though they had no way of realizing it, those Jews who elected to become colonists were being handed a fortuitous stroke of luck: they would be far from Jerusalem when the Hasmonaeans established themselves.

Antiochus III was now at the zenith of his powers. All that remained was the reconquest of certain portions of western Asia (most notably Parthia), and, on the Greek mainland, Thrace, and his realm would have those boundaries established by the progenitor of his august house.

Then came his collision with the Romans.

Legend tells us that Rome was founded at a few minutes before eight o'clock on the morning of April 21 in the year 753 B.C. by Romulus and Remus, the twins born to the goddess Rhea Silva nine months after her sexual abuse at the hands of the war god Mars.

History tells us that Rome rose from a group of settlements confined to what is today the Palatine Hill; and that after a century and a half of intermittent warfare involving a number of volatile neighboring tribes including their reputed ancestors the Etruscans, the Romans began to found colonies and spread out from the Seven Hills. Their march to ascendancy, begun around 450 B.C., was checked temporarily sixty years later when the Gauls sacked and burned the city. After the Gauls had glutted themselves and moved on, the Romans came out of the hills,

---

* Josephus adds (Ant. XII. IV. 4) that Antiochus showed his respect for Jewish tradition by forbidding Gentiles to enter the Temple on pain of death, and his respect for the Levitical Code by banning the introduction into Jerusalem of "unclean animals."

rebuilt their city, and began a period of military expansion that, by 290 B.C., saw them emerge as masters of central Italy and a decided threat to the various Greek colonies at the foot of the Italian boot. A century later, having established hegemony over the Greek cities of Europe, Rome made the civilized world realize that a new power had arisen in the Mediterranean.

In 197 B.C., three years after evicting the Ptolemies from Palestine, Antiochus the Great crossed over to Europe to evict the Romans from Thrace, to which he held a tenuous hereditary claim. There now ensued a six-year period of cold war. Rome represented itself as the champion of the freedom of the Greek cities and of Egypt and its possessions (Cyprus and Cyrene, today Libya). Egypt had already established diplomatic and trade relations with the Romans and was slowly allowing itself to drift into the status of a client-kingdom of the Roman Senate, which needed the Egyptian granaries to feed its ever-expanding army and empire. Antiochus claimed *he* was the champion of those Greek cities; and as for Egypt, he fobbed off his daughter, Cleopatra I, on the prepubescent Ptolemy V and then instructed his ambassadors to advise the Roman Senate that Egypt now felt little need of Rome's "protection."

The Senate decided it had had enough of diplomatic parrying and thrusting—especially in light of a dynastic marriage that threatened to bring a politically weak though economically vital Egypt under Seleucid control. The cold war turned hot, and Antiochus engaged the Romans at Magnesia. After a disastrous rout, he was obliged to abandon all his Asian possessions west of the Taurus Mountains (in present-day Turkey). It is said that upon returning to Syria, minus half his kingdom, Antiochus expressed his gratitude to the Romans for saving him the trouble of trying to rule so far-flung and thoroughly unmanageable an empire—demonstrating not only his sang-froid but his acceptance of reality.

By the Peace of Apamea, Antiochus agreed (he had no choice)

to pay Rome a 15,000-talent indemnity (upward of two million dollars in today's purchasing power, a formidable sum for the period). Furthermore, as a guarantee that he would make no further trouble in the Roman sphere of influence, he was compelled to send along his younger son—also named Antiochus—to live in Rome as a well-treated hostage. As for his promise not to interfere with spreading Roman influence in the eastern Mediterranean, the Roman Senate need not have fretted: the Seleucid monarch was preoccupied in finding the wherewithal for that crippling indemnity. A year after Apamea, Antiochus met his death while plundering a pagan temple in Elam (in Persia). He was succeeded by his eldest son, Seleucus IV Philopator, a rather nondescript youngster whose inheritance consisted of a truncated kingdom and a bankrupt treasury. It was during Philopator's reign that the first open clash between the Seleucids and the Jerusalem Jews was to occur.

Philopator spent the opening half of his decade-long reign seeking ways to raise revenues and managing, barely, to bring stability to Syria while many of the eastern provinces again declared their independence. The Palestinian Jews had no quarrel with their latest Seleucid overlord, who confirmed all the privileges granted by his father. But toward the end of his reign, with his financial situation an embarrassment, Philopator decided to plunder the Temple. The decision resulted from a quarrel between the Tobiads and Oniads over who was to control the Jerusalem market, a healthy source of revenue; and if the truth be known, the projected plunder was not so much a decision on Philopator's part as an open invitation from the Tobiads.

The pro-Ptolemaic Hyrcanus had fled to the Transjordan (where he eventually committed suicide) when Antiochus III took Jerusalem, and his half brother Simon the Benjaminite was now nominal leader of the Tobiads and civil leader of Jerusalem. Simon's antagonist (and cousin), the reigning High Priest, was Onias III, who had shortly before succeeded his father, Simon the Just. When Onias, not wanting to let go of a good thing, proclaimed that the Jerusalem market was to remain under the firm control of the priests, Simon simply "suggested" to the resident Syrian high commissioner that the king might find in the Temple a panacea for his fiscal problems. Prior to his hasty departure, Hyrcanus had deposited the bulk of his fortune in the Temple for safekeeping. It is logical to assume that Simon hoped to divide the loot, thus enabling the Tobiads to get their hands on some of brother Hyrcanus's fortune; and helping Seleucus Philopator financially could only redound to their advantage.

The king sent his chancellor, Heliodorus, to get the money. Having been reminded that he was to respect the insistence of the Jews that no Gentile enter the Temple's hallowed precincts, Heliodorus politely requested Onias to hand over the treasure. When the High Priest refused on the grounds that the money had been "set aside for widows and orphans" (!), Heliodorus brushed him aside and stomped into the Lord's House. There, according to rabbinic legend (probably derived from II Macc. 3:23 ff.), he was stopped by a trio of heavenly horsemen. Whether or not Heliodorus succeeded in getting the treasure is uncertain. The canonical account claims that the apparition turned him back and, upon his return to Antioch, he told the emperor, in so many words, "Whatever you do, stay away from that Temple!" What is certain, however, is that the Hellenizers were making life difficult for the traditionalists.

Onias III deemed it prudent to hurry north to Antioch, there to plead his case personally before the king. Unfortunately for all concerned, when Onias arrived at Antioch, it was not to solicit Philopator's ear but to attend his funeral. On returning from his alleged encounter with the Lord's steed-mounted angelic messengers, Heliodorus had murdered his monarch and established himself as regent for the young heir-apparent.

It was to be a brief regency. Within months, the child would be sharing the throne with an uncle he had never met (and would probably never really get to know). To history, this uncle is known as Antiochus IV Epi*phanes* ("god-manifest"), while to the Jews of Palestine he was known as Epi*manes* ("the mad-man"). Even in their most dire adversity, the Children of Abraham are not above a delicious pun.

5   The Edict

The Maccabee wars *may* have begun as a God-ordained national crusade to resist the godlessness of the Seleucids, as the chronicler of I Maccabees would have us believe; but it was not long before they had evolved into a class war between the elitists and the masses. Polarization of the Jewish nation resulted as much from the Jerusalem hierarchs' eagerness to accept, and benefit from, political Hellenism as from the Seleucid desire to see it flourish in Palestine. The Hasmonaeans practiced realpolitik; but let it not be inferred that their Maccabee ancestors were concerned less with ideals than with power. They were concerned with both.

Quite conceivably, had Judah Maccabee been satisfied, after winning back for his people the right to practice their religion unmolested—*a concession the Syrians were not only willing but eager to grant*—and not turned a religious cause into a political crusade, the tragedy that ensued may well have been avoided. But if Judah Maccabee is to be "condemned" for his actions, he must not stand alone: he could no more have succeeded without the assistance, whether active or passive, of his people than could any other leader, for good or for bad.

Seleucus Philopator had sent his second son, Demetrius, to take the place of his brother Antiochus as Rome's Seleucid hostage. The Roman Senate could have sent Demetrius home to claim his slain father's throne, if only on behalf of his quasi-captive brother. But militating against Demetrius was his youth.

Though the Romans had no doubt but that Heliodorus would eventually murder the boy-king and usurp the crown, there was no guarantee that young Demetrius would fare any better. And if by chance Heliodorus were to be overthrown, there was always the risk that another usurper would establish himself behind Demetrius. The latter's uncle Antiochus had spent his formative years in Rome and had become a complete Romanophile. Also, Antiochus was a mature man. Reasoned the Senate: if anyone was going to depose the deposer, they preferred that it be an adult impressed with Rome's way and Rome's might. Thus, by keeping the rightful heir as hostage, the Senate was tacitly putting forth its own candidate. They would not help Antiochus gain the throne, but they would not hinder him either.

Historical sources reveal that Epiphanes was energetic, capable of leadership, and of a high intellectual bent; after showing an early interest in the Stoic school of philosophers, he had converted to Epicureanism, probably as a result of having lived and held public office in Athens, after his period as a hostage in Rome. Even after he became king, he would masquerade in public on occasion, the better to observe popular reaction to his Romanized policies regarding civil administration—policies for which he had a healthy respect. In short, he was not "mad." (Some scholars have hypothesized that he eventually succumbed to a clinical disorder as a result of a fever contracted during the course of his imperial peregrinations; if so, tertiary syphilis is as good a guess as any.)

Epiphanes was forty years old and living in Athens at the time of his brother's assassination. A number of factors mitigated against his claiming the throne. He had not been seen by the Antioch citizenry since his youth, and there was no great outcry for his return: he represented, after all, the junior line in descent from Antiochus III, and though Heliodorus was the regent, he was regent for the legitimate heir. Even had there been a clamoring for his return, Epiphanes was in a bind: he lacked an army. He did, however, have two things going for him: a driving thirst for kingship and a fortuitous knack for friendship. The thirst was congenital; the friend was Eumenes II, king of Pergamum, a former Seleucid vassal state and now Rome's best friend in western Asia.

Eumenes deemed it politic to have on the neighboring Syrian throne a monarch who would be well disposed toward him, should he ever incur the hostility of the Roman Senate. Therefore he put a powerful army at Epiphanes's disposal, and when the pretender (as indeed Epiphanes was) landed at Antioch, he was able to rally to his side the citizenry and, more consequentially, the military. Deposing Heliodorus presented no problem for Antiochus, but deposing his nephew-king was another matter: though too young to command an army, the royal child was not too young to command a fair share of loyalty. It has been deduced, on the basis of coinage dating from his reign, that Antiochus ruled jointly with his young nephew—until he felt secure enough to have the child murdered.

Simon the Benjaminite had passed on at about the same time as Seleucus Philopator (though the two events were unrelated), and Onias III—anti-Hellenistic and fiercely defensive of priestly prerogatives—now had another antagonist with whom to contend. His brother, Jason.

While Onias had been at Antioch, Jason allied himself with Simon's successor Menelaus, who had assumed leadership of the Tobiads. These staunch Hellenizers had been insidiously eroding the power of the priests, but had not yet won over the masses; they realized that this could be accomplished only through an open alliance with the Oniads, whose hold on the populace was similar to that enjoyed by the Church in any one of a half-dozen Latin American nations. Therefore they turned to Jason, scion of the High Priestly line, and a political opportunist who saw no conflict between religion and politics—so long as it redounded to his advantage. After a hurried conference and exchange of ideas with Menelaus, Jason set out for the Syrian capital. (At this juncture, nomenclature may be simplified: the Tobiads and Oniads became, to all intent and purpose, one party—the Hellenizers.)

No sooner had Epiphanes established himself at Antioch than he was asked to grant an audience to Onias III. When the High Priest entered the imperial chambers—and quite probably gave the new king his first sight of a Jew—he immediately swore the fealty of his nation. He also advised Epiphanes of his legitimacy as High Priest of Judaea, and expressed the hope that the new emperor would follow the example set by his illustrious father, Antiochus III, and not interfere with Judaea's internal structure. Epiphanes advised Onias that he had no intention of rescinding the privileges granted by his august sire. Since he had been informed that Onias had always been prompt in delivering Judaea's tax revenues, he expressed himself as eminently satisfied with Onias's leadership and wished him a long and healthy High Priesthood.

With his latest overlord's best wishes, Onias was about to return home when he learned that brother Jason had arrived in Antioch and been granted an interview with the emperor, during which Jason had offered Epiphanes lavish bribes and firm assurances that he would further the cause of Hellenism at Jerusalem—provided he was recognized as his brother's successor. Onias rushed to the palace and protested most vehemently that Jason was in effect usurping an hereditary office that was not yet vacant. Caring less for assurances than for bribes (money was always a problem with the Seleucids) Epiphanes quite conveniently allowed shekels to speak louder than legitimacy. Onias now saw only futility in trying to fight the issue—especially on being informed that Jason had the backing of the less conservative priests, not to mention those powerful aristocrats. Onias decided to remain in exile at Antioch, where a sizable Jewish community had been flourishing. Jason returned to Jerusalem to fulfill his promises to Epiphanes (and to gather together the monies for the bribe).

The Holy City now became a Greek city. The former Council of Elders—based on the traditional Seventy Elders who assisted Moses in governmental administration during the Exodus—was converted by Jason into a *boule*, a municipal senate, conforming with Greek procedures and confined in membership to men of good standing in the Hellenist party. As I Maccabees informs us, many of the Judaeans "intermarried with Gentiles, and abandoned themselves to evil ways." A Greek-style gymnasium was instituted wherein, to the horror of the orthodox faithful, the progressive young men as well as some of the more athletic priests "abandoned themselves" by indulging in sports contests, especially the favorite Greek sport of wrestling, and otherwise exercising—in the buff. We learn from II Maccabees (4:13–15) that "Hellenism reached a high point. . . . As a result, the priests no longer had any enthusiasm for their duties at the altar, but despised the temple and neglected the sacrifices; and in defiance of the [Mosaic] law they eagerly contributed to the expenses of the wrestling-school whenever the opening gong called them." Not only were the priests partaking of the Hellenistic fun-and-games, they were also subsidizing them with funds from the Temple treasury.

There were, it is only right to assume, some within the priesthood who did not, as the text was wont to reiterate, "abandon the faith of their fathers," but these were negligible in number. There is no indication that they were not tolerated by the Hellenizers. This would lead us further to assume that these conservatives put up as best they could with a rather sordid situation, making their sacrifices and stoking the sacred flames with a forbearance bordering on abject stoicism.

Their apostate confreres, led by Jason, did not, however, go to the extreme of worshipping pagan gods—yet. But they came close. When the quinquennial festivities were held at Tyre, Jason sent an embassy bearing three hundred drachmas in cash with which to purchase sacrifices to the pagan god Hercules. The messengers, fearful of committing such a blasphemy, "considered that it should be spent otherwise." Instead of purchasing the sacrifices to Hercules, they devoted the funds to the less compromising task of building ships for Antiochus Epiphanes's navy (II Macc. 4:18–20). A passage in the biblical text claiming that all citizens were "registered as Antiochenes" suggests that the name of the Holy City may well have been changed to Antioch, a common practice throughout the Seleucid realm.

Three years after coming to the throne, Antiochus Epiphanes paid a visit to Jerusalem before taking his army into winter quarters in Phoenicia and was "lavishly welcomed by Jason and the city and received with torchlight and ovations" (II Macc. 4:22). The Syrian monarch pronounced himself eminently pleased with the Hellenized state of his Judaean province, as well he should have been.

For the traditionalists, the situation had become intolerable. Not only were they incensed over Jason's obnoxious Hellenization policy, they thought it excessive that a High Priest should be appointed by a foreigner, and a Gentile king at that. But there was little they could do about it. As for the less conservative among the faithful, they managed to find some consolation in the knowledge that Jason was at least genealogically entitled to the office; and since his brother Onias III had wisely elected to remain an exile at Antioch, Jason was acceptable if only by default. Thus, and ironically, Jason's strongest opposition did not come from the orthodox community. Rather, it came from his own supporters among the nonpriestly aristocrats who felt that his policy of Hellenization was not radical enough! The step they wanted Jason to take was the one he would under no circumstances have considered: surrendering his High Priestly office to one of their own. Lacking any alternative, the apostates decided to take the office; Menelaus was put forward as their candidate.

Because Menelaus was of the tribe of Benjamin and not of the sacerdotal tribe of Levi, were he the holiest man in all Israel he would not have been acceptable; his followers knew they could never force him on the nation without running the risk of precipitating a popular uprising—one that would be led by Jason and the other apostate Levite priests. Perhaps, they reasoned, opposition might be finessed were Menelaus to be established in office by their Syrian overlord whose hegemony was by now universally accepted, if not universally applauded. A powerful Syrian garrison was stationed in the city; should Epiphanes name Menelaus to the High Priestly office, the dissenters would be forced to accept him.

Unwittingly, Jason played into Menelaus's hands. When it came time to deliver the yearly payment on his bribe to Epiphanes, he accepted Menelaus's kind offer to make the arduous journey in his stead. Menelaus seized the opportunity to offer a still larger bribe (he "outbid Jason by three hundred talents in silver") and was sent back to Jerusalem as the new High Priest. In defense of the Syrian monarch, he probably did not know Levites from Benjaminites; and we may assume Menelaus did not deign to tax his imperial mind with such genealogical trivialities.

Jason was not about to take this passively as had his deposed brother. Though he had incurred the wrath of the traditionalists, he was able to win their support, plus the support of the accredited Levites, with the argument that even though he might be, to their way of thinking, a dismal High Priest he was at least a legitimate one. Riots broke out, and Epiphanes was forced to send troops into Jerusalem to augment the Syrian garrison in propping up Menelaus (an indication that Epiphanes was not one to go back on a bargain). Jason fled with a band of his followers to the Transjordan, there to bide his time, while Menelaus—who managed to win the begrudging recognition of the less intransigent Levites as their High Priest—faced still another problem: how to meet the bribery payments to Epiphanes. While Menelaus turned his attention to raising the necessary revenues, Epiphanes turned southward to Egypt.

A tragicomic chain of circumstances was now set into motion that was to result in the outbreak of the Maccabee wars.

Epiphanes's sister, Cleopatra I, had transferred her loyalties from Syria to Egypt following her arranged marriage to young Ptolemy V. When Ptolemy was assassinated in 181 B.C. by some of his courtiers (quite possibly at the demand of his Syrian wife), Cleopatra assumed the role of queen-regent for their son Ptolemy VI Philometor ("mother-lover"). During the decade-long regency that ended with her death (presumably from natural causes), Cleopatra guided the politically weakened nation in a pacifist policy toward Syria. But immediately following her death, a cabal led by two former slaves who had risen to eminence at court determined to retake Coele-Syria.

Fortunately for Antiochus Epiphanes, the situation was not perilous: all he had to do was move an army south toward the frontier and the Egyptians beat a hasty retreat. With Egypt subdued and Judaea firmly under the control of Menelaus and the Hellenizers, the Syrian king now felt secure enough on his southern flank to attend to troubles in Cilicia where the cities of Tarsus and Mallus were in rebellion against having been assigned as appanage to Antiochus's current mistress, Antiochis.

Before marching off to put down the fractious Cilicians, Antiochus ordered his regent at Antioch to call Menelaus to task for having failed to pay the promised bribe. Aided by his brother Lysimachus whom he delegated to act as High Priest during his absence, Menelaus looted the Temple of its sacred treasures, some of which he sold to raise cash while others were used to curry the regent's favor. Riots again broke out in Jerusalem as a result of this blasphemous looting, with Menelaus held personally responsible by the regent. And as if the High Priest did not have enough problems, a delegation of Jewish elders journeyed north to Tyre, where Antiochus Epiphanes was now encamped, to complain against the apostates. Epiphanes dismissed the deputation and sent word to his regent to put an immediate end to what he considered an insignificant, if not incomprehensible, local squabble.

In the meantime Lysimachus had managed to raise a small army of mercenaries, and with the aid of the Hellenizers and the Syrian garrison troops, he quelled the riots, losing his life in the attempt. Through further bribes to the right Seleucids, Menelaus was reconfirmed in his office. Pausing only long enough to engineer the murder of the still-popular Onias III, Menelaus returned to a dissension-torn Judaean capital. As Menelaus was rushing back to Jerusalem, Antiochus Epiphanes was rushing back to Egypt. Those two ex-slaves had mounted another invasion of Palestine.

Epiphanes routed the Egyptian army at the border and then moved up the Nile to Memphis (thus becoming the first Macedonian since Alexander to penetrate successfully Egypt's hitherto impregnable defenses). The court at Alexandria panicked and young Ptolemy Philometor tried to escape by sea, but was captured by his uncle Antiochus. Philometor's younger brother, Ptolemy VII Physcon ("fat-paunch"), was immediately enthroned by the Alexandrians. Posing as the champion of the "rightful" king, whom he held at Memphis, Epiphanes then moved down to Alexandria to depose his other nephew. There he was met by the ambassadors from Athens and the various other Hellenistic states, all of whom tried desperately to mediate. Fearing the wrath of Rome, the Greek states felt that the quarrel between Syria and Egypt should immediately end; in essence, they did not want Epiphanes to disturb the status quo.

Rome's victory over Macedon (at Cynoscephelae) and Syria (at Magnesia) had deeply impressed the eastern Mediterranean states: that Rome was eager to spread her sphere of influence as far eastward as possible was a foregone conclusion. By now her grip on the ancient world was such that, even when intervention was *not* expected, any party to a dispute wanted the Roman Senate to know its official version, in order to be the first to enlist

Roman support. Prior to his Egyptian campaign, Antiochus Epiphanes had sent a legate to convince the Senate—by argument if possible, by bribery if necessary—that Egypt had been the aggressor. But he knew he was on shaky ground. Therefore he allowed himself to be convinced by the Hellenistic ambassadors that Rome would intervene in Egypt if necessary, that Seleucid authority would not be tolerated there, and that only by his agreeing to a settlement of the dynastic issue would Roman armies be kept out of western Asia.

Epiphanes agreed to a diplomatic solution—but on his terms. Philometor would reign in Memphis, the fat Physcon in Alexandria.

Instead of resolving the problem, Epiphanes simply compounded it: Egypt now had a brace of young kings who happened to be mutually antagonistic into the bargain. Nevertheless, Epiphanes felt free to withdraw from his nephews' divided domain, assuming that the country would be so paralyzed by dynastic rivalry as to preclude any threat to Coele-Syria. And there was, for Epiphanes, an added dividend: he would not be open to Roman censure for maintaining a Seleucid presence there.

While Antiochus was negotiating in Egypt, a false rumor spread north that he had been murdered. The rumor drifted as far as the Transjordan, from which Jason led his small army into Jerusalem, exterminating all those who had remained loyal to Menelaus. Again Jason managed to win over a large segment of the populace—he was, after all, the only legitimate hereditary High Priest available. Menelaus sought refuge in the Temple, but the priests declared openly for Jason. Making his way to the Akra, the Syrian garrison on a western hill near the Temple Mount that constituted a fortified city within a city, and with the aid of the Syrian troops, Menelaus managed to drive Jason out of Jerusalem and into the pages of history. ("He fled from city to city, hunted by all, hated as a rebel against the laws. . . . In the end the man . . . died in exile . . . unmourned; he had no . . . resting place in the grave of his ancestors." Thus is recorded Jason's fate in II Maccabees 5:8–10, a fate that can be neither confirmed nor denied but which, considering the source, can at least be questioned.)

Unfortunately, when Epiphanes heard of the Jerusalem riots he interpreted them as evidence that the Judaean province had switched its loyalty to Egypt. He immediately raced north and put down the anti-Menelaus faction. II Maccabees claims "the king had the audacity to enter the holiest temple on earth, guided by Menelaus, who had turned traitor both to his religion and his country. He [Epiphanes] laid impious hands on the sacred vessels; his desecrating hands swept together the votive offerings which other kings [that is, of Israel] had set up to enhance the splendour and fame of the shrine [after which he] carried off eighteen hundred talents from the temple and hastened back to Antioch" (5:15–21). Here the chronicler seems to have interpolated some of Epiphanes's actions which actually occurred during the subsequent desecration of the Temple; historical facts are telescoped and susceptible to scrutiny. Epiphanes's course of action at this juncture was simply to prop up Menelaus as High Priest, thus restoring order; he had come to Jerusalem not to desecrate the Temple but to nip an incipient insurrection in the bud. As for those "eighteen hundred talents from the temple," this was in all probability a bribe on the part of Menelaus to appease the king and hasten him on his way.

The orthodox masses were willing to go along with the Hellenizers and accept Syrian suzerainty (not that they had much choice)—provided Menelaus were removed from office. But the Hellenizers would not turn their back on him. The mobs soon became quite ugly, and riots again broke out, precipitating a potentially explosive situation with which even the Syrian garrison was unable to cope. Epiphanes, who was now back at Antioch, could not attend to the situation personally, nor could he spare many troops: he was preparing to reconquer the Parthians. (Trying to bring these mavericks back into the imperial herd had become a Seleucid cause; failing to do so was becoming a Seleucid effect.) Therefore he ordered one of his most capable lieutenants, Apollonius, commander of the Mysian mercenaries, to put down the riots and restore authority to Menelaus and the Hellenizers.

Having been advised by the Hellenizers that the truly pious insurgents would not violate the Sabbath even to defend themselves, Apollonious arrived in Jerusalem with his mercenaries on a Friday afternoon, under the pretense of hoping to reach a peaceful settlement between the contending factions. On the following day the slaughter began. With the Hellenizers standing by benignly, many of the orthodox laity (and a number of the conservative priests) were killed, their wives and children deported into slavery; the city was set to the torch, and the city walls all but razed. After reinforcing the Akra garrison, Apollonius and his Mysians departed Jerusalem—which now lay exposed, its walls breached, like a cadaver subjected to a bungled autopsy.

Epiphanes was about to set out for Parthia when he received news that caused him to race back to Alexandria. His nephews Physcon and Philometor had put aside their differences—temporarily—to unite against their Syrian uncle. The decision had been instigated, in large measure, by their shrewd sister, Cleopatra II—who, like her mother, Cleopatra I, had become loyal to Egypt, and who, following the Ptolemaic pattern, had married Philometor, elder of the rival kings. Egypt was too weak to forestall an invasion, and Epiphanes encountered little or no resistance—until he reached the outskirts of Alexandria. It was the year 168 B.C. and the Romans, having established their mastery over so much of continental Europe, were at last free to mount a war in North Africa—but only if such a move were unavoidable.

Although the Treaty of Apamea between Epiphanes's father and the Roman Senate did not expressly forbid Seleucid expansion at the expense of the Ptolemies, the Senate had no intention of allowing Egypt—the major source of their food supplies—to slip into the Syrian orbit. Much of Rome's success can be attributed to her rarely, if ever, fighting a war that was not of her own choosing, at her own time, and on her own terms. It was Roman policy, wherever feasible, to send in an envoy instead of an army. Popilius Laenas was sent by Rome to demand that Epiphanes evacuate Egypt.

Halting the invader in the Alexandrian suburb of Eleusis, Laenas told him in no uncertain terms to get out and stay out. Laenas's position was, on the surface, highly insupportable: Epiphanes had a large army with him, whereas the envoy was surrounded only by his small, well-dressed suite. Laenas pointedly reminded the Syrian king of the power he represented and advised him that, if necessary, Rome would send in a few of its legions to enforce his withdrawal. When Antiochus asked for time to consider, Laenas drew a circle in the sand around the king's feet and coolly told him not to step outside that circle until he had made his decision! Epiphanes stepped out of the circle—and out of Egypt. (Thus the "conquest" accredited to Epiphanes by the chronicler of I Maccabees.) With their country now under the "protection" of Rome, the royal siblings began a troubled tripartite rule. The Roman Senate nodded appreciatively; it had halted Seleucid pretensions without being dragged into a war.

It now behooved Epiphanes to guarantee the unqualified loyalty of Palestine as a buffer state to Rome's client-kingdom—a buffer state whose most viable component province, Judaea, had become too fractious. Had the Judaeans accepted only minimal cultural Hellenism (language, dress, and so forth) and remained a tribute-paying temple-state, such fractiousness could well have been obviated. While it is true that the very concept of theocracy is odious, it had "worked" for the Palestinian Jews, it had been accepted by the people. As had the Ptolemies, and his own immediate Seleucid ancestors, Antiochus Epiphanes would not have interfered with Judaea's internal affairs so long as they remained docile to his authority. But the Jewish hierarchs had opted for political Hellenism, and in so doing had divided the nation. Popular objection to this polity was rampant, and in the emperor's thinking, the only way the turbulence could be reduced was to complete the job begun by the Hellenizers; if their religion were extirpated, reasoned Epiphanes illogically, the traditionalists would have no "excuse" to resist the Hellenizers upon whose support he knew he could depend.

It was then that the Temple was desecrated and the New Order proclaimed: Judaism was proscribed in the Jewish province, and all were obliged to "convert" to the Greek religion and traditions on pain of death. It was, as time and events were to prove, a sad miscalculation on Epiphanes's part. The majority of the people had been content, if not to embrace then certainly to accept the gradual Hellenization of their nation; in addition to adopting Greek names, the Greek language, and Greek dress, many males had gone to the extreme of having themselves "uncircumcised," as the Greeks found mutilated penises aesthetically offensive. But now, with their religion proscribed, their loathing of the Seleucids knew no bounds. And the Jerusalem hierarchs, who had been able to foster Hellenism by pointing to political concessions to be won through accommodation with their overlords, were looked upon as collaborationists and ousted from public favor (though not from public office).

But there seemed little the masses could do short of submitting in light of the dire consequences which might result from open objection: the Hellenizers controlled the nation's purse strings, and were in a position to bring in hired mercenaries, if necessary, to keep the peace. For those who could not in all good conscience submit, the only answer was flight. Many headed for refuge in the mountains and desert—there to pray that the Lord would come to their rescue. Still others went farther afield, swelling the numbers in the Jewish communities of the Diaspora. For those who neither fled nor sided with the Hellenizers, there seemed little choice but to accept their fate with the pernicious passivity that can infect a people browbeaten by foreign oppressors down through the centuries.

There was, however, at least one Jew who, as I Maccabees so succinctly informs us (2:62), did not "fear a wicked man's words"—an egregious understatement, as events were soon to demonstrate. . . .

6 Mattathias— The Beginning

In addition to ordering the profanation of the Temple, Antiochus Epiphanes decreed that all shrines throughout Judaea were to be renovated in like manner: idols were to be installed at the altars upon which swine would be offered in sacrifice. (That these shrines existed when the Judaeans were near the Temple, to which they enjoyed free access, would suggest they were actually synagogues; but this is doubtful, as worship had not yet become so decentralized among the Palestinian Jews. What is more probable is that the suburban communities had become disenchanted with the Jerusalem priesthood.) When a Syrian delegation arrived at the frontier village of Modin, about seventeen miles northwest of the capital city, the first step toward revolt was taken by one Mattathias, "a priest of the Joarib family from Jerusalem, who had settled at Modin" (I Macc. 2:1).[1]

As religious leader of the community, Mattathias was asked by the Syrian commander to set the example by being the first to make the heathen offering. The aging priest was promised that were he to do so, he and his sons would be rewarded with the honorific "Friends of the King." Mattathias was not looking for such friendship. He had heard of the tragedy at Jerusalem and had told his people that dying in defense of their religion was infinitely preferable to being forced to live without it; he appears to have been motivated by a sincere religiosity, and should not be condemned for the actions of his descendants.

Instead of making the required sacrifice, Mattathias made an impromptu speech, the conclusion of which was that "I and my sons and brothers [here alluding to all Israelites] will follow the covenant of our fathers. Heaven forbid we should ever abandon the law and its statutes. We will not obey the command of the king, nor will we deviate one step from our forms of worship" (I Macc. 2:20–22; it is interesting to note that Mattathias is not mentioned in the II Maccabees account).

At that point one of the villagers, a squealing piglet under his arm, stepped forward to make the sacrifice. Then the infuriated Mattathias and his sons fell upon the Syrians, slaying, in addition to their commander and the unnamed apostate, some enemy mercenaries and other apostates among the villagers who were slow in getting out of range. He then overthrew the obscene altar and cried out for all those who were faithful to the Mosaic Law to follow him. Whereupon he literally "took to the hills" (I Macc. 2:28)—the foothills north of Jerusalem—with his five sons: Caddis, Thassi, Judas, Avaran, and Apphus, to give them their Greek names, or as they are better known to history, and henceforth in this narrative: John, Simon, Judah ("the Maccabee"), Eleazar, and Jonathan—all of whom were to die violently (and in the case of Eleazar, most extraordinarily). A number of villagers followed Mattathias and his sons.

Thus began the revolt of the Maccabees and the gestation of the Hasmonaean Dynasty.

When Appollonius learned of the incident at Modin, he ordered his constabulary to track down the miscreants—and to attempt to reason with them. To Apollonius it was all simply a Judaic tempest in a Syrian teapot. He had no desire to compound matters by starting a wholesale slaughter. Most of the Jerusalemites who had not fled had accepted, albeit quite unwillingly, the Epiphanean Edict; and Apollonius had been charged by his monarch with preventing an insurrection, not starting one.

I Maccabees (2:32 ff.) tells of one group of refugees who were overtaken—on the Sabbath—by a Syrian force whose commander, following orders that bloodshed was to be avoided at all costs, tried to get them to "repent." Standing outside the cave where the zealots, numbering a thousand and including women and children, had taken refuge in the Judaean wilderness, he guaranteed that if they came out and obeyed the king's commands their lives would be spared. To this the Jews replied from the innermost recesses of the cave: "We will not come out; we will not obey the king's commands or profane this sabbath." The Syrians then attacked, "but the Israelites did nothing in reply; they neither hurled stones, nor barricaded the caves. 'Let us all meet death with a clear conscience,' they said."

They did.

On hearing of the massacre, Mattathias gathered about him his small band of followers and delivered a major pronouncement: henceforth, all Jews would fight on Saturdays—if attacked. Such a flagrant abrogation of the Mosaic Law was not well received by the highly orthodox (who, like fundamentalists of all faiths, hewed to a line that precluded acceptance of anything rational as well as logical). The abrogation came from a truly religious man who was fighting their battle as well as his own; yet it was a forecast of the antagonism to which the Maccabees were to be subjected by the more pious among their followers.

The zealous priest and his band "then swept through the country, pulling down pagan altars." In addition to altars, they were also, in a manner of speaking, pulling down trousers for they forcibly circumcised "all the uncircumcised boys found within the frontiers of Israel" (I Macc. 2:45–47)—that is, sons of Hellenizers who had abandoned this most basic of Hebrew traditions. Also subjected to attacks in this vein by Mattathias were those adult Jews who had "uncircumcised themselves" in order to avoid being embarrassed in the eyes of their Hellenized companions. (Sources fail to enlighten as to how the already circumcised managed to conform with Grecian aesthetic sensibilities.)[2]

The revolt attracted little concern on the part of the Jerusalem authorities since the rebels confined their activities to the outlying areas and their ranks were insignificant in number. Also, they received little support even in the suburban villages: those who were sympathetic with their aims were also fearful of retaliation by the Syrians as well as the Hellenizers within their midst. At the outset, Mattathias's efforts represented little more than a minor guerrilla insurrection destined for an early extinction. It was only when the Hasidaeans came over to their side that the movement gained numerical strength and, of greater import, a religious cachet.

The Hasidaeans ("pious ones") were a loosely knit group of orthodox laymen who had first opposed the Hellenized priesthood during the reign of Onias III. They were soon to emerge as the most potent—and for the Maccabees, the most frustrating—of the major sects in postexilic Judaism. Included in their number, and probably the most cohesive as a group, were the Scribes (Heb., *sopherim*), that class of religious teachers who dominated Jewish theological thought during the Intertestamental period. Originally mere transcribers of Holy Scripture, their familiarity with the Law enabled them to become the arbiters of religious legality. It was the Babylonian Exile that provided the greatest impetus for their development as a class: with the Temple in ruins and the ritual suspended during the Exile, the Law became virtually the sole bond, other than their common heritage, that linked the deported Israelites. Since responsibility for reproducing accurate copies of the Law and for interpreting abstruse or conflicting points of that Law devolved upon these Scribes, they tended to form a class that assumed many of the prerogatives of the temporarily eclipsed Temple priesthood.

When the Exile ended and worship was resumed in the reconstructed Second Temple, the Jewish religion became divided: the Levitical priesthood, still the official arbiters of Judaism, were concerned with ritual requirements; the Scribes, on the other hand, interpreted the requirements of the Law as it affected the day-to-day lives of the people. The fact that the priests allied themselves with the elitist aristocrats, whereas the Scribes assiduously resisted succumbing to Hellenism, earned the Scribes the greatest influence with the common people, thus furthering the schism between the classes. But this was a social factor, and the Scribes were more concerned with the influence they might exert in the religious sphere. Realizing the increased stress placed upon the Law, and the vital importance of avoiding the violation of any of its tenets however inadvertently, they constructed around the Law a fence of sorts, a myriad of lesser restrictions that came to be regarded as equally binding with the Law itself.[3]

By the time of the Seleucid period, the Levitical priesthood had come to represent an old and already outmoded form of Judaism organized around the concept of Israel as a political entity focused on a physical center of worship, the Temple; in effect, a turning back to the premonarchy concept of national organization. The Scribes, on the other hand, freed Judaism from reliance on a particular political institution, forming instead a community of worshippers bound together primarily by their observance of the Law. They saw it as their ancillary goal, in a statement ascribed to the aforementioned Simon the Just, to "train many scholars." While the enthusiasm that had accompanied the completion of the Second Temple undoubtedly lessened the influence of the Scribes as a class, this was only temporary. The postexilic religious reforms of Ezra,[4] commingled with the corruption and outdatedness within the priesthood, served to recast the Israelites into a religious community organized around the Law (which Ezra had made accessible to all people; hitherto it had been accessible only to the priests).*

As the Maccabees began to enjoy some measure of success against the Epiphanean program, the Hasidaeans—considering

* It was only at the outbreak of the Maccabee wars that the Scribes—predecessors of the rabbis who were to form the patriarchate of Jewry following the collapse of the nation in the Roman period—became identified with the Hasidaeans. This group in turn evolved into the Pharisees who, during the Hasmonaean period, stood in opposition to the Sadducees—the sect that evolved out of the Temple hierarchy to form a coalition of vested interests ("Oniads" and "Tobiads") in both the religious and commercial spheres.

the rebels to be fighting on the side of God—sought them out. They saw the revolt as purely a religious one (as did Mattathias, for that matter). As will be shown, once their religious freedom was secured, the Hasidaeans would return to their Torahs, disabusing themselves of any notions regarding involvement in the secular life of their nation. So imbued were they with religious fervor, they cared little about *who* was in political control of their land. Conversely, every time their religious freedom was threatened, they would be the first to offer their services to the Maccabees—only to abdicate from the nationalist cause when a religious "victory" had been secured, and, worse, making almost as much trouble for their former allies as did their mutual enemies, the Hellenizers and Syrians.

The Syrians were soon to realize how ill-advised Epiphanes had been in attempting to suppress a religion and a people that has always been—and will always be—unsuppressible. While the Syrians did not want to obliterate the Judaeans, they *did* want to obliterate the Maccabees. Ironically, they could easily have done so.

The numerical strength of the many Syrian armies pitted against the Maccabees, as reported in the canonical books, borders on the dismissible; the statistics are as inflated—and as ridiculous to accept—as the figures given out by the American government on enemy losses in the Vietnam War. This is not to imply that the Maccabees were not always outmanned and outweaponed. They were. And as if they did not have troubles enough with the Syrian adversaries before them, they were forced to contend with their apostate coreligionists, the Hellenizers, to the rear. But as was the case when the Israelis achieved independence in 1948 despite the overwhelming Arab forces thrown against them; as was the case, when, in 1967, those same numerically inferior Israelis thoroughly humiliated their Arab adversaries (and their Russian suppliers of war matériel); as was the case when Arab lunacy led to the "Yom Kippur War" late in

1973; and as will undoubtedly be the case should the Arabs again attempt to "push the Jews into the sea," the secret of the Maccabean successes—a quite open secret—was that they were literally fighting for their lives. Like the man who finds himself actually lifting a two-ton automobile that has pinned a loved one, when a numerically inferior people find themselves achieving what is ordinarily physically impossible, it is old-fashioned adrenaline that turns the tide.

But there are limits beyond which even adrenaline cannot carry a man, or a nation. Had the Syrians thrown the full weight of their military capability against the Maccabees in one overall concerted drive, the rebels would have been destroyed. Fortunately for the Maccabees, the Syrians were more preoccupied with trying to hold together a collapsing, unrealistic empire.

Judah Maccabee was often able to rouse his men with the theological argument that "With heaven it is all one, to save by many or by few" (I Macc. 3:18). But to take victory in battle as the index of divine favor would be rather illusory: in Palestine of the second century B.C., as in other lands in other centuries, "heaven" has usually been on the side of the nation fielding the strongest army. Or to translate it into contemporary terms: had the Allied Powers during World War II depended less on productivity and coordinated manpower than on divine grace, it is quite reasonable to assume that a number of theologians and dedicated deists would have quickly found themselves in the highly embarrassing posture of having to "explain" what charms Hitlerism may have held for the Lord.

After a few months of guerrilla fighting, altar razing, and wholesale circumcision in the Judaean hinterlands, Mattathias died (166 B.C.). Since the sources do not indicate otherwise, it is safe to conclude that he passed on either from old age or total exhaustion. The further prosecution of the seemingly unrealistic anti-Syrian revolt was left to his five sons and his approximately 5,000 followers.

7 Judah Maccabee— The Religious War

Leadership of the revolutionary band fell to Mattathias's third-born son, Judah, whose cognomen "Maccabee" (Gr., *Maccabaeus* from the Heb. *Hamahkabi,* possibly "hammerer" or "hammer-headed") made him the family's and the movement's eponym. I Maccabees describes Judah as "a lion in his exploits, like a lion's whelp roaring for prey" (3:4). Since this is the only description of him on record, it shall have to suffice; however, his prowess as a military chieftain bore out this rather fanciful encomium, as his intransigence gave justification to his nickname. No mention is made of his private life; he left no known heirs. We do not know when he (or his father and brothers, for that matter) was born, though the year and manner of his death have been recorded.

Initial Syrian dismissal of the movement as a futile exercise in guerrilla warfare limited in scale and doomed to an early extinction was shared by the Hellenizers in Jerusalem, with whom the revolutionaries had yet to come into contact. But when Judah went on to lead his band in a series of victories throughout the hinterlands, and word started drifting down into the capital city, the authorities at Antioch—encouraged in their thinking by the Hellenizers—deemed action was warranted.

Apollonius, now serving as Epiphanes's military commander in Samaria, was ordered to stop the insurrection before it got out of hand. With a detachment of Syrian troops whose ranks were augmented by a number of Samaritans only too eager to flatter their Seleucid overlords by fighting their coreligionists, Apollonius moved south. In the battle that ensued, he was killed and his forces routed—a victory which not only won the Maccabees more followers but which gave them much needed weaponry. The ancient Syrian soldiers, like their present-day counterparts, had developed to a fine art the practice of abandoning their military hardware whenever set to flight—which was often. After helping themselves to the enemy spoils (Judah "took the sword of Apollonius, and used it in his campaigns for the rest of his life"), the Maccabees retreated in order to prepare for what Judah must have instinctively realized would be a retaliatory attack from Antioch.

In order to understand fully the ability with which Judah Maccabee's men so often worsted the numerically superior and better-equipped Syrian armies sent against them, it is necessary to rid oneself of the assumption that the Jews of this period were unwarlike, given only to sedentary pursuits and the handling of money—a stereotype that developed during the Dark and Middle Ages when the Christian world barred the Hebrew people from, among other professions, that of bearing arms. The Jews of second-century B.C. Palestine were not known for their aptitudes in the areas of trade and finance; as Josephus was led to remark, in his moving defense (and exegesis) of his people, *Contra Apion* (I, 60): "We are not a commercial people."[1] While the main occupations of the Palestinian Jews were agriculture and stockbreeding, they were also in great demand as mercenary soldiers, as witness: the powerful Jewish garrison at Elephantine in Upper Egypt dating from the fifth century B.C.; the fact that the Ptolemies settled Jewish military allotment-holders throughout Palestine (as did Antiochus III in the Seleucid realm); and the fact that a number of Ptolemies, most notably Cleopatra II and Cleopatra III, had armies commanded by Jewish generals. If one were to accept that the Jews as a people have always been of the mold into which the Christian world cast them, one would be hard put to "understand" how the Israelis not only regained their ancestral homeland in 1948 in the face of incredible odds, but went on in short order to establish their tiny nation as the most politically, economically, socially, and, yes, *militarily* viable nation in western Asia. This is hardly to imply that all Jews are by nature bellicose. There are to be found proportionately within the "Jewish nation"—world Jewry—as many dedicated pacifists and abject cowards as are found within all nations of the world. We Jews have more in common with others who inhabit our planet than many, not excluding some of our own number, would care to accept.

The next Seleucid move was entrusted to Seron, commander of one of the Syrian home armies, who "said to himself, 'I will win a glorious reputation in the empire by making war on Judah and his followers, who defy the royal edict'" (I Macc. 3:14). Seron set out to win his glorious reputation at Beth-Horon ("place of caves"), a dozen miles northward of Jerusalem. There he was joined by a contingent of Hellenizers who had rushed from the capital city to help put down what they were now coming to regard as a threat to their hold on the emotions of the masses—a hold which was tenuous at best: though the Maccabees had yet to come near Jerusalem, word of their success over Apollonius had already penetrated the city's walls.

Judah may have been short on men and arms, a chronic problem, but he was rather long on locker-room oratory. When his followers demurred at taking on a superior force, Judah addressed them in rousing tones: "Many can easily be overpowered by a few. . . . Victory does not depend on numbers; strength comes from Heaven alone" (I Macc. 3:18–20). Whether the strength they needed truly came from Heaven or from the conviction they held in the righteousness of their cause is academic. The small band was able to launch a surprise attack, and the glorious reputation Seron had sought to win became a glorious rout. (As recent history has shown, Jews are better offensive than defensive fighters.)

Antiochus Epiphanes was furious when he heard these tidings.

He had been making plans preparatory to his eastern campaign against the Parthians, assuming Judaea safely under the control of the Hellenizers, only to learn that a rather moth-eaten band of religious zealots had scattered two of his powerful home armies. The king was about to postpone the Parthian campaign in order to deal personally with the Maccabees—until he realized that his treasury was deficient: tax payments had been held up due to insurrections in a number of the eastern satrapies. Without doubt, had Epiphanes led his large army into Judaea, that would have been the end of the Maccabees. But now, in light of his financial embarrassment, he deemed it wiser to head east immediately, there to bring the recalcitrant provinces to heel and thus renew the flow of tax monies into his depleted treasury.

Before leaving Antioch, he ordered Lysias, one of his closest lieutenants, to end the revolt in Judaea. Lysias was also named as regent at Antioch and guardian over the young heir-apparent. Too, Epiphanes allegedly transferred to Lysias "half the armed forces, together with the elephants, and told him all he wanted done . . . to the population of Judaea and Jerusalem." Also, if we are to believe the I Maccabees account (3:35–37), Lysias was commanded to "break and destroy the strength of Israel and those who were left in Jerusalem, to blot out all memory of them from the place," and "to settle foreigners in all their territory, and allot the land to settlers" from other portions of the Seleucid realm. (It is likely that so large an army—but hardly "half the armed forces"—was left to Lysias, not to be used exclusively against the Maccabees but to maintain imperial order throughout Coele-Syria.) After delivering his charge, Epiphanes took "the other half" of the Syrian army and set out from Antioch in 165 B.C. for Parthia—and oblivion.

In keeping with what had long been a penchant among the unknown chroniclers of the Old Testament to inflate the numbers of ancient Israel's numerous enemies, the writer of I Maccabees claims "forty thousand infantry and seven thousand cavalry" were sent to devastate Judaea. It is patently ridiculous to believe such a force would have been deployed: the Maccabees were not yet considered so formidable an enemy (less than a fifth of that number would have been sufficient); Syrian troops were needed to man garrisons throughout Syria proper and Phoenicia, plus the other western provinces; and the Syrians realized they could count on the Hellenizers at Jerusalem to give any assistance needed. Suffice it to say, a sizable force was sent against the Hammerer and his brethren.

Remaining behind at Antioch, Lysias ordered two detachments, commanded by the generals Nicanor and Gorgias, to march down the Philistia (Mediterranean) coast and enter Judaea from the more hospitable west. Judah Maccabee was thoroughly outmanned. His only hope for success lay in dividing the enemy army. But this classical stratagem was beyond his ability to effect. Fortunately—thanks either to divine will or Syrian stupidity—the substantial combined army of Gorgias and Nicanor divided itself!

The Syrians encamped at Emmaus,[2] west of the capital city, preparatory to their assault on Jerusalem. That night Gorgias, guided by some of the Hellenizers who had learned that the Maccabees were encamped just to the south, set out from Emmaus with 6,000 men to launch a surprise attack. When Gorgias reached the Maccabee camp, he found it deserted. He then searched in the hills, assuming the rebels had been forewarned and taken flight. In fact, it was Nicanor's detachment that had taken flight. For while Gorgias had been moving toward the Maccabee encampment, Judah and his band had taken a parallel route in the opposite direction—the two opposing forces may well have passed like ships in the night—and attacked at Emmaus. The following morning an advance patrol of Gorgias's contingent reached Emmaus and saw that Nicanor's army had hastily departed, the camp was afire, and the Jews were in command of the plain. They reported back to Gorgias, who was still in the hills looking for Maccabees. Gorgias took the word of his scouts, and left for the Philistia coast.

On learning of this latest Syrian debacle, Lysias decided to move south in order to ascertain personally what was required to put down the revolt. The biblical account would have us believe he marched an army of 65,000 into Idumaea where, at Bethsura south of Jerusalem, they were attacked by 10,000 Maccabees; and that after losing 5,000 men and seeing the remaining 60,000 flee into the hills, Lysias fled back to Antioch to collect an even larger force of mercenaries with which to return to Judaea. Responsible historians have concluded that the "army" Lysias led into Judaea was actually no more than a small reconnaissance force. Bethsura commanded an open approach to Jerusalem; from here he was in a better position to apprise the overall situation, to determine what was needed to end the insurrection. There is little doubt the Maccabees scored a victory, and over a superior force (as there is much doubt that the Maccabee forces numbered anything near 10,000). But Lysias's return to Antioch came *after* he had arrived at a diplomatic solution to the "Jewish problem."

Such a solution made much more sense to Lysias than a military one. Antiochus Epiphanes was committed with the bulk of the Syrian army in the eastern provinces. The regent hoped to pacify Syria's southern flank—and preclude the necessity of committing large numbers of troops into the area that were needed elsewhere—by weaning away from the Maccabees many of the war-weary moderates among the Judaeans. Toward that end, he called for a truce; the two commanders met to arrive at an understanding. It was not within Lysias's power to abolish the Epiphanean proscriptions against the Jews but, realizing that his monarch had gone too far, he did promise to petition for an abrogation. Meanwhile, he proposed, if the Maccabees would lay down their arms, they would be permitted to take up residence in Jerusalem.

The Hellenizers were not ecstatic at having the rebels in the Holy City, but their apprehensions were allayed when Lysias reminded them that the Syrian garrison force in the Akra would keep the peace. For his part, Judah was not thrilled with the idea of the Hellenizers remaining in Jerusalem (or in Judaea, for that matter), but there was little he could do about that—for the present. And as for having to tolerate that Akra garrison—well, on the basis of subsequent actions, it is safe to assume he had planned a little countermove of his own.

As Lysias returned to Antioch, Judah led his rebels into Jerusalem—it was the fall of 164 B.C.—and immediately seized the city. In this he was helped by many of the more militant Hasidaeans, whose hatred for the Hellenizers was now a matter of public record—and who thought that Judah Maccabee was only intent on restoring religious freedom. Unable to seize the Akra, to which the Hellenizers had fled in panic, the Hammerer did the next best thing under the circumstances: he put it under siege. Lysias in the meantime arrived back at Antioch satisfied that the revolt had been ended, unaware that the edicts which he could not nullify were rapidly being nullified by Judah Maccabee.

The Mosaic Law was reestablished as the law of the land, and the Council of Elders was purged of the Hellenizers. As for the priesthood, the Hammerer managed to find enough anti-Hellenist candidates to fill its ranks. (Josephus claims Judah grabbed outright the all-powerful office of High Priest, but he stands alone in making such a claim; it is logical to assume Judah would not have thus antagonized the Hasidaeans and the conservative priests.) But these changes came about after he had attended to the most important business at hand: purifying and rededicating the Temple.

Single-handedly (if the biblical account is to be considered accurate), Judah razed the altar which had been profaned by offerings to the Zeus Olympios, overthrew the pagan idol, and cleansed the entire area of the stains of roasted pork and the debris of countless orgies; then he erected a new altar made of rough stones, a harking back to the first of the many altars raised by the patriarch Abraham after finding God in the barren stretches of western Palestine. With all signs of pagan worship obliterated and the sanctuary and interior cleansed and purified, Judah commanded that new accouterments, including sanctified holy vessels, as prescribed by the Law, be set up in their proper places. After which, on the twenty-fifth day of Kislev (December), 164 B.C.—three years to the day after Antiochus Epiphanes had completed its desecration—the purified Temple "was rededicated, with hymns of thanksgiving, to the music of harps and lutes and cymbals. All the people prostrated themselves, worshipping and praising Heaven that their cause had prospered. They celebrated the rededication of the altar for eight days; there was great rejoicing as they brought burnt-offerings and sacrificed peace-offerings and thank-offerings. They decorated the front of the temple with golden wreaths and ornamental shields. They renewed the gates and the priests' rooms, and fitted them with doors. There was great merry-making among the people" (I Macc. 4:54–58). The occasion is celebrated to this day by world Jewry as *Hannukah*, the Festival of Dedication, also known as the Festival of Lights.[3]

After eight days of hymns of thanksgiving, prostrating, worshipping, praising, celebrating, and offerings of sacrifices, the Hasidaeans redirected their attention to their collective Torah, while Judah Maccabee turned to more earthbound considerations. Specifically, he "encircled Mount Zion with high walls and strong towers to prevent the Gentiles from coming and trampling it down as they had done before" (I Macc. 4:60). He thus commanded that a nationalist fortress be built in the vicinity of the Temple Mount—close enough to protect the Temple, but not so close as to antagonize the conservatives.

Judah Maccabee's subsequent activities, which are so often overlooked in the recounting of his accomplishments, more than suggest he may well have made the decision at that time to transform the fight for religious freedom into a struggle for political independence from Antioch; were this indeed his intent, then surely he must have realized he was treading on thin ice. The

Hasidaeans, having gotten what they wanted, had returned to the exclusive pursuit of their monotheism, thus not only reducing his ranks but, of more consequence, stripping the movement of its religious justification; worse, they had exploited the hold they maintained over the masses to discourage further popular support for the nationalist cause. And while he had managed to shunt aside Menelaus and the Hellenizers (who were hiding in the besieged Akra), Judah must surely have realized that if he went beyond his agreement with Lysias to the point of active aggression outside Judaea, much less in Jerusalem itself, he would be issuing what was tantamount to an open invitation for the Syrians to return en masse.

The Apocrypha claims that "when the Gentiles [here read Syrians] round about heard that the altar had been rebuilt and the temple rededicated, they were furious, and determined to wipe out all those of the race of Jacob [that is, the Jews] who lived among them. Thus began the work of massacre and extermination among the people" (I Macc. 5:1–12). Here again an historically supportable demur must be entered: it was not the rebuilding of the Temple that had infuriated the "Gentiles," but the campaigns upon which Judah now launched his Maccabee band; "the work of massacre and extermination among the people" was begun, not by the Syrians but by Judah Maccabee himself.

North, south, east, west—Judah struck in all directions. Brother Simon was sent north into the Galilee region to "break the resistance of the Gentiles" and to bring back to Judaea "the Jews . . . their wives and children, and all their property." Meanwhile, with brother Jonathan, Judah crossed east into the Transjordan where he raised hell among the Arabs, putting "all males to the sword" and plundering "all their property." Then he "marched out with his brothers and made war on the descendants of Esau to the south" (that is, the Idumaeans), and followed up this campaign by rushing west to Philistia where he "pulled down their altars, burnt the images of their gods, carried off the spoil from their towns." The Maccabees "won a great reputation in all Israel and among the Gentiles, wherever their fame was heard, and crowds flocked to acclaim them" (I Macc. 5:3–68).

If, as the apocryphal account would have us believe, Judah undertook these campaigns in order to help his fellow Jews scattered in small communities throughout Palestine, he would have helped them better by staying home. To quote from F. E. Peters: "Judah and the Maccabee faction were now in control of the seat of power in Judaea, and the fighting took on a new savagery on both sides. The Syrian communities outside his immediate reach—which was growing longer—took reprisals against the Jews who dwelled in them, while Judah for his part struck across the land murdering non-Jews and putting the temples of the Greek and Syrian gods to the torch. . . . What had begun as an insurrection had become a veritable jihad."

Far from setting himself the task of winning complete political independence for his nation, the Hammerer was now out to Judaize all of Palestine!

Judah's activities were probably no secret to Lysias. But the regent was having problems of his own.

Antiochus Epiphanes had died, as had his father, the Great One, while plundering a pagan temple in Elam.[4] It seemed that prior to his death, he had allegedly named his good friend Philip, a Phrygian, to be regent over the young heir who was in Antioch with Lysias. (There is always the possibility that his having been named regent was a manufactured claim on the part of Philip, who was now in command of the dead emperor's powerful field army and thus had the wherewithal to back up such a claim.)

While awaiting Philip's move, Lysias was visited by a deputation of hysterical Hellenizers. Judah Maccabee had tightened the siege on the Akra, hoping to starve out the Syrian troops as well as the Hellenizers who had taken refuge there. During the siege, a number of these had managed to escape and make their way to Antioch, where they now implored Lysias to come to their aid.

The last thing Lysias needed was a strong army antagonistic to him on his southern flank, especially in light of his anticipated showdown with Philip over the regency; there was always the possibility that Philip would make concessions to the Maccabees, thus putting Lysias in the position of having to fight a war on two fronts. The Hellenizers promised that if Lysias were to put down the Maccabees once and for all, there would be no further problems in Judaea. Lysias moved south.

The biblical claim that his army numbered 120,000 can be dismissed as a fanciful exaggeration, unless his infantry and cavalry were augmented by camp followers, merchants, mendicants, and wizards—which is extremely doubtful: Lysias was a military chieftain, not the manager of a traveling carnival. Nevertheless his forces were considerable for he was able to invest the vital fortress of Bethsura overlooking Jerusalem and then move on to the capital city. Judah Maccabee led his band to meet the enemy, but was forced to fall back to Jerusalem, where his position became quite untenable. Not only did he have a veritable fifth-column of Hellenizers behind him, augmented by the Syrian garrison troops who had broken out of the Akra when Judah called off the siege to meet the oncoming enemy—he also had to contend with the Hasidaeans who, in concert with the conservative priests, made it palpably clear that there would be no fighting whatsoever within the Holy City. The Maccabees moved out to Beth-Zechariah, a mountain village south of the city, there to regroup their forces and prepare for what appeared to be an imminent fight to the death.

For one of the Maccabee brothers it was indeed just that. It was at Beth-Zechariah that the first of the five sons of Mattathias was to pay the supreme penalty. Traveling with Lysias, presumably to learn the "art" of putting down anti-Seleucid insurrections—and certainly as physical evidence that Lysias still considered himself the regent, notwithstanding Philip's questionable selection—was the nine-year-old heir-apparent. It was this royal apprentice who was inadvertently responsible for the death of Judah Maccabee's younger brother, Eleazar—the only human in recorded history to be killed by a dead elephant!

As it is so eloquently chronicled in I Maccabees (here in the unmatchable prose of the King James Version): "Perceiving that one of the beasts, armed with the royal harness, was higher than all the rest, and supposing that the [heir] was upon him," Eleazar immediately "ran upon [the elephant] in the midst of the battle," and after scattering the enemy forces "so that they were divided from him on both sides . . . he crept under the elephant and thrust him under [with a sword] and slew him: whereupon the elephant fell down upon him, and there he died" (6:43–46). With what may be specious justification for Eleazar's extraordinary escapade, some apologists have theorized that the beast had somehow become disoriented while trundling round the busy battlefield in quest of its young royal master—who had, to be sure, been removed to the sidelines for his own imperial safety—which would indicate that perhaps Eleazar was justified in "perceiving" as he did.

Tragic to report, while Eleazar's sacrifice was a noble one, it was also futile: the Maccabees, thoroughly routed, were forced to retreat as best they could to Jerusalem, with Lysias and the Syrian army in hot pursuit.

The Maccabees managed to make their way to the fortress they had only recently constructed atop Mount Zion. This Lysias immediately put under siege. Though the defenders held out bravely against the enemy siege-engines, they were doomed. Militating against them—in addition to a strong Syrian army, the Hellenizers who were all for a Seleucid victory, and the Hasidaeans who did not care who won just so long as the Temple Mount was spared this indignity—was their own Mosaic tradition. For as luck and the calendar would have it, this was the year following the septennial Festival of the Sabbatical Year;

according to the Law, the one year in seven during which the Jews were specifically enjoined from harvesting crops. Worse, the city was cluttered with refugees from outlying communities fleeing persecutions by their Gentile neighbors in retaliation for those previous Maccabee raids. Also, many of Judah's staunchest followers—for the most part, those Jews who had been brought back to Jerusalem from Galilee and Samaria during earlier raids—had fled the city. It was only a matter of time before the sadly depleted nationalists would either be starved into submission or killed to a man.

A miracle was wanted.

A miracle was granted.

The "miracle" came in the form of a runner from Antioch who arrived with tidings of extreme urgency for Lysias: Philip had returned from the East with Epiphanes's army and had entered the Seleucid capital, thereby challenging Lysias for the regency. Lysias had no choice but to return home with the crown prince and their army as rapidly as their elephants could carry them.

This marked the first time—but certainly not the last—when a victorious Syrian commander found himself in the curious, and humiliating, position of having to announce to an all but defunct nationalist movement's leader in Judaea that *he* was suing for peace!

Lysias's terms: Judaism was to be allowed to continue unmolested; with Epiphanes dead, Lysias felt empowered to rescind the proscription (a rather gratuitous move, since Judah Maccabee had already taken that step). An amnesty would be granted the Maccabee brothers and their followers. And to pour Seleucid oil on troubled Judaean waters, the hated (and illegitimate) Menelaus would be removed as High Priest. (He was carted back to Antioch and beheaded—less out of concern for Hasidaean sensibilities than because of his failure to Hellenize the nation more securely and for having gotten Lysias into this hellish mess in the first place.) Lysias thus preempted any cause for the continuance of a rebellion for religious freedom. That freedom was now being handed to the Judaeans on a Seleucid salver.

In return for these concessions, Lysias demanded a few of his own. A pro-Hellenist High Priest was to be installed. Though the candidate, Alcimus, had been one of the leading apostates in the Jerusalem priesthood, his selection was acceptable to the Hasidaeans because his genealogical credentials were impeccable. For his part, Alcimus vowed not to interfere with orthodox rites in the Temple, nor would he or his followers attempt to proselytize on behalf of Zeus and the other Olympians (this was more to appease the conservatives than the Maccabees). Judah also agreed to Lysias's demand that the nationalist fortress on Mount Zion be dismantled (he could always build another), and to the continuance of a Syrian garrison force in the Akra (which he could always put under siege again, if necessary). Hands were shaken all around, and Lysias and the crown prince departed with their army for Antioch and the showdown with Philip and *his* army.

As has been indicated, it was never Seleucid policy to interfere with local religions: Epiphanes's edicts, his motivation notwithstanding, were the exceptions that proved the rule. That Lysias had been magnanimous only because it was to his advantage cannot be denied; but Judah Maccabee's presumed assumption that once the dynastic situation at Antioch was resolved the Syrians would return to destroy Judaism is extremely doubtful. A defense of Judah's thesis that religious freedom under the Seleucids could never be secure until political freedom as well had been achieved could be submitted, but such a defense would be highly speculative at best. Judaea's importance in the Syrian scheme of things was geographical, rather than cultural. Antioch wanted a tranquil nation on its southern flank, not a contentious one. So long as that nation was loyal, the manner in which and to what or whom a segment of the populace prayed was to the Syrians a matter of supreme indifference. Antioch already had the loyalty of the Jerusalem Establishment; and this Establishment—the Hellenized aristocrats and priests—obviously had no intention of suppressing the Hasidaeans or the few remaining conservative priests. There was no need to. The Hellenizers had what they wanted: economic, social, and political control of the nation. The Hasidaeans had what they wanted: religious freedom. The conservative priests had what they wanted: permission to continue roasting cattle and collecting *t'rumahs*.

Whether the sanctimoniousness that permeated the Maccabee movement began with Judah or was waiting to bloom through the actions of his brothers Jonathan and Simon and the latter's descendants is undeterminable: a good argument can be advanced to support either attitude. The purpose here is not to derogate Judah Maccabee's motivation and heroism so much as to put them into proper perspective. Notwithstanding the willingness of the Hellenizers, the Hasidaeans, and the war-weary Judaean populace, as well as the Syrians themselves, to settle for the status quo ante, and despite the fact that his party had been severely depleted in manpower as well as justification, Judah Maccabee, on the basis of evidence at hand, seems to have suspected that perhaps the time could not be more fortuitous to pursue the somewhat fanciful goal of complete independence from Antioch.

The Syrians were involved in a monumental dynastic convulsion.

It would prove to be but the first of many. . . .

8 Judah Maccabee— The Political War

Lysias had no difficulty in disposing of Philip and winning over the loyalty of the army or in placing on the throne the young heir as Antiochus V Eupator (the name means "of a good father," but in light of his tragic fate, "transitory" might be deemed a more appropriate cognomen). Shortly thereafter, young Eupator's cousin, the twenty-five-year-old Demetrius, arrived at Antioch to claim the throne. That's when Lysias's difficulties began.

From this point on until the empire's self-inflicted demise, the history of Syria under the Seleucids is one of hotly contested infighting between the "Antiochan" and "Demetrian" factions for the throne—the former representing the junior line, the latter the senior line in direct descent from Antiochus the Great. Every time the Jewish nationalists were on the verge of being defeated irrevocably on the battlefield by the Syrians, another chapter in the dynastic farce-tragedy would be played out: the Syrian armies and their mercenaries would be drawn off to fight each other, and the day would be saved for the Jews. Though, as we shall see, the Judaeans finally did achieve political independence, largely through the unintended offices of their Syrian overlords, it was an independence doomed to failure. From the long range of history, it is safe to conclude that the Palestinian Jews might well have met with better fortune had they decided that, instead of periodically going into battle with the Syrians, they should maintain a low profile while the Syrians went into battle with themselves.

It will be recalled that when Antiochus Epiphanes assumed the throne of his murdered brother the Roman Senate kept his nephew Demetrius from asserting his more legitimate claim. On learning of Lysias's assumption of the regency, Demetrius pleaded in vain with the Senate that he be allowed to return home. The Senate's refusal was based on its desire to maintain the instability of the Seleucid house. The Romans had no love for Lysias, who had made it evident that he was ruler of Syria in all but name; while undertaking a program of consolidation in order to secure his position, Lysias had inadvertently murdered a Roman envoy. But it was never Rome's practice to be dragged into wars not of its choosing. (Lysias managed to mitigate Senatorial displeasure by giving the slain envoy a grand funeral and sending a gift-laden embassy to the Senate.) Rome realized that Lysias was unpopular with his subjects, and preferred to let it go at that. Allowing Demetrius, whose return was now being openly demanded by the Antioch mobs, to assert his dynastic claim would hardly be consonant with Rome's desire to keep the fragmenting Seleucid Empire in a state of flux.

Demetrius did the next best thing under the circumstances. He escaped from Rome. Though political prisoners and hostages were carefully watched by the Romans, they were usually given the run of the city and were permitted a wide margin of liberty. Demetrius was aided in his escape by the Greek historian Polybius (himself a political prisoner), who had managed to cultivate the friendship of a number of Rome's influential citizens— including a Senator or two. Demetrius had spent more than half his life in Roman custody, and, as had his uncle Epiphanes, become thoroughly "Romanized." However, he had acquired a reputation as a playboy; the Senate had good reason to underestimate his abilities as a leader. Thus when his escape become known, the Senate was not too upset. Lysias still had the army behind him; all that Demetrius had was a dynastic claim. A struggle for power in Syria could probably create even more flux than the Senate had initially dared anticipate. (Indeed, were the reader to suspect that the Roman Senate as a body had covertly engineered the escape, he would probably not be too wide of the mark.)

Following Demetrius's arrival on the Phoenician coast, the Syrian army abandoned its loyalty to Lysias and, along with the Antioch populace, quickly rallied to his cause. (Lysias and young Eupator were put to death, probably on orders of Demetrius.) A strong Seleucid was now on the throne, giving slight concern to the Roman Senate. This concern was quickly mitigated when Timmarchus, satrap of Babylonia, declared independence from Syria and proclaimed himself Great King over the Babylonians and Medians. Demetrius wanted Rome to accept his kingship over the entire Seleucid Empire, while Timmarchus was eager to have Roman support for his own rather tenuous claim. The Senate was not yet willing to recognize Demetrius, who had quickly proved himself to be an able and enterprising young king; conversely, it did not want to commit itself to Timmarchus either, mainly because Timmarchus was to the Romans an unknown quantity. The best policy was to let the two fight it out between themselves—at the same time hoping that others among the Syrian satraps would raise the standard of revolt. Therefore the Senate gave Timmarchus verbal recognition, but told him not to expect any material assistance. The Syrian Empire was now split in two. Rome was delighted.

Meanwhile Judah Maccabee had been consolidating his position. He had simply pushed aside the High Priest, Alcimus—an act which served to antagonize not only the nation's elitists but the Hasidaeans as well. Shortly after Demetrius had enthroned himself at Antioch (161 B.C.), Alcimus led a deputation of Hellenizers north to pledge their allegiance to this latest Seleucid overlord—and, as Josephus recounts it, to complain that the Maccabees "had slain all his [the king's] friends and that those in his kingdom that were of his party . . . were by them put to death; that these men [the Maccabees] had ejected them [the

Hellenizers] out of their own country, and caused them to be sojourners in a foreign land" (*Ant.* XII. X. 1).

Demetrius ordered Bacchides, a lieutenant under Antiochus Epiphanes who had prudently transferred his loyalty to the new king, to escort Alcimus back to Jerusalem with a sizable military force and to reconfirm him as High Priest—if necessary, over the dead bodies of the nationalists. It was not the king's plan to interfere with the practice of Judaism, but rather to reestablish the Hellenizers and thus, hopefully, restore tranquillity in the Judaean province. But as a result of stupidity on Alcimus's part, commingled with Maccabean ambitions, civil war soon broke out.

Assuming that the Hellenizers were again in control and having propped up Alcimus by ordering the Syrian garrison in the Akra to help the apostate High Priest "keep the country in obedience," Bacchides felt free to return to Antioch to report the conclusion of a successful mission. The mission had also been a bloodless one: Judah Maccabee had wisely opted to lie low until Bacchides's departure.

No sooner had Bacchides left Jerusalem than Alcimus ordered the slaying of sixty of the Hasidaean leaders, assuming that this action would break the back of the growing conservative opposition to his Hellenizing ways. This tactical blunder made it easy for Judah to convince the Hasidaeans that their hopes for religious freedom lay only in political freedom. Alcimus then led the Akra garrison force and the more bellicose Hellenizers "all over the country, and slew all that he could find" of the nationalist party. The Hammerer retaliated in kind: "he also went all over the country, and destroyed those that were of the other's party" (*Ant.* XII. X. 3). As more and more of the Hasidaeans came over to the Maccabee cause (temporarily, to be sure), Alcimus found it necessary to scurry back to Antioch for assistance in putting down the bloodbath he had helped start.

Demetrius was preparing to move east to put down Timmarchus and thus force Rome to recognize his kingship over all of the empire as a *fait accompli*. Being "already of the opinion that it would be a thing pernicious to his own affairs to overlook" the growing power of the Maccabees, the emperor "sent against him Nicanor, the most kind and faithful of his friends [and] gave him as many forces as he thought sufficient" to put down the Jewish revolt (*Ant*. XII. X. 4).[1]

It will be recalled that Nicanor already had experience fighting the Maccabees: his was one of the two Syrian armies routed so embarrassingly during the early days of the insurrection. This time "he did not resolve to fight" if need be, "but judged it better to get [Judah] into his power by treachery" (*Ant*. XII. X. 4). On arriving at the outskirts of Jerusalem, he sent the Hammerer a message of peace, conceding that there was no necessity to resort to needless bloodshed, and could they not settle the entire problem amicably? Inexplicably, Judah and his brothers fell for the ruse, and with a small escort they came out of Jerusalem to parley with Nicanor. At a signal, the Syrians tried to seize the Maccabees, but they managed to escape. The infuriated Nicanor marched his troops to engage the nationalists where they had encamped near Capharsalama (a suburban Jerusalem village no longer extant), and with what must surely have struck contemporary observers with a feeling of *déjà vu*, the numerically superior Syrians were routed.

But this time the Syrians did not flee to the Philistia coast. Instead, they followed Nicanor to Jerusalem, where they were heartily welcomed by the Hellenizers—who obligingly closed the city gates before the pursuing Maccabees. Nicanor now decided to accomplish through psychological threat what he had failed to effect through military deed. Or so he hoped. From the safety of the reconstructed nationalist fortress atop Mount Zion which had come into the hands of the Hellenizers, Nicanor warned the conservatives that unless Judah Maccabee surrendered, bringing the promise that the independence party would dissolve itself, and remain dissolved, he would raze the Temple.

This turned out to be Nicanor's second mistake (his first was in coming into Jerusalem). Whereas he had reasoned that the Hasidaeans—by now a powerful force to be reckoned with, claiming the support of the majority of the people—would do anything to spare the Temple, even to capturing and delivering the man who had "cleansed" it of its Epiphanean pollutions, the Hasidaeans suspected, however unjustifiably, that the Syrians would destroy the Temple even if the Maccabees were captured. Also, reasoned the more bellicose Hasidaeans, here was a God-sent opportunity to rid the nation once and for all of the Hellenizers and to get Judaea out of politics and back into religion.

Unlike so many generals down through the ages who have littered the literary marketplace by peddling their *apologias* thinly disguised as autobiographies, Nicanor did not live long enough to put quill to scroll. Thus we shall never know what agency—short of egregious self-confidence—could possibly have induced him to withdraw to suburban Beth-Horon, there to pitch camp and await the priests' reply. True, ancient sources inform us that an auxiliary Syrian force had rushed down from Antioch. (Demetrius realized he had not "thought sufficient" the numbers needed by his "most kind and faithful of friends" to put down the Maccabees.) But why, instead of having that force come into the capital, did Nicanor go outside the city to join it? There is, of course, the acknowledged fact that the Hasidaeans, along with the conservative priests, drew the line at allowing any harm to come to the Temple, however inadvertently. But Nicanor still controlled the city, and with the help of the obliging Hellenizers would have kept out the Maccabees; the auxiliary task force could have engaged the rebels on the outside, and Nicanor could have attacked from the rear. In the event, as Nicanor was marching his large army out of Jerusalem, Judah Maccabee was sneaking his small army in!

Judah Maccabee now found himself in a rather indefensible position. He was outmanned by the Akra garrison and the Hellenizers; nor could he count on any assistance from most of the Hasidaeans, who assumed that the crisis had passed. Also, a number of his loyal followers were outside the city. While Nicanor was waiting at Beth-Horon for the response to his ultimatum, Judah and his small band secretly marched out of the city past the Akra garrison and the screaming Hellenizers, and marshaled their forces at Adasa (or Edasa), a small village near the enemy camp. Josephus claims the nationalists totaled a mere thousand men; I Maccabees triples this number. Be that as it may, the nationalists were hopelessly outnumbered. It was time for Judah to deliver another of his pep talks in which he concluded that Nicanor was to be judged "as his wickedness deserves."

The armies joined battle—and Nicanor was indeed judged as Judah had promised: he was the first to fall. "When his army saw [this] they threw away their arms and took to flight. The Jews, sounding the signal trumpets in the enemy's rear, pursued them as far as Gazara, a day's journey from Adasa. From all the villages of Judaea round about, the inhabitants came out and attacked their flanks, forcing them [the Syrians] back upon their pursuers. They all fell by the sword; there were no survivors [a bit of an exaggeration here]. The Jews seized spoil and booty; they cut off Nicanor's head and that right hand which he had stretched out so arrogantly, and brought them to be displayed at Jerusalem. There was great public rejoicing and that day was kept as a special day of jubilation. It was ordained that the day should be observed annually, on the thirteenth day of Adar" (I Macc. 7:43–50).[2] "After which," Josephus informs us, "the Jewish nation was, for a while, free from wars, and enjoyed peace." Josephus then goes on: "but afterwards they returned to their former state of wars and hazards" (*Ant.* XII. X. 5).

When the victorious Maccabees reentered the Holy City, the Hellenizers went underground and the Hasidaeans again climbed off the nationalist bandwagon. En masse. Their Temple remained standing in all its Solomonic splendor, but the Hellenizers had been stripped of their hold on the nation. Temporarily.

Concomitantly, more and more of the general populace now

allowed themselves to be convinced that the fever of nationalism was not the worst malady that could befall a people. Winning political independence from Syria seemed so *easy*.

Judah Maccabee was the man of the hour. That he was already moving in the direction of a totally independent Palestinian state, with himself as its temporal leader may be deduced from the fact that as Alcimus and his cohorts were sneaking out of Jerusalem and heading north to Antioch, an embassy from Judah Maccabee was scurrying west to Rome. . . .

Demetrius had, in the interim, defeated Timmarchus and regained the loyalty of the Babylonians and Medians (who acclaimed him as their savior, thus his cognomen "Soter"), and by the following summer (160 B.C.) the Roman Senate had little choice but to grant him formal recognition in his kingship. But with that recognition went increased ill will: Demetrius was getting too strong for the Romans, who were eager to keep Syria weak, if only to protect their investment in Egypt. The playboy had proved himself adept at kingship. Rome was not pleased. Judah Maccabee was aware of Rome's displeasure at the turn of events in Syria (when Rome was displeased, everyone in the civilized world was apprised of it). He hoped that an affinity between the Jews and Romans would suffice to keep Syria off Judaea's back.

After proffering suitable gifts, Judah's ambassadors informed the Roman Senate that "the Jewish people have sent us to you to conclude a treaty of friendship and alliance with you, so that we may be enrolled as your allies and friends"—and so that, though the message was by implication, Judah Maccabee would be recognized as Judaea's leader. Impressed with the apparent ability of the Jews to keep Demetrius busy on his southern flank (Rome always kept abreast of what was happening around the eastern Mediterranean), the Senate found the proposal eminently acceptable. The envoys were sent back to Jerusalem with a bronze tablet upon which was inscribed the terms of the treaty.

After calling for "Success to the Romans and the Jewish nation by sea and land for ever!" (the "by sea" was rather one-sided, since Judaea was landlocked), and expressing the hope that "sword and foe be far from them!" the Senate allowed that

> if a war breaks out, first against Rome or any of her allies throughout her dominion, then the Jewish nation shall support them wholeheartedly as occasion may require. To the enemies of Rome or of her allies, the Jews shall neither give nor supply provisions, arms, money, or ships; so Rome has decided; and they shall observe their commitments, without compensation. Similarly, if war breaks out first against the Jewish nation, then the Romans shall give them hearty support as occasion may require. To their enemies there shall be given neither provisions, arms, money, nor ships; so Rome has decided. These commitments shall be kept without breach of faith. These are the terms of the agreement which the Romans have made with the Jewish people.

The Senate also informed Judah that it had dispatched a letter to Demetrius demanding to know "Why have you oppressed our friends and allies the Jews so harshly?" and going on to warn the Syrian that "if they make any further complaint against you, then we will see that justice is done them, and will make war upon you by sea and by land" (I Macc. 8:20–32).

The treaty between Rome and Jerusalem was, like so many treaties the Senate entered into with powers who were the enemy of their enemy, all shadow and no substance. Rome certainly had no intention of being dragged into an Asian war—yet. And Demetrius, sitting securely on his throne, knew this full well, as he knew that Rome's threatening letter was less a statement of intent than an outrageous (and somewhat amateurish) bluff. Therefore when Alcimus arrived at Antioch with the latest news from the southern front, the king felt in secure enough a position to ignore the Roman threat. Bacchides was sent back into Judaea with 22,000 picked troops to finish off the job of which Nicanor had made such an unmitigated mess.

With orders to destroy the nationalist movement for all time, to reestablish Alcimus as High Priest, and to assure the docility of Judaea as a loyal province by handing it back to the Hellenizers, Bacchides marched his troops south along the Gilgal road, laid siege to Messaloth west of the Sea of Galilee and, after capturing this vital Maccabee outpost and inflicting heavy losses, moved on toward Jerusalem. Again not wishing to antagonize the Hasidaeans by allowing the battle to be fought within the Holy City, Judah led his band of about 3,000 out of Jerusalem and prepared to meet the Syrians at Elasa.

When the Maccabees saw the size of the enemy army before them, they were dismayed. As in previous campaigns, Judah tried to encourage them through persuasive argument. But this time his oratory failed him, and many deserted. The mere 800 who remained loyal tried to dissuade Judah in his zeal, arguing that it might be best to retreat back to Jerusalem or into the hills. To this Judah replied in indignation: "Heaven forbid that I should do such a thing as run away! If our time is come, let us die bravely for our fellow-countrymen" (I Macc. 9:10).

Judah was as good as his word. He died bravely for his fellow-countrymen.

Bacchides had divided his cavalry into two detachments, with the slingers and archers ahead of the main force. The Syrian phalanx came toward the nationalists in two divisions, and the battle was joined. When Judah realized, toward evening, that Bacchides and the main strength of the Syrian force were on the right flank, he led his small band in a suicidal charge that broke the flank. As the Syrians fled, the Maccabees followed in hot pursuit. Unfortunately, the Syrians on the left flank, apprised of the fate that had befallen their comrades, turned and followed on the heels of the Maccabees, attacking them in the rear. The pursued right flank, now regaining courage, made a *volte-face*, and the Maccabees were caught in a pincer. Judah fell, and his remaining followers dispersed quickly in all directions.

After entering Jerusalem amid the applause of the Hellenizers, Bacchides announced that the orthodox would be permitted to practice their religion unmolested. However, he insisted that Alcimus be recognized as High Priest. To this the sacerdotal conservatives brooked little objection: Alcimus might be a horror, but he was a horror with an authentic pedigree. As for the Hasidaeans, they simply washed their hands of the priesthood, cast their collective pox on everyone's house, and told the masses to resume study of the Law and worship of the One God. Bacchides now felt confident enough to send his victory message to Demetrius: Judaea was at last completely Hellenized. The independence movement had died with Judah Maccabee.

A strong sense of relief settled over the area. The status quo ante was an incontrovertible reality; this foolhardy notion of political independence was done with, once and for all; Judaism was no longer proscribed; that was all that really mattered. There would be no more warfare. Judah Maccabee was dead and buried.

But his younger brother, Jonathan, was still very much alive. . . .

9   Jonathan— High Priest

Jonathan—youngest of the five sons of Mattathias—had an extraordinary faculty for exploiting dissensions among his enemies; and, God knows, he had plenty to exploit. Our sources do not indicate why he, youngest of the three surviving Maccabee brothers,* succeeded Judah as leader of the insurgents, though it can be presumed he had shown prowess while fighting at the side of his adored and much lamented brother. From all accounts Jonathan did not seek leadership of the independence movement. There was no movement to lead.

After reinstating Alcimus and placating the nation as a whole, Bacchides established himself temporarily at Jerusalem in order to oversee the complete garrisoning of Judaea and to kill off every last Maccabee sympathizer. In this latter endeavor he was aided by the Hellenizers who, Josephus relates, "caught the friends of [Judah] and those of the [independence] party, and delivered them up to Bacchides, who when he had, in the first place, tortured and tormented them at his pleasure, he, by that means, at length killed them" (*Ant.* XIII. I. 1). But there still remained a few—in hiding, and away from Jerusalem—who, nurturing the idea of independence, sought out Jonathan and begged him to revive the movement: "Since your brother . . . died, there has not been a man like him to take the lead against our enemies, Bacchides, and those of our own nation who are

* The eldest Maccabee son, the unbellicose John, was murdered by Arab brigands while leading the band's herds into the Transjordan for safekeeping, an act which Jonathan subsequently avenged.

hostile to us" (I Macc. 9:29). Jonathan allowed "that he was ready to die for them" (*Ant.* XIII. I. 1). The rabid nationalists took him at his word. Then, realizing that their best move would be to put as wide a berth as possible between themselves and the Syrian-supported hierarchs at Jerusalem, Jonathan led his band into the wilderness—probably the marshy areas along the west bank of the Jordan River, though sources are unclear on this point.

When Bacchides learned from some anxious Hellenizers that a small group of revolutionaries was coalescing around Jonathan, he set out with a task force to eradicate them. Catching up with the Maccabees in the Jordan marshes, he waited until the Sabbath to attack, assuming, as had so many of his predecessors, that the Jews would not defend themselves on that holy day. Apparently Bacchides had not been advised that the Maccabees had long since contravened that particular (and peculiar) piece of Mosaic legislation. When the Syrians struck, Jonathan and his band were waiting; after a fierce fight in which two thousand Syrians are believed to have perished, Jonathan led his band into the river for a fast swim to the eastern bank and into the Transjordan. (There is no account of the Maccabee losses, which must have been negligible, as their entire force was itself negligible.) Bacchides chose not to pursue, assuming they had fled Judaea for good. Instead, he returned to Jerusalem "and fortified with high walls, gates, and bars a number of places in Judaea," including the vital fortresses of Jericho, Emmaus, Beth-Horon, and Bethel, in all of which "he placed garrisons to harass Israel." He also "took the sons of the leading men of the country as hostages and put them under guard" in the Akra (I Macc. 9:50–53). These "leading men" were probably sympathizers with the Maccabee cause who had been betrayed by the Hellenizers.

Shortly thereafter, in the following spring (159 B.C.), Alcimus decided to "renovate" the Temple along more Hellenistic lines. The traditional-minded priests made violent protests to Bacchides. Not wishing to antagonize the Hellenizers, Bacchides told the plaintiffs it was not within his power to stop the apostate High Priest, who went on to commit the ultimate horror: breaking down the wall that separated the outer court from the sacrosanct inner court, the Holy of Holies. The frantic conservatives prayed to the Lord, and this time He was listening: "at the moment when he began demolition, Alcimus had a stroke which put a stop to his activities. Paralyzed and with his speech imperfect, he could not utter a word or give final instructions" (I Macc. 9:55–56). The stroke, which soon proved fatal, was looked upon by the faithful as an act of Divine Retribution.

But with Divine Retribution came Divine Confusion. The Jewish nation now found itself in the rather curious position of being without a legitimate High Priest. Apparently the Aaronic line had finally died out. The Hellenizers among the priests were all for changing the Law in that one respect, but the conservative priests were adamant: they, along with the rest of the nation, would rather tolerate no High Priest than an illegitimate one. While there were many of the tribe of Levi, there was none who could prove his descent from Aaron. The Hellenizers, who were in complete control of the nation, decided not to make an issue of it; and that Judaea was now without nominal leadership posed no problem to the conservatives, who were quite willing to ad lib the sacrifices until, by chance, a truly qualified candidate should happen along. Meanwhile, his garrisoning of Judaea complete, Bacchides returned to Antioch, and a two-year period of tranquillity settled over the troubled nation.

Probably acting on the strong advice of his worldly and pragmatic brother Simon, Jonathan refrained from any overt acts. Though there is no evidence that Jonathan used this period to build up his forces, the strength he exhibited when the Syrians eventually returned most definitely suggests this to have been the case. The Maccabees maintained a low—and distant—profile; so far as the Hellenizers and Syrians were concerned, Jonathan and his small band had decided to live in peace far from Jerusalem, east of the Jordan.

Two years went by.

And then some of the Hellenizers in communities near the west bank of the Jordan heard rumors that Jonathan had returned. After fleeing Bacchides, Jonathan and Simon had avenged their brother John's murder at the hands of the Transjordanian Arabs, helped themselves to a large haul of booty, and returned to western Palestine. The Hellenizers, on learning of this, became nervous; they felt that so long as one Maccabee remained alive, their hold on the nation was threatened. " 'Look,' they said, 'Jonathan and his people are living in peace and security. Let us bring Bacchides here; he will capture them all in a single night' " (I Macc. 9:58). They hastened north to Antioch to "bring Bacchides."

For Bacchides, capturing Jonathan had become a cause: he had never forgiven the Maccabee for eluding him in the Jordan marshes. Assuming that he could, as the Hellenizers had promised, "capture them all in a single night," Bacchides moved south with a small task force, first sending letters ahead to all suburban Hellenizers and Syrian garrisons to seize the rebels for his final disposition. Fortunately, one of the letters fell into the hands of some Maccabee sympathizers, and when Bacchides arrived at the site where "Jonathan and his people" were alleged to be "living in peace and security," he found a hastily vacated encampment. After slaying the fifty Hellenizers who had led him there, Bacchides set out with renewed determination to track down the rebels.

But he had no idea where to find them.

Jonathan and Simon had led their band into the out-of-the-way village of Beth-Hoglah, southeast of Jericho near the northern end of the Dead Sea, which they proceeded to fortify with watchtowers and hastily erected walls. Word got around, and soon many of the more nationalist-minded citizens scattered around Judaea were encouraged to make their way south to the fortress. Bacchides, in the meantime, had been seeking out the elusive rebels in western Palestine; he began to wonder if perhaps the Hellenizers had brought him down from Antioch on a wild-goose chase. As he was about to return home, he heard rumblings of a minor exodus toward Beth-Hoglah: Jonathan's activities had become the worst kept secret in all of Israel. Finally catching up with his quarry, Bacchides put the encampment under siege.

Though he had many ardent followers, Jonathan had few really qualified militiamen; with his forces outnumbered, his only hope lay in following the time-worn dictum that the best defense is a good offense. Therefore he left brother Simon to supervise the beleaguered settlement, and with a small group slipped past the Syrian siege-engines. Coming up behind the main enemy encampment, he attacked under cover of darkness. When Simon learned of Jonathan's success in harassing the Syrians from the rear, he organized a suicide task force, broke out of the encampment, and drove headlong into the enemy midst, setting the siege-engines afire and starting a stampede that soon saw Syrian soldiers fleeing pell-mell in all directions.

Bacchides was enraged: he was surrounded on all sides by Jonathan's followers, and his own troops were deserting him.

Bacchides was also anxious: he had received an urgent message from Demetrius to settle the Judaean problem at once and bring the army back home with dispatch.

The Syrian commander made two decisions: he would hastily withdraw from the area and make his way back to Jerusalem; and he would attempt to arrive at some rapprochement with this detested Maccabee who had made such a damn fool of him.

From the sanctuary of the Akra garrison, Bacchides sent word that he would welcome an embassy from Jonathan. The Maccabee suspected a trap. But when he learned of Demetrius's difficulties and of the Antioch government's eagerness to curtail commitment of large numbers of troops in Judaea, he agreed to a parley. As Jonathan's ambassadors set out for Jerusalem, Bacchides—while cursing himself for having failed in his initial mission—slaughtered those Hellenizers who had dragged him into so compromising a mess in the first place.

In exchange for the release of all prisoners taken in previous campaigns, Bacchides insisted that a number of pronationalist hostages be sent to the Akra, as a guarantee that Jonathan would not further harass the Hellenizers—or, for that matter, the skeletal garrisons Bacchides left in the Syrian fortresses throughout Palestine. And in return for Jonathan's promise to stay away from Jerusalem, he was allowed to occupy the city of Michmash. Jonathan agreed readily to this bargain: he was not yet ready to take on the Jerusalem hierarchy—nor, for that matter, the Hasidaeans, the conservative priests, and the war-weary populace, all of whom wished that he would simply disappear. Also, Michmash ("hidden" or "hidden place") was of inestimable strategic value: tucked away in a gorge about 2,000 feet above sea level approximately seven miles north of Jerusalem, it commanded the approaches to all of Judaea from the Syrian frontier.

After a mutual agreement not to make further war on each other, hands were shaken all around, and Bacchides departed for Antioch with the bulk of Syria's army in Palestine in tow. The skeletal garrisons throughout the area were told to leave Jonathan alone, so long as he left them alone.

A period of tranquillity again descended upon Judaea. The Hellenizers assumed that Jonathan was completely satisfied now, that there would be no more trouble from that quarter.

So involved did Jonathan become in his own endeavors—quietly welcoming the growing numbers of nationalist-minded citizens who wended their way daily and covertly toward Michmash—he could not have possibly foreseen that divine fortune was about to come his way shortly through no less a personage than the *soi-disant* bastard son of Antiochus Epiphanes. . . .

The curious troika Epiphanes had established at Alexandria—his niece Cleopatra II, her brother-husband Ptolemy Philometor, and their horribly obese younger brother Polemy Physcon—had lasted little more than five years when Cleopatra "divorced" Philometor and in tandem with Physcon forced Philometor to flee to Rome. At the insistence of the Senate, a compromise was worked out: Philometor was sent back to rule at Alexandria and Cyprus, while Physcon was to be king of Cyrene. Cleopatra accepted Rome's decision, albeit reluctantly, as did Physcon who set out to Cyrene, there to bide his time. (It is not certain whether the agreement included Cleopatra's divorcing her second, deposed brother and remarrying her first, reinstated sibling, nor does it really matter.)

Prior to his return to Alexandria (163 B.C.), Philometor had, while living in Rome, become a carousing companion of his cousin Demetrius, then being held hostage. This would not, of course, have kept Philometor from pursuing the traditional Ptolemaic goal of trying to reestablish hegemony in Palestine. Any man who would turn on his own brother (a congenital affliction among the Ptolemies) would hardly entertain any qualms when it came to betraying a mere cousin. But Rome had made it quite explicit: Egypt was to remain within its own borders—not so much for the safety of the Seleucids as for the safety of the Ptolemies themselves. Besides, Philometor still entertained a fondness for cousin Demetrius—until cousin Demetrius showed that *he* was not above turning on an old fellow-roisterer by trying to seize the Ptolemaic appanage of Cyprus.

Demetrius Soter's attempt to take Cyprus was a manifestation of his avarice as a man and his deficiency as a conciliatory monarch—attitudes that became apparent just as Bacchides was arriving at his détente with Jonathan. For by then Demetrius had alienated his three most powerful dynastic neighbors: Attalus II of Pergamum, Ariarathes V (who was also a cousin) of Cappadocia, and of course, cousin Philometor. And the fact that he was not too popular with Rome certainly did not stand Demetrius in good stead when he cast his eyes on Pergamum, one of the wealthiest kingdoms, as well as Rome's closest ally, in western

Asia. Since Attalus's brother, Eumenes II, had helped Antiochus Epiphanes take the Seleucid throne, Pergamum felt its interests prejudiced when the Epiphanean line was replaced by the elder line in the person of Demetrius. Too, Pergamum feared that a war precipitated by Demetrius's attempt to regain lost Seleucid territory in western Asia (which territory included Pergamum and Cappadocia) could well turn their Roman allies into their Roman overlords.[1]

That Demetrius was indeed trying to regain those lost territories became apparent when he chose to involve himself in the dynastic rivalry for the Cappadocian throne. Attalus of Pergamum supported one contender, while Demetrius supported the other; and when Demetrius's candidate was defeated (156 B.C.) and fled to Antioch for refuge, the victor joined with Attalus in what was rapidly evolving as a powerful anti-Demetrian coalition. To complicate matters, the Demetrian candidate, Orophernes—who was also a grandson (through his mother) of Antiochus the Great—abused the laws of hospitality by attempting to replace cousin Demetrius on the Syrian throne.

Though he was successful in putting down the attempted usurpation, Demetrius began to suspect that if so many Syrians were willing to side with Orophernes—as had been the case— then perhaps his popularity with his own subjects left much to be desired. But Demetrius should not be dismissed out of hand as a complete bungler. As Bevan points out: "Demetrius Soter had evidently some of the qualities of a great ruler—energy and high courage. But he seems to have been deficient in the gift of conciliating. . . . He became unpopular with the populace at Antioch." Bevan concedes, however, that "the fault may not have been altogether his. The Greek or Hellenized population of Syria was of very degenerate fibre: perhaps Demetrius had good enough reason to despise them, for his contempt will have been more bitter, inasmuch as his schemes for regenerating the kingdom must have required some good quality in the human material, and he saw them fail for want of that. At any rate, he could not conceal his contempt, and his subjects hated him for it."

Perhaps as a mark of the man, Demetrius withdrew into the seclusion of his imposing palace on the outskirts of Antioch, there to divide his time between imbibing the philosophy of the Epicureans and the produce of his vineyards. The monarchs of Pergamum, Cappadocia, and Egypt—with a none-too-subtle wink from the Roman Senate—decided the time was ripe for stirring up the Seleucid dynasty. They realized they could count on that faction of the populace, a considerable one, whose loyalty to the junior (Epiphanean) line had never wavered. But the plotting monarchs, acting on the advice of Rome, had to move cautiously: they dared not replace Demetrius with a strong man, who just might conceivably unite the Syrians. (The fact that there was no known heir for the Epiphanean line was a factor they dismissed summarily.) Rather, what was wanted was a weakling, preferably of the contemptible variety, who would be more involved in establishing control over a fractious Syria than in attempting to regain control over those former Syrian domains—a rationale with which the Roman Senate was in eminent accord. The problem: where to find that contemptible weakling.

Attalus of Pergamum came up with an eminently acceptable candidate.

Living in Smyrna was a young man named Balas who bore a remarkable physical resemblance to Antiochus Epiphanes. Whether Balas originally claimed to be Epiphanes's bastard or whether he took his cue from Attalus is both unascertainable and immaterial. After giving his young discovery the illustrious name Alexander, Attalus moved him into Cilicia close to the Syrian frontier. When word got out that the "rightful heir" to the Seleucid diadem had been discovered, there flocked to Balas's cause the "Antiochans," who were either convinced of his credentials or unconcerned with his ancestry, and a large number of "Demetrians," who preferred even a bastard from Smyrna to the bastard now sitting on their throne. Demetrius did not become too concerned—until he learned that Balas had been granted recognition by the Roman Senate as "the rightful king of Syria." Rome had no intention of supporting the venture other than with verbal recognition. But that was enough. The anti-Demetrian monarchs took their cue; returning to Asia Minor after his "confirmation" at Rome, young Balas was pleased to learn that he could count on the support of the Ptolemies.

Philometor had no intention of becoming involved—yet. Though furious with Demetrius for having tried to grab off Cyprus, Philometor had no guarantee of Balas's success; if he supported Balas openly, and Balas lost, Philometor would be faced with the threat of invasion by a vengeance-ridden cousin Demetrius. Exhibiting a tact that was hardly consonant with Ptolemaic thinking, Philometor covertly promised Balas that *if* he succeeded in deposing Demetrius he would be given one of Philometor's daughters in marriage. That was good enough for Balas. Some time around the fall of 152 B.C., he moved on to Ptolemais, a vital port city in northern Palestine where Ptolemaic influence was strong. From there he sent out sorties preparatory to invading Syria proper.

Demetrius now realized his precarious position: not only were his immediate neighbors antagonistic toward him, but most of the Antioch populace as well. Casting about for friends, he turned to—Jonathan!

During this period (157–153 B.C.) Jonathan's power and influence had slowly but steadily increased, as had the numbers of those who openly supported Judaean independence. He had kept his part of the bargain and stayed away from Jerusalem. Nevertheless, the hierarchs were having a difficult time of it, holding on to the emotions of the peasants and middle class (exclusive of the Hasidaeans and their more orthodox supporters) in whose collective breast the fires of nationalism were being stoked. Nor could the Hellenizers at Jerusalem be of much help to their brethren in the provinces, who were now at the mercy of

Jonathan. The small Syrian garrisons stationed throughout the country were apparently quite willing to stand by as Jonathan "began to govern the people, rooting the godless of Israel" (I Macc. 9:73); so long as Jonathan did not bother them, they would retaliate in kind.

That Demetrius chose to woo Jonathan indicates—aside from the obvious fact that the king had no other immediate neighbors even remotely interested in allying themselves with him—Seleucid recognition of the Maccabee as de facto leader of the Jewish nation, as well as tacit acceptance of that leadership. Demetrian selection of Jonathan as a possible ally also indicates Demetrian pragmatism: the Hellenizers might still be in control of the capital city and the Temple treasury, but Jonathan was in control of what passed for the military establishment. While the Hellenizers had been busy running the Jerusalem market, collecting t'rumahs, and indulging in games at the gymnasium, Jonathan had been busy training soldiers. And when an Epicurean dynast is in dire need of friends, he woos soldiers instead of priests and fun-loving merchants.

Demetrius sent word to Jonathan that he was prepared to make a deal: all Jewish hostages still being held in the Akra were to be released; also—and most extraordinary—Jonathan was empowered (legally) to raise and equip troops; in effect, to function as a licensed revolutionary (though, to be sure, on behalf of Demetrius). Jonathan did not say yes. Nor did he say no. What he did say was that he was amenable to a deal—which Demetrius eagerly took to mean yes. As Demetrius mustered his forces to fight the Pergamum-led coalition, Jonathan moved his headquarters from Michmash to Jerusalem. There, without bothering to disabuse Demetrius of the notion that he had in Jonathan a staunch ally in the forthcoming contest with Balas, the wily Maccabee prepared to await what he suspected—rightfully, as it turned out—would be a "deal" from Balas enlisting Jewish support. Both contestants realized it was vital to have Judaean support in their respective causes—if not to fight beside them in battle, then certainly to keep them from siding with the opponent. Judaea's geographical importance was not to be taken for granted by either of the contenders.

While awaiting a message from Balas, Jonathan took control of Jerusalem (to the consternation of the Hellenizers), fortified the Temple Mount area (further alienating the Hasidaeans), and purged the polluted priesthood (which earned him the gratitude of the conservatives, though they wished he would have built his fortifications in another part of town). He then sent expeditionary forces throughout Judaea to oversee the withdrawal of all Syrian troops from those areas previously garrisoned by Bacchides, a task which involved a minimum of effort on Jonathan's part: the garrisons had been called home by the king, and they were anxious to fight by his side against the Antiochan pretender. However, two garrisons could not be evicted. One was at Bethsura, where the more intransigent Hellenizers had entrenched themselves and were prepared to resist. Jonathan merely ignored them and, returning to Jerusalem, turned his attention to the other recalcitrant garrison: the Akra. Demetrius had insisted that a pro-Syrian mercenary force be maintained there; they had been joined by the Hellenized priests fleeing the wrath of the conservatives. Instead of wasting his time trying to evict them, Jonathan simply encircled the Akra with a task force and dared those within—now virtual prisoners—to come out. The dare was not accepted.

Having taken full advantage of the terms Demetrius offered, but feeling no obligation of loyalty should Balas come up with a better offer, Jonathan sat back to await Balas's anticipated bid for support. It came in the form of a letter appointing Jonathan to the office of High Priest of Judaea!

The idea of being High Priest of his nation was one that even Jonathan had never dared entertain. Though the office had been vacant seven years since the death of Alcimus, and even though he had by now won the support of the majority of the people—including a number of the more rational Hellenizers who saw in him a winner—the Hasidaeans and conservative priests violently opposed the appointment to that august office of a non-Aaronic warrior (not that Jonathan pretended to be otherwise), and, into the bargain, by a Gentile bastard.

Jonathan could afford to say yes to Balas's bid for support, if only because the pretender was in no position to make trouble should he say no. And for essentially the same reason, Jonathan could inform Demetrius not to count too heavily on Jewish assistance in the upcoming struggle for his throne. But Demetrius, now desperate, was not about to give up; even Jonathan must have foreseen this, or he would hardly have dared offer his services to the rival contestants in so outrageously auctioneering a manner.

Demetrius Soter's move to outbid Balas came in the form of a "Dear Jonathan" letter. After forgiving the Maccabee's duplicity (as if he were in a position to do otherwise!), he tendered an even more extraordinary bribe: Syrian subsidies for the upkeep of the Temple, plus Syrian funds to finance reconstruction of Jerusalem's bruised walls; surrender of the Akra; restoration of all Judaean territories that had been grabbed off by prior Seleucid monarchs; and, *mirabile dictu*, exemption from Syrian taxation for the Jews. The anxious Soter's letter ended with protestations of enduring friendship—and bore the implied caveat that if Jonathan double-crossed him again, and assuming that he would defeat Balas, Demetrius would personally come to Jerusalem and slaughter the Maccabee in cold blood.

Clearly, Jonathan could only ally himself with one of the contenders, in whose cause he had to commit troops. Equally clear was the realization that he had to wind up on the side of the eventual winner. Whether because of shrewd guesswork, innate prescience, or even divine inspiration—it was hardly because he distrusted Demetrius; he also distrusted Balas—Jonathan made what proved to be the right decision: he threw in his lot with Balas. As the pro-Demetrian Hellenizers burrowed in further, all the while praying for an anti-Antiochan victory, they vociferously hurled epithets at Jonathan for taking Soter's bribe and then welshing on it—bleatings which, to Jonathan, were beneath his High Priestly contempt.

Thus by some outrageous twist of fate, Jonathan Maccabee was now in league with the son, bastard or otherwise, of the very man whose policies had caused the Maccabees to revolt in the first place. And what is perhaps more ironic, through sheer diplomacy plus a soupçon of fortuitous luck and a dash of *chutzpah,* Jonathan was winning for his people what his poor dead brother Judah had been unable to achieve on the battle-field: recognition by the Syrians of Judaean autonomy. The nation was still a province of Antioch. But the first concrete steps had been taken toward complete independence.

For Demetrius the end came swiftly. Pergamum and Cappadocia sent task forces into Syria from the north, a number of Demetrian generals defected to Balas, the people of Antioch rose up against him, and even Ptolemy Philometor felt confident enough to send a small army up from Alexandria. When Balas killed Demetrius and mounted the throne of Syria and Babylonia, he proved that, while he might be a bastard (self-proclaimed or otherwise) to his own people, he was far from a bastard to the Jews. To everyone's surprise, and the Jewish nation's great relief, Balas did not renege on his bid for their support. Having named Jonathan to be religious as well as temporal leader of Judaea, Balas confirmed all the concessions Demetrius had promised. And then, to seal the bargain, Balas made Jonathan a Prince of Syria. Judaea was now recognized, and respected, as an autonomous province of the Seleucid Empire.

Balas did not go so far as to proclaim independence for the Jews. Nor did Jonathan make any such demands; he realized full well his position. For the time being, Jonathan was quite satisfied to reign over his people as a servant of the Antioch government, responsible directly to the new emperor for his actions. Such a situation—being in both religious and temporal control of his own land—was one he could well exploit through shrewdness and skillful diplomacy (plus a bit of luck). Jonathan was obviously aiming for complete independence from Syria. But first he must strengthen his own position, which involved building up an army and extending his territories beyond the rather narrow geographical limits of Judaea.

To demonstrate further his appreciation for Jonathan's having sided with him and led Jewish soldiers into battle on his behalf, Balas invited Jonathan to be his personal guest at his marriage to Philometor's daughter, Cleopatra Thea ("goddess")—unarguably and demonstrably one of the most fascinating shrikes of ancient history. In a somewhat hectic career that spanned thirty brief years, this daughter of Philometor by his sister-wife, Cleopatra II, was to marry three Seleucid monarchs (two of them brothers); usurp the Syrian throne; and become the mother of, among assorted spawn, four kings, the third of whom she was to murder in cold blood, before the last one murdered *her* upon learning she had consigned him to a like fate.

After the great wedding, which was celebrated riotously at Ptolemais in early 149 B.C., Jonathan returned home to build up his nation, while Balas set out to lose his.

The fact that Balas spent most of what remained of his five-year reign whoring at Ptolemais instead of ruling at Antioch suggests that either he was unsure of his popularity among his new subjects or that he allowed himself to become subordinate to his Ptolemaic father-in-law. Before long, the Demetrians were on their way back in, the Antiochans were on their way out, and Jonathan was afforded new enemies and dissensions to exploit.

10   Jonathan— "First Friend"

The bride whom Jonathan had toasted at Ptolemais not many months before was soon to emerge—albeit unwillingly, and certainly unintentionally—as one of the Maccabee's long-term benefactresses. Cleopatra Thea, not unlike the heroine of some dismal television soap opera, lost her virginity and became pregnant at one and the same time. To Balas she bore a son, whom she seems to have abandoned as a cat would an unwanted kitten, and of whom we shall be hearing shortly. Immediately thereafter, she cultivated an intense detestation for her whore-mongering mate. While Thea may have been but a child herself, she was mature enough to perceive that in her arranged marriage to the Epiphanean bastard lay the possibility of the Ptolemies reasserting their hereditary claim to all of Coele-Syria. Thea was also mature enough to realize that the first step could not come from within her family; rather, her in-laws would have to create the chaos that she and her kin would willingly exploit to their own ends.

The Seleucids cooperated, above and beyond all expectations. A dividend of that cooperation was, for the Jews, political independence from Syria.

Balas had delegated authority and mistakenly put his complete trust at Antioch in Diodotus Tryphon and Hierax, two generals who had defected from Demetrius. Tryphon and Hierax immediately put to death young Antigonus, the Demetrian heir (after which Tryphon had Hierax killed). Whether the regicide/infanticide had been carried out at Balas's specific request is not known. But what is known is that in the following spring (147 B.C.), Soter's second son, also named Demetrius, suddenly appeared on the frontier of northern Syria in the company of an army of Cretan mercenaries commanded by one Lasthenes. Prior to going into battle with Balas, Demetrius Soter had sent his two younger sons to Cilicia to be out of danger, leaving his older son and heir, the ill-fated Antigonus, in Syria. Apparently Demetrius felt confident he would retain his throne, but there was a limit to that confidence: should he lose (as he did), and the heir be murdered (as he was), there would be at least two others to continue the line. Demetrius Junior, the elder of the brothers, had only recently arrived at puberty, so that it was probably Lasthenes who masterminded the campaign to depose Balas and reinstate the more legitimate Demetrian line.

Hastening north to defend Antioch, Balas left one Apollonius behind as governor of Coele-Syria. Apollonius immediately declared for the young Demetrius—a disaster not only for Balas but for Balas's "First Friend" Jonathan. But Jonathan remained loyal to Balas. When fighting broke out in Palestine, he succeeded in capturing—ostensibly on Balas's behalf—the important cities of Joppa, Ashdod, and Ascalon, and in pushing Apollonius's forces back to the Mediterranean coast. (In one instance, at Azotus, Jonathan burned the temple of the Philistine god Dagon in which a number of refugees had sought asylum. Jonathan had learned well at the side of his brother Judah.) When Balas, who was meeting with some success in the north, learned of Jonathan's victories, he promoted him to the highest order, "Kinsman," and awarded him the militarily and economically vital city of Ekron as a personal appanage.

Balas assumed that Jonathan had taken those cities on the king's behalf. Obviously Balas did not know Jonathan. After pushing Apollonius back to the coast, Jonathan occupied the captured cities (and a few others that fell to him by default) and established his authority therein. Thanks to this latest turn in what had by now become a sort of Syrian Wars of the Roses, Judaea was, overnight, doubled territorially!

At this point Ptolemy Philometor, deciding to intervene, headed north with a strong army. Jonathan's first reaction was that the king was coming to quash him; but he soon relaxed when he realized that Philometor's intervention was precipitated, not by Jonathan's military excesses but by Balas's ineptitude—an ineptitude which, according to Ptolemaic thinking, was the sign from the gods that Coele-Syria was destined to be again under their hegemony. As he pressed on toward Syria along the coast, establishing garrisons loyal to Apollonius (and by extension to the young Demetrius), Ptolemy avoided any confrontations with Jonathan's armies—who wisely stayed out of the Egyptian army's path. I Maccabees claims Philometor intervened with the express purpose of overthrowing his contemptible weakling of a son-in-law, Balas. Extrabiblical sources, including the writings of Diodorus and Josephus (both of whom probably drew on the account set down by Polybius), maintain Philometor's intention was to support Balas against the legitimate pretender. Since Philometor and Thea were great opportunists, it is quite probable that they had not decided which of the two factions they would support, allowing future events to determine their course of action.[1]

Father and daughter settled at Seleucia, the great city built by Seleucus Nicator a few miles north of the mouth of the Orontes as a fortress and port city to serve and protect Antioch which lay on the left bank. By now Philometor controlled, to one degree or another, the major coastal cities of Palestine. Having ascertained in which direction the Seleucid wind was blowing, he concurred in daughter Thea's opinion that the cretinous Demetrius (as history would prove him to be) and his Cretan mercenaries would triumph—with just a small assist from the Egyptian army. Openly accusing Balas of having attempted to assassinate him (!), Philometor announced his support for Demetrius. Thea then stepped forward and announced that she had divorced Balas and was engaged to marry the fourteen-year-old Demetrius—a piece of news of which both the ex-husband and intended groom had not yet been apprised.

Balas fled to Cilicia, there to raise an army of mercenaries; Thea and Philometor entered Antioch, there to await the victorious Demetrius. And Jonathan, after securing his defenses all along the line, hastened back to Jerusalem, there to dispatch an embassy to Rome advising the Senate of what was happening— and to offer a propitiatory prayer while awaiting the latest news from the north.

The Ptolemies were welcomed at Antioch as true saviors. Even those who had supported Balas strictly out of distaste for Demetrius I now transferred their allegiance to Demetrius II. Tryphon led out of Antioch and into the hills what remained of the pro-Balas faction. Soon, thanks to Thea's captivating manner, her father became so popular with the Antioch canaille that they invited *him* to accept their throne, notwithstanding their professed loyalty to young Demetrius. The heir, who had not yet arrived, was, after all, a mere child and an unknown quantity; Philometor was not only a known quantity but was also a lineal descendant of Antiochus the Great.

The offer was a tempting one. It would have put Philometor in control of all of Syria as well as Egypt. But against Thea's argument that here was the golden opportunity the Ptolemies had so long sought was Philometor's logical thesis that were he to assume the throne, Rome would be provoked beyond measure— chiefly because Rome had no assurances that Egypt could hold on to Syria. The Senate strongly suspected what the Ptolemies stubbornly refused to concede: the Egyptians would not only be unable to maintain their claim to the area, they would probably be forced into a war in order to retain their own land. Rome had no intention of being dragged into the military posture of having to pull Egyptian chestnuts out of a Syrian fire. Thus, from a position of self-induced belief in the strength of his nation, and still maintaining a pragmatic approach, Philometor, in his best avuncular manner, persuaded Antioch to accept Demetrius II as their rightful king. When the youth entered the Syrian capital at the head of his band of Cretan mercenaries, he was acclaimed Nicator ("conqueror").

He was also introduced for the first time to his "Egyptian" bride.

The royal nuptials had barely been celebrated when word was received that Balas was returning with an army of Cilician mercenaries. Jonathan, suspecting an erosion in Balas's strength, wanted to keep his options open; he sent word to his military commanders to sit this battle out.

Philometor's forces, along with his newest son-in-law's Cretans, scored a decisive victory over Balas on the banks of the Oenoparas River in northern Syria (June, 145 B.C.); as a reward, he was handed Balas's severed head. Sad to relate, Philometor had little time in which to enjoy his victory: five days later he fell from his horse and broke his neck. Philometor's poor horsemanship was the signal for the next round in the continuing series of hair-raising, and blood-splattering, family quarrels among the Ptolemies. Ordering that a contingent be left with Thea at Antioch, the sister-queen-widow, Cleopatra II, hastily recalled the bulk of the Egyptian army to Alexandria. She had just learned that her other brother, Physcon, was marching from Cyrene to depose her.

Jonathan was aware that Cleopatra II was kindly disposed toward her Jewish subjects at Alexandria, while the Egyptian Jewish community was on the closest of terms with their brethren in Judaea. In the withdrawal of the Egyptian army from Syria, Jonathan saw the removal of a powerful force that might have proved to be an ally to his people, whose primary enemies were the Syrians. Jonathan also began to wonder whether he might have blundered in openly supporting Balas against the man whose heir was now sitting on the Seleucid throne.

Demetrius Nicator had no trouble ascending the throne; but he did have trouble staying on it. His problems stemmed less from his youth than from his inability to keep in check the rapacious Cretans, who now embarked on an orgy of looting and pillaging in Antioch and the immediate environs. This not only alienated the citizenry, it drove the Egyptians who had remained to guard Thea to pack up and return home, despite her shrill command to the contrary; and as the Egyptians departed the strife-torn Syrian capital, Diodotus Tryphon prepared to enter it, bent on exploiting the explosive situation to his own advantage. Meanwhile, with Demetrius ascending his late father's rather wobbly throne, Jonathan decided it was time to ascend his metaphorical fence and engage in a little heavy straddling.

The first thing Demetrius chose to remember was that the Jewish leader had supported Balas against his father Soter; the first thing Jonathan chose to remember was that he had better demonstrate his good intentions toward this latest Syrian overlord. To show what passed for good intentions, he resorted to the outrageous ploy of pretending to put the Akra under siege, suspecting that Demetrius would be forced into making concessions in order to have the siege lifted. (And here it should be remembered that, unbeknownst to Nicator, the Akra—with its Syrian detachment and anti-Jonathan sympathizers—was already under siege!) Because the Cretans were running amok at Antioch, Demetrius and Thea established their court at Ptolemais; it was there that Jonathan was commanded to report in person and explain the "siege." Ordering his troops to double the guard at all Judaean outposts and offering up a few hasty sacrifices, Jonathan and an escort—well armed and expensively costumed—set out for the temporary Seleucid capital with lavish gifts for the royal couple. Immediately on being ushered into the imperial presence, Jonathan promised to break off the siege—*provided* Nicator would continue the Jews in all concessions made by his predecessors.

Nicator was visibly impressed with Jonathan's audacity and display of affluence and power. Realizing that the Seleucid dynastic struggle was bound to rear its horrendous head anew,

Nicator determined he had better keep in the good graces of a man, albeit a Jewish man, who commanded so powerful an army on Syria's southern border (and who, Nicator deduced on the basis of Jonathan's suite, was wealthy enough to dress his men so becomingly). He accepted Jonathan's lavish presents—and re-affirmed Judaean autonomy. Whereupon Jonathan magnani-mously offered 300 talents as down payment on the taxes owed the Seleucids before Nicator's father had granted remission. (So far as Jonathan was concerned, that "down payment" was to be *total* payment.) So taken was he by Jonathan's "sincerity" and panache, Nicator immediately raised him to the exalted rank of "First Friend of the King." Jonathan magnanimously accepted the raise, and proffered the proper expressions of gratitude and fealty.

Then, thus elevated, Jonathan felt in a more tenable position to suggest tactfully that if Nicator were to count on him for more than minimal support in what was already shaping up as the next round in the Antiochan-Demetrian hassle, the young monarch should ascertain that his "First Friend's" military posture in Palestine was that much more secure. Nicator saw the wisdom of this suggestion, and Jonathan was immediately given permission to annex three districts contiguous to Judaea that belonged to the Samaritans (who were in no position to object). Jonathan—now convinced that he was negotiating with an imbecile—made an-other magnanimous offer: a Jewish battalion would be detached to form part of Nicator's royal bodyguard.

After the two had shaken hands and sealed their pact with an exchange of toasts, Jonathan returned to Jerusalem where he proceeded to lift the siege of the Akra (by erecting a wall around the fortress, prisoners and all!)—while Demetrius returned to Antioch where he proceeded to lose his throne.

On arriving back at the capital, hopefully to arrive at some understanding with Lasthenes and thus curb the Cretan excesses, Nicator found himself in the middle of a full-scale insurrection: the Antioch mobs were trying frantically to evict the Cretans.

When word got about that Nicator had returned, the mobs went looking for him: it was his fault that the city was overrun with rapacious mercenaries in the first place. In the fighting that ensued, there was a great massacre of anti-Cretans (ergo, anti-Demetrians), in which massacre Jonathan's Jewish Brigade took an active role on the young monarch's behalf. Now the Antioch mobs, calling openly for the dethronement of their latest king, sought someone to lead them toward that goal. Tryphon, who had been hiding in the hinterlands awaiting a propitious moment, entered Antioch with a surprise package in his arms. The surprise: Thea's and Balas's infant son, whom Tryphon appears to have found among some Arabs into whose safekeeping the infant had been delivered (probably by Balas, certainly not by Thea). Tryphon had little difficulty in rallying the Antioch mobs, who would accept anything, even the bastard Balas's miserable issue, as a candidate for the throne, so long as it meant ridding the country of the Cretans.

When Thea stepped forward to claim rightful ownership of her son, she was quietly but firmly requested to disappear; Thea had no choice but to return to her spouse, with whom she was rapidly becoming disillusioned. The two hastily fled back to Seleucia where they maintained Nicator's legitimacy to the throne, while Tryphon established himself as regent for the royal infant at Antioch.[2] By October of that same year (143 B.C.), Syria had two kings—an inept youth and an ignorant infant—whose only common bond was that the unloving wife of the former was the disinterested mother of the latter. From Seleucia, Nicator still maintained control over most of the seaboard areas as well as the Babylonian portion of the realm; Tryphon controlled the entire Orontes valley. Demetrius Nicator immediately mounted an invasion of Antioch to depose Tryphon. The Syrian Problem was about to offer Jonathan still further opportunities.

At the height of the battle for control of Antioch, Demetrius received a request from his "First Friend" to withdraw Syrian garrison troops from Bethsura and Gazara, two fortresses over which the Maccabee had yet to gain control. Demetrius was only too happy to oblige: besieged in his own palace, he would do *anything* in exchange for Jonathan's assistance. After overseeing the withdrawal of those Syrian garrisons, Jonathan personally led a force of 3,000 Jewish mercenaries into Antioch, and in a lightning raid rescued the royal couple and delivered them safely back to Seleucia.

It was then that Demetrius felt secure enough to double-cross his "First Friend": all prior concessions made to Jonathan were summarily revoked.

Tryphon was in dire need of a strong Jewish army to further his own ambitions; when news of the revocation reached him, he immediately sent out feelers inquiring if Jonathan had not perhaps taken umbrage at Demetrius's duplicity. Jonathan had indeed. Without hesitation, he transferred his allegiance to the infant Antiochus VI. Tryphon not only showed his appreciation by confirming Jonathan in all concessions and honors previously conferred by Demetrius *and* Balas, he went a step further and named brother Simon to be *strategos* (governor) over all of Palestine, except for Phoenicia, from the Syrian to the Egyptian frontiers.

Tryphon's magnanimous gift was a shrewd one. Demetrius still nominally controlled the area in which Judea lay, but he was able to do little when Jonathan and Simon embarked upon a series of campaigns ostensibly to win territory away from Demetrius for Tryphon (but aimed in reality at furthering their own territorial aggrandizement). After making sure that all the strategically important fortresses within his rapidly expanding sphere of influence were properly garrisoned, Jonathan sent an embassy to Rome to renew the league of amity and "friendship" his brother Judah had contracted with the Senate. Experience had convinced him that material assistance on the part of the Romans would not be forthcoming, the terms of that treaty notwithstanding. But Jonathan was more concerned with the prestige of being an ally of the Senate; he was doing well enough without Roman assistance. The Senate, which had been casting a jaundiced eye on the mess in Coele-Syria, agreed to renew the pact. That the Syrian kingdom was now divided was not what concerned Rome; rather, their concern lay in the possibility that one of the rival contestants might, by some miracle, unify the entire realm and, with Cleopatra Thea now involved, attempt diplomatic or military unification with Egypt. Were that to come about, Rome, though not yet prepared to move into Asia Minor, might be left with no alternative.

Though they had no way of knowing it at the time, the oligarchs who ruled Rome need not have been concerned in the least. For back at Alexandria . . .

When Thea's father, Philometor, fell off his horse and died, her mother, Cleopatra II, assumed the regency on behalf of her and her brother-husband's infant son, an ill-fated waif known to history as Ptolemy Eupator. (No Roman numeral here; he did not live long enough to earn one.) On hearing of his brother's death, the by now horribly obese Ptolemy Physcon returned from Cyprus as fast as his overburdened carriers could transport him. Since no Ptolemaic female could rule without a male consort, Physcon was anxious to finesse the one option still open to his despised sister: raising her baby to the throne. Physcon's strategy was to kill his nephew and thus become king by default.

Civil war broke out in Alexandria.

Fortunately for the Jews of Palestine, Cleopatra II's strongest support, both financial and political, came from the powerful Jewish community at Alexandria. When Onias IV, still considered the legitimate High Priest, fled to Egypt following the assassination of his father by the apostate Menelaus, Cleopatra had turned over to him a disused pagan temple at Leontopolis and had financed its rebuilding along the lines of the Jerusalem Temple. Here Onias IV and his adherents had established a cult for those Egyptian Jews who preferred to adhere to the old Aaronic, nonsynagogue brand of centralized worship. (Though the legitimacy of the Leontopolis temple was never recognized by the Jerusalem priesthood, it continued to flourish as the center of worship for Egypt's Jews until it was ordered closed by the Roman emperor Vespasian about A.D. 73.)

The Egyptian Jews never forgot Cleopatra's act of kindness; when Physcon landed at Alexandria, Jewish support went to Cleopatra. (Some historians suspect that her leading generals, Onias and Dositheus, were the sons of Onias IV; all historians agree that they were Jewish.)

When it became apparent that matters were getting out of hand for all concerned—there was always the danger that the native Egyptians would turn on both contestants for the throne and evict the dynasty once and for all—Cleopatra II came up with a solution: she would marry brother Physcon and the two would rule jointly. Physcon accepted her proposal, a great wedding was arranged, and though husband and wife (sister and brother) cordially detested one another, the civil war was ended. According to the second-century A.D. Christian apologist Justin Martyr, Cleopatra's infant son (Eupator) by her first brother-husband (Philometor) was murdered in the arms of his mother during the nuptial festivities by her second brother-bridegroom. If this is true, Physcon was merely guarding against any ideas his bride might have of killing him off and raising the boy to the throne as her consort. Since there is little historical reason to doubt Martyr's claim, this latest Ptolemaic marriage was getting off to an ominous start. Apparently Cleopatra accepted this rather extraordinary intrusion on her nuptial festivities for the sake of political expediency. Maternal devotion was but one of the many virtues whose practice was alien to the Ptolemies.

(There is also a rather fascinating tale, handed down in the noncanonical Third Book of the Maccabees, undoubtedly apocryphal but nevertheless a fair barometer of the times vis-à-vis the Ptolemies and the Alexandrian Jews. As the story goes, Physcon decided to punish the Jews for having initially supported Cleopatra against him. Toward this end, he sent a herd of elephants into a crowd of Jews—at which point the elephants retreated and trampled the king's men instead. Whether this alleged miracle came about as a result of divine intervention or congenital pachydermal myopia, Physcon got the message; Cleopatra was able to persuade her corpulent consort to abandon his anti-Jewish vendetta.)

Within a year dynastic relationships between the Ptolemies had become further entangled. And though they had no way of knowing it at the time, the Judaeans were to be the ultimate recipients of whatever good was to evolve out of this latest Macedonian depravity.

By her first marriage, to brother Philometor, Cleopatra had borne, in addition to Thea and the ill-fated Eupator, still another daughter who was to wind up in the history books, Cleopatra III. This nubile princess attracted the attention of her uncle (step-father) Physcon, who raped her and then married her.[3] Cleo-patra II suspected her daughter had seduced Physcon with the idea of bearing him a son whom she would raise to the throne as her consort, provided Physcon predeceased both women, and thus shove her aside. (It should go without saying that the two Cleopatras cordially detested one another.) She also suspected that Physcon had agreed to the plot as a means of achieving some revenge, if only from beyond the grave, on the sister-wife whom he absolutely loathed.

Thus Cleopatra II, whether justified or merely paranoic in her reasoning, was all for calling on her Jewish generals again, not as an aggrieved mother who wished to punish the man who had "violated" her daughter, but as a dynastically ambitious harridan who feared that her daughter had, in a manner of speaking, "violated" her. But in her eagerness to depose her coroyals she was dissuaded by her courtiers, who reminded Cleopatra mère of the obvious: since she had no more brothers to marry, nor sons for that matter (nephews and male cousins did not count in the dynastic scheme of things), she had best put up with this latest gambit, at least for the nonce. Swallowing her pride and choking on her bile, she decided to make the best of a dismal situation—though she did serve warning to her closest advisers that this family mess would not be tolerated indefinitely. Such was also the attitude of Physcon, who would have killed off his sister-wife but for the realization that she still held the loyalty of so many among the Alexandrian community—including the military.

Brother and sister finally agreed to a truce; Cleopatra III settled into what was to be a long, action-packed life; and for the second time in their history under the Macedonians, the Egyptians were ruled by an incestuous *ménage à trois*. Meanwhile, back to Antioch . . .

Tryphon had "aspired to be king of Asia. . . . But he was afraid that Jonathan would fight to prevent this, so he cast about for some means of . . . killing him" (I Macc. 12:39–40). Tryphon was no fool: he knew Jonathan would not become involved if he could help it, and he would certainly not ally himself with Demetrius; instead, he would stand aside and hope that the two contenders for the Syrian throne destroyed each other. While enjoying some success in purchasing the loyalty of the eastern satraps still loyal to Demetrius, Tryphon felt that, in time, his program of wearing away at his enemy's strength through attrition would prove successful. But Jonathan was another problem: he had the Jewish nation solidly behind him; and that nation now boasted, if not the largest army threatening Tryphon then certainly the best coordinated and most highly motivated, hence most powerful.

Indeed, Tryphon was not "afraid" of what Jonathan might do. His concern was with what Jonathan had already done. While professing his loyalty to Tryphon and the young Antiochus VI (whom Tryphon had probably by then put to death), Jonathan had conquered a number of cities in areas still theoretically held by Demetrius. These he had fortified in his own name.

In short, the Jewish nation had become too strong for

Tryphon's comfort. Before he could become "king of Asia," he must first become "king of Palestine"—an estate to which he could not hope to aspire as long as Jonathan lived.

The "means" Tryphon decided upon, after a brief spell of "casting about," was—simple treachery. While attending the wedding of Balas and Thea at Ptolemais, Jonathan had reconnoitered the city and been taken with the prospect of establishing control over this port, thus giving the Jews a firm foothold on the Mediterranean. Though he was in no position to attempt a military conquest of the city, Jonathan had made it known that he would give just about anything to control Ptolemais. Tryphon, having learned of Jonathan's obsessive desire, sent word that he was coming south to hand the city over to him, and could they not meet at Beth-Shan ("house of quiet") to discuss the deed of transfer?

Fortunately, Jonathan mistrusted Tryphon. He set out to meet the Syrian with an army of 40,000 picked troops, all well armed and prepared for any exigencies.

Unfortunately, Jonathan did not mistrust Tryphon *enough*.

Panicking at the sight of Jonathan's powerful army as it came into view, Tryphon made an elaborate show of receiving the Jewish leader, going so far as to order his own troops to obey Jonathan as they would himself. Then, having completely caught Jonathan off guard—this being the only instance during the career of the Maccabee brothers when Jewish troops heavily outnumbered Syrians!—the wily Tryphon murmured, "Why have you put all these men to so much trouble, when we are not at war? Send them home now and choose a few to accompany you, and come with me to Ptolemais. I will hand it over to you with all the other fortresses, the rest of the troops, and all the officials, and then I will leave the country. This is my only purpose in coming" (I Macc. 12:44–46).

Believing Tryphon, simply because he wanted to, Jonathan dismissed the bulk of his army and sent them home. Retaining only a mere suite of 3,000 as escort, he journeyed with Tryphon to Ptolemais. As soon as they passed through the city gates, the populace, at a signal from Tryphon, arrested Jonathan and slaughtered those of his retinue who could not effect an escape.

With the exception of the Hasidaeans, who resented Jonathan only because he had agreed to serve in the High Priestly office to which he was not genealogically entitled, the majority of the nation had by now coalesced behind him. Even the more compromising Hellenizers had accepted Jonathan, who did not take his allegiance to Mosaic dogma all that seriously and was pragmatic enough to realize that his acceptance of the Establishment could only redound profitably and politically to his success as the nation's leader. When news of Tryphon's treachery reached Jerusalem, brother Simon was immediately named as Jonathan's successor by popular acclaim: not only was he still *strategos* of Palestine, he was the only survivor of the original five Maccabee brothers.

Simon strengthened Jerusalem's fortifications in anticipation of a siege and then moved north to confront Tryphon, who in the meantime had marched south from Ptolemais with his highly-prized hostage in tow. The two met at Adida—ironically, in the vicinity of the Maccabee town of Modin where it had all started a generation before—and negotiations were undertaken. Simon was highly suspicious of Tryphon's offer to release Jonathan in exchange for 100 talents of silver and the handing over of two of Jonathan's sons (names unknown) as hostages. But he feared that, were he not to comply, he would stand accused before his people of having caused their beloved leader's death. Lacking any choice, Simon sent the money and the nephews to Tryphon—who, as Simon had anticipated, refused to surrender Jonathan.

Instead, the Syrian made a quick forced march down to Idumaea, hoping to attack Jerusalem from the less impregnable southeast. He knew there was little Simon could do to stop such an attack since the Jewish army was scattered in garrisons throughout Palestine. Tryphon was eager to get to the capital city, not only to score a psychological advantage over the now thoroughly demoralized nation, but also to relieve the Syrian garrison still walled up in the Akra, along with a number of the fiercely anti-Maccabee Hellenizers, all of whom were literally starving to death. Too, Tryphon had heard of the fabled treasures to be found within the Temple. (The plundered coffers had long since been replenished, thanks in large measure to those Diaspora Jews who never missed a payment on the yearly tithes.)

As ill luck would have it for those hungry prisoners in the Akra, and good luck for the Judaeans, a heavy snowstorm suddenly fell on the Promised Land (the more intransigent traditionalists would have us believe the Lord had pulled off another of His celebrated theophanies), and Tryphon was unable to move his army toward Jerusalem: the elephants, unused to maneuvering in slush, were literally bogged down.

In a fit of pique at having been stopped by the elements, and fearing that the Jewish garrison forces would soon be converging on him from all directions, Tryphon hastily aimed his army in an easterly direction and retreated across the Jordan. There, after putting Jonathan to death out of sheer frustration, he returned to Antioch.

Tryphon assumed that with their brilliant and popular leader dead, the Jews posed no further threat to his ambitions; as soon as the situation allowed, he would return to Jerusalem and conquer the nation. (If Tryphon revoked Simon's appointment as *strategos* over Palestine, it must be assumed that Simon simply dismissed the revocation out of hand.) Feeling confident enough to impose himself on the Antioch populace, Tryphon proclaimed that the boy-king had been deposed and that he was now emperor of Syria. So hasty was he in pushing toward his overall (and highly unrealistic) goal—"to be king of Asia"—in his blind greed and reckless avidity he failed to comprehend that his murder of Jonathan had made the Jews his mortal enemies;

worse, from the Syrian point of view, he had united the nation as it had not been united since the days of Ezra and Nehemiah.

Judah Maccabee had won religious independence for the Jews, and then, perhaps, made the mistake of seeking national independence. But times, and Seleucids, had changed, and brother Jonathan had succeeded in making Judaea at least an autonomous nation. With brother Simon, the aspirations were to be carried through to their inevitable conclusion: complete political independence from a fragmented and dissension-torn suzerain power. Given the political conditions that obtained as Simon assumed leadership, it is not too difficult to justify the Palestinian Jewish nation's taking that ultimate step. But what is difficult to justify is why the nation, having finally achieved that independence, labored so assiduously to throw it away.

11 Simon— High Priest and Ethnarch

For eight years (142–134 B.C.) Simon ruled over a Jewish state in Palestine which owed its independence as much to this particular Maccabee's consummate leadership and the dynastic rivalries of its immediate neighbors to the north and the south as to the willingness of the Judaeans to lay aside—temporarily—their religious and philosophical rivalries and reconcile their differences. There was no interference with those who preferred to pursue the path of strict orthodoxy. Prosperity abounded. The Jews were quite capable of defending themselves militarily. The *gymnasia* had probably fallen into disuse; circumcision had long since been resumed. And with the fall of the Akra to Simon, the Hellenizers ceased to exist as a political force. The nation was, to be sure, a Hellenized one, but only politically. And as their contacts with the surrounding Hellenistic rulers increased, Judaea's rulers assumed the characteristics of neighboring monarchs.

Illustrative of this is the case of Simon himself. Though he was a strict adherent of God and the Law, and ruled wisely and equitably, the sad fact remains that it was this same Simon who set the life style by which his descendants were to live—and were to destroy their nation into the bargain. Simon established a court where his family dwelt in an Oriental splendor the Jews had not tolerated since the balmy, and eventually disastrous, days of King Solomon a millennium before. Also in the manner of a Hellenistic monarch, Simon amassed an enormous private fortune, though to his credit he used much of it (but by no means all) for the public weal. As Russell has observed: "The state which Simon and his brothers had done so much to establish was yet to pass through many troubled times. For the next seventy years or so . . . it enjoyed independence so hardly won, until another world-power, greater even than that of the Seleucids, once more brought it into subjection. But from the beginning the foundations on which it had been built were none too strong. The victory of the Jews under the Maccabees was essentially the victory of a particular party within the nation, even though it included the greater part of the people. . . . The Jewish state, though now politically independent of Syria, was nevertheless part and parcel of the Hellenistic world in which it had to live its life. . . . Even when allowance is made for the idealized picture of [Simon's] reign in I Maccabees, it is clear that he was regarded by his subjects as a great and wise ruler, essentially a man of peace, who took seriously his High-Priestly office and was devout in his observance of the Law. It is equally clear, however, that he and the members of his family lived in considerable splendour and amassed wealth which dazzled even the envoys of the Syrian king . . . , Simon himself using much of his private fortune for public benefactions and fitting out the army at his own expense, after the style of a typical Hellenistic king. . . . These characteristics, and others less attractive, were to become much more pronounced in the lives of his successors and were yet to cause grave concern among the people, some of whom were convinced that the descendants of the Maccabees had betrayed their God-given trust." (Only *some* were convinced?)

There are those who adhere to the Tolstoyan thesis that the times create the man, while others believe the opposite; thus it is probably a philosophical question as to whether the tragedy that carried Palestinian Jewry from its high state under Simon to the depths of misery under his grandsons and their sons can be attributed solely to the inevitability of history or to the actions of the Hasmonaeans themselves. Nevertheless, the record of these kings suggests rather convincingly that, had the Hasmonaeans been of stronger moral fiber, the Jewish nation might well have been able to ride out the Mediterranean political maelstrom that saw all the neighboring nations fall before the might of the emerging Roman Empire.

After seeing that Jonathan had been given the proper funeral rites, Simon sent an embassy to Seleucia offering Demetrius Nicator the support of the Jews—most especially their powerful army—in the latter's attempt to reclaim western Syria from "King" Tryphon. Whether Simon would have committed troops to battle on Nicator's behalf is extremely doubtful; Demetrius had shown himself to be politically inept and insensitive. But Simon was aware that Tryphon had managed to usurp the Syrian throne by stuffing the pockets of the Antioch military establishment; the citizenry resented a regicide who was not to the purple born. Tryphon, for his part, was not yet prepared to commit troops to battle; he needed them to reinforce those areas of the empire which he held in thrall. Rather, he was hoping to wear away Demetrius's strength through attrition; Demetrius still held the loyalty of Babylonia despite Tryphon's frantic bid to bribe the satraps to his cause. If, by chance, the contending factions were to meet in battle, Palestine would be the battlefield. What loyalty the Jews now held for Demetrius was predicated solely on their intense hatred for Tryphon. Thus Simon's renewed vows to Demetrius, who had stupidly revoked his prior concessions to Judaea, were less a firm commitment than a calculated risk: that Demetrius would ultimately triumph over Tryphon, being the only legitimate Seleucid available.

There was, of course, the well-grounded fear on the part of the Jews that, should Demetrius by chance win back his throne, he would again turn on them. But Simon was playing for time—time to fortify completely his nation, which had now more than doubled in size. Should Demetrius attempt a reconquest, the Jews would be in a more tenable position to cope. Thus Simon's confidence was most assuredly *not* rooted in a "we'll jump off that bridge when we come to it" attitude. He knew that the

Ptolemies would fight to keep their Seleucid in-laws out of Palestine, but would not attempt to reconquer the buffer state for themselves; the Romans would see to that. And he took no small comfort in the knowledge that Cleopatra II was kindly disposed toward the Judaeans for a variety of reasons, among them: the large and prosperous Alexandrian Jewish community, which was one of the major stanchions of her power base; her armies were commanded by Jewish generals, who also served as her military and political advisers; her nation was in no position to undertake a major war, even should Rome desist from checking any proposed aggrandizement north of the Sinai Desert; the Jews of Palestine posed no territorial threat to Egypt. And then there was the time-worn dictum of which even the Ptolemies were cognizant: "the enemy of my enemy is my friend."

Simon's ambassadors presented Demetrius Nicator with a magnificent golden crown and palm branch—and the message that the Jews had "rebuilt the fortresses of Judaea, furnishing them with high towers and great walls with gates and bars."[1] Demetrius was also casually reminded that "Judaea" now embraced decidedly much more territory than Jerusalem and the surrounding communities, its territorial limits at the beginning of the Seleucid period. In exchange for their loyalty, Demetrius was politely requested to grant the Jews release from taxation, thus recognizing Judaea as an independent state. Fearful lest Simon ally himself with Tryphon, Demetrius had little choice but to grant this great concession, as he made quite explicit in a letter to "Simon the High Priest and friend of Kings, and to the Senate and nation of the Jews." After expressing profoundest greetings, and without attempting to apologize for his prior duplicity, the Syrian king acknowledged receipt of the golden goodies Simon had sent, and then allowed as how

> we are ready to make a lasting peace with you and to instruct the revenue officers to grant you immunities. All our agreements with you stand, and the strongholds which you built shall remain yours. We give a free pardon for any errors of omission or commission, to

take effect from the date of this letter. We remit the crown-money which you owed us, and every other tax formerly enacted in Jerusalem is henceforth cancelled. . . . Let there be peace between us (I Macc. 13:33–40).

There was.

Now all that remained was the extirpation of that Akra garrison. This presented no problem: the Syrian troops and the apostates therein "were prevented from going in and out to buy and sell food in the country: famine set in and many of them died of starvation. They clamoured to Simon to accept their surrender, and he agreed." In May 141 B.C., the nationalists entered the Akra "with a chorus of praise and the waving of palm branches, with lutes, cymbals, and zithers, with hymns and songs, to celebrate Israel's final riddance of a formidable enemy" (I Macc. 13:49–52).

Thus was proclaimed, rather noisily, the independence of Judaea.

Simon had automatically assumed the office of High Priest following Jonathan's murder; now, with peace throughout the land, the Hasidaeans and those few priests who had resisted the Hellenizers reminded him that he was fulfilling this divine office without divine authorization. Simon did not wish to antagonize the traditionalists by dismissing their arguments as minor technicalities; and being by nature a pacifier, he did not want to automatically "inherit" the office to which his brother had been named by a Gentile king. Too, one would like to assume Simon might have accepted in this office a legitimate heir of the Aaronic line; but seek as they might, the traditionalists could not come up with a candidate. The Jews as a whole had been content to go along without a High Priest during the seven-year hiatus between Alcimus's fatal stroke and Jonathan's appointment to that office. But conditions had changed: the Jews were more unified and Simon realized it would be inimical to that unity if a High

Priest were not found in some manner that would be totally acceptable to all concerned.

Simon solved the problem by calling a great convocation of "priests, people, rulers of the nation, and elders of the land" on the eighteenth day of Elul (late August) 141 B.C., on which occasion he had

> the following facts placed on the record. Whereas our land had been subject to frequent wars, Simon . . . and his brothers risked their lives in resisting the enemies of their people, in order that the temple and the law might be preserved, and they brought great glory to their nation. Jonathan rallied the nation . . . and then was gathered to his fathers. Their enemies resolved to invade their land to destroy it, and to attack the temple. Then Simon came forward and fought for his nation. He spent large sums of his own money to arm the soldiers of his nation and to provide their pay. He fortified the towns of Judaea . . . and on the boundaries of Judaea . . . formerly occupied by the enemy. There he settled Jews, and provided these towns with everything needed for their welfare.

Though the I Maccabees account (14:27 ff.) is, of course, the "official" Hasmonaean history, and many implied questions went unanswered—where, for instance, did Simon get those "large sums of his own money to arm the soldiers of his nation and to provide their pay"?—the message was loud and clear. Simon was graciously requested to accept the office of High Priest "in perpetuity until a true prophet should appear." Simon, with equal grace, accepted the High Priesthood, as well as the temporal office of Ethnarch.[2] (For the record, a certified "true prophet" has yet to "appear.")

The assemblage also decreed that Simon was to "be their general, and to have full charge of the temple; and in addition to this the supervision of their labour, and of the arms and fortifications was to be entrusted to him. He was to be obeyed by all; all contracts in the country were to be drawn up in his name. . . . None of the people or the priests [were to have] authority to abrogate any of these decrees, to oppose commands issued by Simon or convene any assembly in the land without his consent . . . on pain of severe punishment."

Thus was Simon endowed with more powers than had ever been granted even to kings David and Solomon. Those were merely temporal rulers. Simon embodied in one person both temporal and religious sovereignty, and by the will of the people —twenty-five years after he had entered history as the unknown son of an intransigent village priest.

All that remained was acceptance by Rome. Immediately upon entering his dual offices, Simon sent an embassy to the Senate with a large gold shield (according to Josephus, "worth a thousand minas") to reaffirm the Maccabean "alliance" with Rome. Preoccupied with the third (and last) of the Punic Wars whereby the power of Carthage was destroyed and the Roman province of Africa created, the Senate—only too happy to have a strong ally between a divided Syria and an enfeebled Egypt— readily confirmed the previous leagues made with Simon's sibling predecessors. Simon understood Rome's terms—verbal acceptance without material assistance; however, this was of little concern to Simon, whose people were quite capable of protecting themselves.

The Senate also sent a letter (quoted in I Macc. 15:19) to "the various kings and countries [that is, the principal kingdoms and city-states of western Asia] requiring them to do no harm to the Jews, nor to make war on them or their cities or their country, nor ally themselves with those who so make war." The Senate was aware that "the various kings and countries" were too involved in their own problems to be concerned about a powerful Jewish nation whose only desire was to solidify its borders for its own protection. The letter was but another Roman exercise in diplomatic bluff.

The situation in which the Jewish nation now found itself is reflected, in a somewhat idealized fashion, in I Maccabees (14:8–15):

They farmed their land in peace, and the land produced its crops, and the trees in the plains their fruit. Old men sat in the streets, talking together of their blessings; and the young men dressed themselves in splendid military style. Simon supplied the towns with food in plenty and equipped them with weapons of defence. His [Simon's] renown reached the ends of the world [a quaint exaggeration here]. He restored peace to the land, and there were great rejoicings throughout Israel. Each man sat under his own vine and fig-tree [a common biblical metaphor here], and they had none to fear. Those were days when every enemy vanished from the land and every hostile king was crushed. Simon gave his protection to the poor among the people; he paid close attention to the law and rid the country of lawless and wicked men. He gave new splendour to the temple and furnished it with a wealth of sacred vessels.

The *t'rumahs* were made faithfully and the Mosaic Law followed most scrupulously in all its often sordid ramifications—by those who were so inclined. But the power of the priesthood had been drastically weakened, its authority now vested in a national leader who, while following the more rational precepts ascribed to Moses, realized that times had indeed changed since the laws had been promulgated. It is reasonable to assume that the money previously derived from the sacrifices now found a more logical outlet: the money with which Simon "supplied the towns," etc., had to come from *somewhere*. Also, tithes were flowing in with regularity from the Diaspora Jews for the "upkeep" of the Temple, and since these communities were thriving, logic would dictate that the "upkeep" had quite probably reached the saturation point.

To say, however, that much of this money, as well as the revenue derived from increased international commerce, found its way into Simon's pockets would be to discredit his intentions. Simon had no desire to establish a monarchy; rather, he wanted to establish a powerful, independent, quasi-theocratic nation within the context of its traditional bounds. Nevertheless, he was not averse to enjoying some of the perquisites to which by position he undoubtedly felt entitled, if we are to judge from a passage in the Apocrypha (I Macc. 15:32) to the effect that when a Syrian emissary arrived at Jerusalem and "saw the splendour of Simon's establishment, the gold and silver vessels on his sideboard, and his display of wealth, he was amazed."

But no one was complaining.

With all due regard for the industry and tenacity of the Jews, it must be recognized that their growth from a provincial temple-state to a major power within a generation had been contingent upon events involving surrounding powers. By the time of Simon's assumption of leadership, the Judaean nation had come through a dazzling series of ordeals by fire. With Simon now in firm command, and the nation united and flourishing, the Judaeans assumed, quite understandably though perhaps naively, that those ordeals had ended.

They had, in fact, only begun.

The Syrians were at it again (rather, still), only this time the old theme had taken on a new variation: a pretender who was Demetrian in spirit yet Antiochan in name had come forward to claim the tarnished Seleucid diadem.

Cleopatra II had found it intolerable having to share the throne with her brother-husband, Physcon, and her daughter/stepdaughter/sister-in-law, Cleopatra III. Regardless of the Ptolemaic tradition that no female could reign alone, she was frantically determined to depose her coroyals and rule *in absoluta.* Knowing how popular she was with the Alexandrian community, she assumed that the proscription against consortless queens could somehow be overcome. But Cleopatra would have to operate covertly, lest her reins be checked by the Romans, who all but went into collective apoplexy whenever Egypt decided to become rambunctious. Once she had accomplished her goal, which included, incredible to relate, reestablishing Ptolemaic hegemony over all of Coele-Syria including Syria itself, she would, assumed Cleopatra naively, be in a position to present

Rome with a *fait accompli*. (And here it should be noted that of all the post-Alexandrian dynasties, the Ptolemies were the only ones who never took up arms against Rome; this goes a long way toward explaining why this particular dynasty, one of the most thoroughly inept in the entire Hellenistic world, proved to be the most durable.) Before undertaking her various projects, further reasoned Cleopatra, it was necessary to have the support of Syria, which was now divided between those loyal to her son-in-law Nicator and those loyal to the deposed boy-king Antiochus VI who was, in fact, her own grandchild.[3] Once she had gained Syrian support and overthrown her comonarchs, believed Cleopatra, she would be better able to overthrow the *Syrian* monarch. Given the situation among the Seleucids, it all sounded quite plausible—to the highly ambitious Cleopatra II. In fact, it was as plausible to believe she could succeed as it is to believe that pigs can fly.

Opting to support her son-in-law, probably because his claim to the Syrian throne was more legitimate, Cleopatra ordered daughter Thea to prop up the desperate Demetrius. Thea had no army to offer her husband, but she did have some sound advice. The Babylonian provinces, which had been loyal to Nicator, had suddenly been overrun by the Parthians. Though Nicator had been marshaling his forces for another invasion of Antioch, Thea advised—quite logically—that his best hopes lay in first recovering those eastern provinces, whose troops, matériel, and much-needed (and long overdue) tax revenues would better enable him to oust Tryphon and reclaim the loyalty of the western provinces. Thea also pointed out that Nicator need not fear the Parthians; they would most certainly be held from overrunning Syria proper by the threat of Roman intervention. Although the Parthians had by now become Rome's major adversary in Asia, there was a westward point past which even they dared not move.

Demetrius led his army across the Euphrates and into battle against the Parthians. Not only did he succeed, in amazingly short order, in pushing them back to their own borders, he also enjoyed renewals of fealty from his Babylonian subjects—totally ignorant of the fact that the Babylonians, fearing the mighty Parthians but certainly not the weak Syrians, were offering a fealty that bore no remarkable degree of permanence. The campaign was a rousing success. Thea's advice had paid off. On learning of her husband's victory, Thea sent a fleet-footed messenger with the request that he return to Seleucia quickly and press on to Antioch.

Demetrius pressed on—but in the opposite direction. Having expelled the Parthians from his eastern provinces, and now quite carried away with himself, Demetrius decided to fulfill the Seleucid dream of bringing Parthia back into the realm once and for all time. He pressed on to the Iranian plateau—and into the hands of the Parthian king. It was for the Syrians both a military and a political disaster of the first magnitude. The king, Mithridates I, shrewdly decided not to put Demetrius to death, but to keep him as a pawn. The Parthian persuaded his prisoner, by force, to marry his daughter, the princess Rhodogune, and then installed the bridegroom in a magnificent Parthian palace—as a well-treated and well-guarded prisoner.

Back in Seleucia, Thea was livid.

She was also immured. When word was received that Demetrius had followed up his Babylonian victory with a Parthian disaster, Tryphon had sent his troops to occupy Seleucia. Thea had hastily taken refuge in the royal palace, surrounded by a guard loyal to Demetrius, which palace Tryphon put under siege. Thea offered to negotiate with Tryphon, playing on the fact that the deposed infant-king was her own child. The gesture was a futile one: not only had Tryphon probably murdered the child by this time, Thea's reputation had preceded her. Tryphon had no intention of becoming involved in any of *her* deals.

But Thea was not about to give up. On learning that Tryphon had made himself detested by so many of his followers including the military, she gave out the news that a true heir of the old

Seleucid house was still alive and available. Furthermore, she announced, were the Syrians to come over to her side, she would help place the legitimate heir on the throne and depose the tyrannical Tryphon.

Thea was not lying; nor was she referring to her incarcerated husband as the "legitimate heir." There was indeed a royal candidate: her brother-in-law. Everyone seemed to have forgotten—everyone but Thea, that is—that Demetrius Nicator's younger brother had also been sent out of Syria for safekeeping when their father, Demetrius I Soter, lost his throne (and his life) to Thea's first husband, Balas. The youngster, whose regnal name was to be Antiochus VII Euergetes Eusebes Soter ("benefactor, pious savior"), but who was more popularly known as Sidetes (from Side, his place of birth), had also entertained royal aspirations of his own. Indeed, he had thought seriously of overthrowing Tryphon *and* his own brother Nicator, but he lacked a power base.

Sidetes had been wandering around western Asia these past few hectic years, waiting for a miracle. When word came from Thea that she could guarantee support of Tryphon's defectors if he would come to her aid, it seemed to Sidetes that his miracle had come to pass. Thea also added the enticing fillip that she would divorce his imprisoned brother and marry Sidetes immediately, if only he would *hurry*. Sidetes hurried. Thea felt no qualms about divorcing Nicator whose stupidity she blamed for her current predicament, partly because he had married, albeit against his will, his captor's daughter, partly because feeling qualms of any nature was a grace to which Thea never aspired.

Simon became alarmed when he learned of Thea's plot and the coming of Sidetes. Was the peace his nation had been enjoying to be shattered by still another Seleucid dynastic war? Though he should not have been disappointed to learn someone was en route to depose the hated Tryphon—who had made it quite explicit that as soon as he controlled all of Syria he would return to deal with the Jews—Simon was now faced with an unknown quantity. With Tryphon unpopular among the Syrians, and Demetrius Nicator in Parthian captivity, Judaea's position was most tenable. But, God forbid, should the latest Seleucid heir unite the kingdom. . . .

Simon immediately ordered his army on full alert throughout Palestine, urged everyone to double the sacrifices in hopes of inducing the Lord to pull off another of His miracles on behalf of His Chosen People, and waited. He did not have to wait long; nor was it even necessary for the Lord to get into the act. Thea had suggested that her new husband ingratiate himself with the powerful Judaean nation. Her mother, Cleopatra II, had advised her most urgently *not* to antagonize the Jews, whose brethren in Alexandria were among her chief supporters; and mother Cleopatra needed all the support she could muster for her attempt to depose her coroyals.

Before long, Simon received a communication from the latest Antiochus, allowing "Whereas certain traitors have seized my ancestral kingdom, I have now decided to assert my claim to it, so that I may restore it to its former condition."[4] Sidetes went on to inform Simon that he had "raised a large body of mercenaries and fitted out ships of war," and that he intended immediately "to land in my country and to attack those who have ravaged my kingdom and destroyed many of its cities." Then Sidetes got down to the business at hand:

> Now therefore I confirm all the tax remissions which my royal predecessors granted you, and all their other remissions of tribute. I permit you to mint your own coinage as currency for your country. Jerusalem and the temple shall be free. All the arms you have prepared, and the fortifications which you have built and now hold, shall remain yours. All debts now owing to the royal treasury and all future liabilities thereto shall be cancelled from this time on forever. When we have re-established our kingdom, we shall confer the highest honours on you, your nation and temple, to make your country's greatness apparent to the whole world (I Macc. 15:2–9).

Sidetes was not asking Simon to fight with him; he was tacitly and tactfully asking Simon not to fight *against* him. In addition to being, as we shall soon learn, an exercise in flagrant lying, the communication was in many respects rather gratuitous: Simon had since ceased any tribute payments to Syria, and it is quite possible that he had already begun to mint his own coinage. Nevertheless, Simon was happy to receive the letter, and was willing to accept it at face value, especially on learning that Tryphon's popularity had reached a low point with the Antioch mobs, all of whom were eagerly awaiting the arrival of the legitimate king.

The twenty-year-old Sidetes had little trouble in capturing Antioch and putting Tryphon to flight. When Thea arrived at the capital toward the end of that year (139 B.C.) to meet her new husband (and to learn for the first time that her son by Balas had been put to death), she did not even pause long enough to enjoy a honeymoon (or a memorial service for her slain child), so concerned was she with establishing a climate that would lead to unification between Syria, under her personal aegis, and Egypt, under the aegis of her mother. Thea had already borne Demetrius Nicator a brace of heirs, and was soon to carry in her womb, by Sidetes whom she had thoroughly enchanted, the future Antiochus IX Cyzicenus. Yes. Thea had plans. And they did not augur well for Simon and his people.

Within a few months of his hasty flight from Antioch, Tryphon, now deserted by his most loyal troops, was tracked down by Sidetes and forcibly encouraged to commit suicide. Safely enthroned at Antioch, Sidetes now realized—at the instigation of Thea, and against the urgent advice of his mother-in-law—that an independent and powerful nation on his southern border must not be tolerated. Sidetes was convinced that Judaea posed a threat to his realm. Thea was convinced that a powerful state between Syria and Egypt posed a threat to her dynastic ambitions. Cleopatra II may have known what was best for Egypt, but Thea knew what was best for Thea.

For Simon, the first hint of Sidetes's intentions, that letter of amity and promise notwithstanding, had come when the High Priest and Ethnarch sent 2,000 well-equipped Jewish troops to assist the Syrian king while he was besieging the fortress at Dor where Tryphon had taken refuge. Sidetes refused the offer and sent the soldiers back to Jerusalem. For Simon, the second hint came when Sidetes sent Athenobius, one of his chief lieutenants, to Jerusalem with a message:

> You are occupying Joppa and Gazara and the Akra in Jerusalem, cities that belong to my kingdom. You have laid waste their territories, and done great damage to the country, and have made yourselves masters of many places in my kingdom. I demand the return of the cities you have captured and the surrender of the tribute exacted from places beyond the frontiers of Judaea [i.e., of the cities in those areas outside the original postexilic territorial limits] over which you have assumed control. Otherwise, you must pay five hundred talents of silver on their account, and another five hundred as compensation for the destruction you have caused and for the loss of tribute from the cities. Failing this, we shall go to war with you (I Macc. 15:28–31).

It was difficult to ascertain whether Sidetes was soliciting blackmail, trying a bluff, or manufacturing an excuse for hostilities; though by heritage a Greek, he would appear to have been, on the basis of this outrageous *aide-mémoire,* by rationale a Syrian.

Simon reminded Athenobius that the seized areas contiguous to Judaea were in fact "the inheritance of our ancestors"—territory that had belonged to the Jews ever since Joshua's, and later King David's, conquests, and which had been "unjustly seized for a time by our enemies." He then added, as diplomatically as he could, that the Jews had simply "grasped our opportunity and claimed our patrimony." Then Simon, most affably and ever the diplomat, conceded that Joppa and Gazara *might have* belonged properly to the Syrians, but that he had been forced to capture them as "these towns were doing a great deal of damage among our people and in our land." To settle the issue, he suggested most equitably that the Syrians forget about trying to retake these two vital cities, but accept instead a payment of one hundred talents in compensation.

Without answering, the enraged Athenobius stormed out of Jerusalem. Upon learning the outcome of his mission and of Simon's "splendour and all the things" the envoy had seen, the furious Sidetes and the avaricious Thea went into tantrums of bellicosity. Egged on by Thea, Sidetes immediately ordered one of his armies into Palestine. In the ensuing battle, the Syrians were repulsed by a numerically inferior but highly motivated Jewish army commanded by Simon's second-born son, the future John Hyrcanus, who drove the invaders out of Judaea and into a disorganized rout toward the Syrian frontier.

Thea, in a furious rage that bordered on a *grand mal* seizure, urged Sidetes to lead personally every Syrian soldier and mercenary he could purchase down into Judaea. But Sidetes, realizing it was more imperative that he secure his own position in the eastern satrapies, prevailed: he would await a more propitious moment to deal with the Jews. . . .

The threat of war was again laid to rest in Judaea—but for Simon, time had run out. The end came, not at the hands of a Syrian but at those of his own son-in-law, Ptolemaeus, commander of the Jewish armies in the Jericho plains. In February of 134 B.C., Simon, in the company of his sons Mattathiah and Judah, arrived at Jericho to inspect the area, which was of vital importance to Judaea's defenses. Jericho itself—dating back seven thousand years, and today the world's oldest city still inhabited—was located at the southern end of the Jordan valley, on the west bank, approximately five miles from the northern end of the Dead Sea. As such, it served as the nation's main bastion of defense against marauding Arab tribes from the Transjordan, as well as against any Syrian or Egyptian attempts to invade Jerusalem from the east. The first city captured by Joshua after the Israelite invasion of Palestine, it was also the last city the Jews could afford to lose.

A persuasive man as well as a devious one, Ptolemaeus had enlisted a number of malcontents in his plot to usurp his father-in-law's High Priesthood and Ethnarchy—with the aid of Sidetes (who was, it must be admitted, quite ignorant of the harebrained scheme). While entertaining his in-laws with a lavish banquet at Dok, his fortress-headquarters, Ptolemaeus plied them with wine and then had them murdered. He then dispatched a messenger to Antioch imploring Sidetes's aid and offering to turn Judaea back to the Syrians as a docile province—on the condition that he be recognized as that province's leader. Thea urged her husband to accept the offer, but he decided to wait and see how far the plot would succeed. Sidetes was not yet prepared to commit more armies to Judaea unless he had a guarantee of success.

After killing Simon and his sons, Ptolemaeus sent some of his coterie of conspirators to kill John at Gazara, where he was head-quartered as commander of the nation's northern defenses. He also sent bribes of gold and silver to John's officers in the hope of enlisting their support. Fortunately, John had been warned by loyal runners who arrived to report the tragedy at Dok. After repelling his malevolent brother-in-law's band at Gazara, he made his way back to Jerusalem where he was immediately rec-ognized by a nervous nation as Simon's successor in all offices. While John had been winning back Gazara and moving down toward the capital city, Ptolemaeus had dashed there in a futile attempt to seize the government. When this proved to be a fiasco, he withdrew to Dok—taking his mother-in-law as hostage. The new High Priest and Ethnarch immediately rushed down to Dok and put the fortress under siege.

According to the account set down by Josephus in both his *Antiquities of the Jews* (XIII. VIII. 1) and *The Jewish Wars* (I. II. 4), the regicide "brought forth [Hyrcanus's] mother, and his brethren,[5] and beat them with rods in every body's sight," after which he threatened that unless John withdrew with his troops, he would toss them over the city walls. But Simon's widow, bearing up with remarkable fortitude under the flailing, "stretched out her hands, and prayed her son not to be moved with the injuries that she suffered to spare the wretch." To her it was better to die at the hands of Ptolemaeus than to see her tormentor go free. Poor John was impaled on the horns of a dilemma: "When he considered the courage of his mother, and heard her entreaty, he set about his attacks; but when he saw her beaten, and torn to pieces with the stripes, he grew feeble, and was entirely overcome by his affection. And as the siege was delayed by this means, the year of rest came on, upon which the Jews rest every seventh year as they do every seventh day. On this year, therefore," Ptolemaus was "freed from being besieged, and slew the brethren of John, with their mother," before fleeing toward the Jordan and into oblivion.

Josephus is the only source of this tragic, and in some respects curious, episode; the biblical account ends only with John Hyrcanus's discovery of Ptolemaeus's treachery (cf. I Macc. 16.22). The "year of rest" refers to the septennial Festival of the Sabbatical Year; apparently this sabbatical year, like the weekly Sabbath, required not only a cessation from all crop-ingathering but a cessation from all extra-Mosaic activities, including wars. John's grandfather, old Mattathias, had already proclaimed that it was permissible to work on the Sabbath if such "work" involved self-defense. However, Hyrcanus, who is referred to in a footnote to the *Antiquities* account as "this excellent high priest," apparently preferred to adhere strictly to the Law. It would seem that Josephus, being of the Pharisee sect, wished to imbue Hyrcanus with a piety that, considering the circumstances, bordered on the inane. Yet in the light of our knowledge that John Hyrcanus was the first of the Hasmonaeans to proclaim openly his anti-Pharisaical biases, the entire account is doubly confusing—if, indeed, it truly occurred. At any rate, the saddened (and orphaned) John returned to Jerusalem, and put to death those who had been associated with the plot. With his formal installation as

High Priest, a new chapter began in the fortunes of Palestinian Jewry.

John Hyrcanus took his High Priestly obligations less enthusiastically than had his father or his uncle Jonathan. By concentrating his energies on temporal problems and prerogatives, he became the first "king" to reign over the Jewish people since the inception of the Babylonian Captivity. (Surviving coins dating from the Hasmonaean period have led scholars to conclude that John's son Aristobulus I was the first to call himself "king.") At this point in their history—four hundred and fifty years after returning from Babylonia—the Jews of Palestine were at long last in a strong enough posture to maintain their independence. The Syrians, their primary antagonists, had already begun their self-immolation through dynastic bloodshed, while in Judaea a viable monarchy had come into being, however surreptitiously. But now, having achieved everything they had fought for, and more so, the nation proceeded—by degrees and with, it must be conceded, some outside assistance—to throw it all away. It was as if, having reached their apogee, some compulsion (perhaps an incipient national suicide complex?) set the Jews on a disaster course toward their perigee as an independent state.

Whereas in the early stages of Maccabee history the nation had divided along class lines with the main "issue" being Hellenism versus Judaism, during John Hyrcanus's stewardship the nation again divided along class lines—only now the issue was Judaism versus Judaism. It was during this period that the philosophical antagonisms among the people found their polarities in two sects, the Pharisees (heirs of the Hasidaeans) and the Sadducees (heirs of the aristocrats and priests). And the inability—more probably, the intransigent unwillingness—of John Hyrcanus and his successors to compromise the differences between the sects, together with the unwillingness of the two sects to reach a mutually beneficial accommodation for the common weal, was to sow the seeds of civil war that consumed the nation when Hyrcanus's miserable grandsons came into their inheritance.

The long reign of John Hyrcanus (134–104 B.C.) was to witness both the halcyon days of Judaea under the Hasmonaeans and the first step along the path that was to lead—slowly, sadly, irrevocably—to its destruction. But before the Judaeans could experience even the balmy days, they had first to contend with a sinister Syrian specter looming hugely on the Hasmonaean horizon.

Antiochus Sidetes was back in town. Literally.

12 John Hyrcanus— End of the Beginning

Overwhelmed by the Syrian forces that poured down suddenly from the north, the major Jewish garrisons at Joppa and Gazara quickly fell; all along the line there was a general retreat of Jewish soldiers and their hired mercenaries to the comparative safety of Jerusalem.* John Hyrcanus immediately dispatched a swift embassy to remind the Roman Senate of its treaty obligation to aid a beleaguered ally. Sidetes had decided to cut short his campaigns in the East and returned to subdue Judaea, now that it had been thoroughly demoralized as a result of the highly popular High Priest Simon's assassination. Almost before the Jews realized what was happening, the Syrian king was standing before Jerusalem with a powerful army whose engineers were hastily assembling their siege-engines. The Roman Senate complied by sending a letter to Sidetes ordering that he return the Jewish cities he had captured and withdraw from Palestine altogether. Sidetes chose to ignore the Senate's warning, at least for the time being. The year-long siege began.

John Hyrcanus's paramount problem was not the physical defense of Jerusalem. Its many towers and well-fortified walls were quite adequate for resisting, indefinitely if need be, the constant pounding to which they were subjected by the enemy engines. Rather, the problem was the growing scarcity of food. The invasion had come on the heels of the Sabbatical Year Festi-

* Hyrcanus was the first Hasmonaean to bring in hired mercenaries, for whose payment he opened and despoiled the fabulous tomb of King David. Many of his subjects never forgave him for spending the money to purchase their defense; they would have preferred to see the treasures lying dormant.

148

val. Though the Jews had been enjoined by Mosaic Law from harvesting crops in the previous year, enough food had been stored for Jerusalem's inhabitants. However, these stores were running low as refugees from the outlying districts flooded the city in advance of the Syrian onslaught. Poor Hyrcanus was, before long, put into the grievous position of having to weed out the nonfighters and physically evict them from the city, retaining, in the words of Josephus (*Ant.* XII. VIII. 2), "those only who were in the flower of their age and fit for war." (Josephus then goes on to paint a vivid picture of the evicted refugees, denied succor by the Syrians and denied entry to Jerusalem, being forced to wander back and forth between the opposing armies until they "wasted away by famine, and died miserably.")

After months of constant pounding and growing hunger, it appeared that even those "in the flower of their age and fit for war" were on the verge of literally starving to death. Hyrcanus asked for—and received—a seven-day's truce. Sidetes was anxious to avoid an extended siege, eager as he was to resume his campaign to restore the eastern provinces to the Syrian realm. When his advisers suggested that he exceed the steps taken by his illustrious predecessor, Antiochus Epiphanes, and exterminate the Jewish masses, deport their leaders, and bring in colonists, Sidetes reminded them of the problems such thinking had led to for the Syrians.

Rather, he preferred to reduce the turbulence, so that his armies would not be tied down in Judaea, while at the same time keeping the quite prosperous nation politically subject to his authority. The best way to accomplish this, reasoned he, would be to permit the Jews to pursue their religion—but as a political tributary. As a mark of his pragmatic program of reconciliation, during the siege the king sent into the beleaguered city "bulls with their horns gilded, and all sorts of sweet spices, and gold and silver cups" for the priests to offer up as sacrifices. They were celebrating the Festival of the Tabernacles—the annual holiday that marks the ingathering of the crops (though in view of the septennial Sabbatical Festival and the resultant catastrophic food shortage, it is questionable as to what crops were actually available for ingathering in *this* particular year; one would hope that the Jerusalemites gave those "bulls with their horns gilded, and all sorts of sweet spices" to the hungry citizens instead of the surfeited priests).

Besides wanting to placate the Jews, Sidetes was anxious to placate the Romans. Though the Senate had not yet sent in troops, nor even an envoy to express Senatorial displeasure (they had no intention of taking either course) the fact that the letter demanding his withdrawal from Judaea *implied* a threat of intervention was enough for the Syrian king. After a series of parleys between the belligerents, it was agreed that Joppa, Gazara, and the other Syrian-occupied Jewish garrison cities would be returned for an indemnity of 500 talents. When Hyrcanus balked at the demand that the Akra be regarrisoned with Syrians, to ensure Judaean tax payments and to preclude any possible resistance to Syrian authority, Sidetes agreed to accept Hyrcanus's show of good faith by turning over a number of prominent hostages, including one of his own brothers. Hyrcanus also promised to field a few Jewish brigades in support of the king. Sidetes then destroyed the city walls and withdrew his army, along with the Jewish troops and hostages, from the devastated and thoroughly famished Jerusalem.

To the Jews it appeared that the few years of independence they had enjoyed under Simon had been but a glorious, all too brief, episode in their tortured history; for while still free to practice their religion unmolested, politically they were again a tributary of Syria. Recent history had more than suggested that Jewish independence was maintainable only when their Syrian overlords were either too busy elsewhere, or too weakened internally, to exercise their authority. The High Priest now led his battered people in praying fervently that history would repeat itself. Their prayers were to be answered, and sooner than even the most optimistic among them had dared hope. Thanks to Sidetes's overconfidence and his wife Thea's machinations, the Seleucid Empire of Syria was about to collapse.

Within a year of leveling Jerusalem, Sidetes had reconquered Babylonia and Media (130 B.C.). Then, as had his brother, Demetrius, Sidetes made his fatal error: he tried to reconquer Parthia. After decapitating Sidetes on the battlefield, King Mithridates decided to release his Syrian son-in-law and send him home to reclaim the vacant Antioch throne. Meanwhile, as Sidetes had been marching into Babylonia, Physcon had been waddling to Cyprus—against his will, and accompanied by his niece/stepdaughter/wife, Cleopatra III. Cleopatra II, with the backing of the Alexandrian mobs, had managed to depose her hated coroyals.[1] But within a year Physcon and Cleopatra III were back in Alexandria; Cleopatra II's hold on the affections of her people was mitigated by her lack of a male consort to raise to the throne. They loved their queen, but tradition was tradition, and though they detested Physcon, he at least was a male.

Demetrius and his mother-in-law, Cleopatra, arrived at Antioch at about the same time: he to claim his inheritance, she to seek exile.

Ten years in Parthian captivity had done little to improve the image of an inept dynast who had never been too popular with his subjects the first time around. Even his ex-wife (and now ex-sister-in-law) Thea was not especially pleased to have him back. She would have preferred Sidetes, a preference rooted less in love (in truth, she despised them both) than in the realization that Sidetes had proved to be a more capable ruler, save for that one blunderous misadventure in Parthia. Also concerning Thea was the fact that Demetrius had sired a few children by Rhodogune; should he manage to stay on the throne this time, there was always the danger that Thea's sons by him would be set aside in the line of succession. Taking her mother's advice, Thea decided to remain at Antioch, but not to divorce Demetrius officially; rather, the two should live estranged. Mother Cleopatra had an idea. . . .

Demetrius and Mithridates had arrived at a mutual understanding. Since both shared a common enemy, Rome, why not arrive at a détente: Parthia would (hopefully) conquer the Romans, but stay outside Coele-Syria, over which Demetrius would (hopefully) regain hegemony. When the two Cleopatras learned of this appallingly illogical (and totally unattainable) goal, they made Demetrius realize the utter stupidity of becoming further involved with the Parthians. Had not Demetrius learned his lesson? Indeed Demetrius had. And when Thea, taking a cue from her mother, "forgave" Demetrius his marriage to Rhodogune and affected a reconciliation, the Syrian king realized that his interests lay outside Parthia. Thanks to the two intrigantes, Demetrius would not be so stupid as to attempt the reconquest of that seemingly invincible land.

He would be even stupider.

He would invade Egypt!

Ptolemy Physcon had thoroughly antagonized the citizenry and military establishment at Alexandria, the two elements among which Thea's mother still had strong support. As presented by the two Cleopatras, the idea of conquering Egypt and reinstating his mother-in-law seemed absolutely delicious to Demetrius, who was casting about for some place upon which to build a power base—a power base for God only knows what. He seems not to have inquired as to what male his mother-in-law would raise to the throne, were Physcon deposed; perhaps he envisioned himself as a likely candidate for the honors.

Upon learning of what his sister-wife and niece were up to, Physcon murmured to the Syrian ambassador at Alexandria that he just might be able to come up with the *legitimate* heir to the Seleucid throne. The ambassador lent an ear: Nicator was being tolerated this go-around by his subjects only because he was the only known adult possessed of that august blood. But if by chance *another* legitimate contender were to be found. . . .

Physcon had really had no intention of getting involved in Syrian politics, especially since his detested sister-wife still posed a threat, albeit a tenuous one, to his own position. If he had his choice, he would have killed her instead of allowing her to escape to Antioch. But Nicator had manufactured a quarrel; and Physcon, egged on by a camarilla at Antioch, decided that, if only to protect himself, he had better fulfill that boast made to the Syrian ambassador. Casting about for a legitimate pretender, he came up with a young man named Alexander, the son of an Egyptian tradesman, whom he fobbed off as the son of Alexander Balas. The ludicrous claim held with the Syrians, and as Demetrius led his army south toward Egypt, Alexander, at the head of a powerful Egyptian army, entered Antioch where he was accepted by an enraged citizenry that would accept *anyone* over Demetrius.

So involved did Egypt and Syria become in the contest for the shabby Syrian throne, they forgot for the moment the Jewish state which divided them territorially. Whether, as the more pious among them contended, the Jews had been granted a Divine Reprieve, or whether, as would seem more logical, it all amounted to a masterful stroke of historical good fortune, the fact remains that John Hyrcanus was able to withdraw from external politics and direct his attention to internal reorganization.

The war dragged on until 125 B.C., when Nicator suffered a defeat at Damascus and pleaded with Thea to give him shelter. Thea suggested that he proceed to Tyre, on the Phoenician coast, until the situation at Antioch had clarified. On arriving at Tyre, the gullible Demetrius was assassinated—on secret orders from Thea. Meanwhile, Physcon was having second thoughts: his protégé, whom the Antioch mobs acclaimed as King Alexander II (tacitly indicating acceptance of Balas, "Alexander I," as his true father), but who became better known as Zabinas, "the bought one," decided that any son of an Egyptian tradesman who can become king of Syria so easily should have little difficulty in becoming king of Egypt as well. In a quick *volte-face*, Physcon supported the claim of his niece/stepdaughter, Thea, as Queen Regent of Syria until her eldest son by Demetrius came of age. Now less afraid of Rome's interference than of her own dynastic ambitions being swept aside, Thea suggested that her mother return to Alexandria and accept the inevitability of again sharing the throne with her brother-husband and daughter/sister-in-law. Physcon was eager to have the elder Cleopatra back, since she still commanded a great loyalty among the Alexandrian community. As for Cleopatra herself, she thought it the lesser of two evils to accept a hateful dynastic (and familial) relationship to living in exile. When she returned, she was welcomed with open arms by her coroyals—whose arms were held open, metaphorically speaking, by the resident Roman legate who had made known the Senate's extreme displeasure at these latest Ptolemaic shenanigans in the north.

Thea usurped the throne of Syria on behalf of her son, whom she managed to have recognized as King Seleucus V in 125 B.C. Syria again had two kings. Financed covertly by Egypt, which had no desire to let the Seleucid throne get out of the family, she rallied the people against Zabinas, who was finally done away with two years after Seleucus V came to the throne. When young Seleucus showed his displeasure at being under his mother's domineering thumb, Thea showed *her* displeasure at this lack of filial loyalty by having him murdered, and then elevated to the throne her second son by Demetrius Nicator. This one, Antiochus VIII Grypus ("hook-nosed," an inherited Ptolemaic trait), attempted to rule as an independent monarch, but this was too much for Thea; in 121 B.C. she attempted to serve him a fatal draught of poison. Grypus forced her to drink it instead.

From that point on, the once mighty Seleucid Empire saw various descendants of Thea contending for what was rapidly becoming less a paralyzed kingdom than an international *plaisanterie*. As Bevan has observed: "These men who called themselves

kings and bore the old dynastic names of the house of Seleucus
. . . were little better than captains of bands, who dominated
now one region, now another, and preyed on the unhappy
country. In this breakup of royal authority, the Greek cities of
Syria acted more and more as independent states and went to
war, or made alliance, with each other on their own account.
Local chieftains, Syrian or Arab, set up principalities of their own
in the less hellenized districts. . . ."

While Syria had been embarking upon its ultimate stage as an
empire—that of total anarchy—John Hyrcanus had been concentrating on fortifying and solidifying his nation; his only political
involvement at the outset of his stewardship had been to declare
his "loyalty" to Alexander Zabinas. By about 123 B.C., with Zabinas
deposed and Syria divided between those loyal to Antiochus
Grypus and those loyal to Antiochus Cyzicenus (Thea's son by
Antiochus Sidetes), John Hyrcanus was ready to expand the
Jewish nation to its traditional territorial limits—at the expense of
the Seleucids. Judaea was surrounded by three "nations" in
whom Hyrcanus saw a decided threat to his own state's independence: the Idumaeans in the south, the Samaritans to the north,
and, in the Transjordan, a plethora of Arab and Greek states all
antagonistic to the Jews. As Graetz has noted, "Hyrcanus therefore considered it his mission to reconquer those lands, and either
to expel their inhabitants or to incorporate them with the Judaeans; for so long as foreign and hostile tribes existed in the
very heart of the country [that is, all of Palestine], its political
independence and religious stability would be in constant
danger. Not only were these hostile people ever ready to join
surrounding nations, and assist them in their greed for conquest,
but they also interfered with the religious worship of the Judaeans, thus frequently giving rise to acts of violence and bloodshed. Hyrcanus was consequently impelled by religious as well as
by political motives to tear up these hotbeds of constant disturb-
ance and hostility."

Whether these peoples "interfered with the religious worship of the Judaeans" is extremely doubtful (even the Samaritans had abandoned all contact with Jerusalem on matters monotheistic); thus, while Hyrcanus's justification for his campaigns on religious grounds is dismissible, his fear that these neighbors did pose a threat to Judean political independence was a valid one. He struck first in the Transjordan, taking the vital city of Medaba after a siege of six months, and then moved on to Shechem, capital of Samaria. Conquering the Samaritans served a potent dual purpose: it gave Hyrcanus control of the Jezreel valley all the way to Mount Carmel, thus securing his northern defenses; and it all but destroyed the Samaritan branch of Judaism, long a sore point with the Jerusalem branch. As was to be his policy in all campaigns, Hyrcanus gave the conquered peoples a choice between submitting to forcible conversion or abandoning their land. This same choice was also given the Idumaeans, on whom Hyrcanus next set his royal sights. These Arab brigands, who had been pushed back to the Negev Desert and had become a nation with which to be contended, accepted, albeit unenthusiastically, their conversion to Judaism. This conversion included compulsory mass-circumcision of all males, something these descendants of Esau were never to forget—especially the Herods, who were to spring from that circumcised stock.

From a traditionalist point of view, Hyrcanus's Idumaean adventure could be justified. According to Genesis, the Idumaeans (Edomites) were descended from Esau, the brother of the patriarch Jacob through whom the Hebrew people trace their descent from Abraham. Because Jacob and Esau were the twin sons of Isaac, the heir of Abraham—again, according to Old Testament tradition, which probably reflects historical fact; Arabs and Jews are of the same Semitic stock—Hyrcanus could reason that he was simply bringing "the lost sons" of Esau back into the congregation. But on a more mundane level, Hyrcanus realized that it behooved him to have the Idumaeans loyal to his authority. Bringing the Idumaeans back into the fold, their unwilling-ness notwithstanding—and they were quite unwilling, though powerless to resist—accomplished a strategic twofold purpose: it finessed a powerful enemy on Judaea's southern flank and increased the population and territorial holdings of Hyrcanus's realm.

No sooner had he completed his conquest of Idumaea than John Hyrcanus had to return to Samaria. That northern area, now inhabited for the most part by Greek settlers, was urged to rebel against Judaean authority by the Syrian kings, Grypus and Cyzicenus, who had united (temporarily) against a common foe. Of these two sons of Thea, Cyzicenus was the more aggressive. He led his armies into Judaea and captured a number of Jewish fortresses along the Mediterranean coast, including the vital port city of Joppa. When Hyrcanus complained to the Roman Senate, which had guaranteed Judaean sovereignty over Joppa, Cyzi-cenus expeditiously withdrew. Now bent on forcing him out of Palestine altogether, Hyrcanus sent a powerful army north, com-manded by two of his sons, Aristobulus and Antigonus (both of whom we shall hear more about shortly). Though Cyzicenus received assistance from Egypt, it was all to no avail. The Syrians were at last evicted from Palestine, the Egyptian armies were sent reeling back toward their own borders in a rout, and Hyrcanus leveled Samaria once and for all time.*

By 110 B.C. John Hyrcanus had assured the total independence of Judaea, "and the country [was] raised to the level of the neighboring states. The enemies who had menaced it from every side, Syrians, Idumaeans, Samaritans, were nearly all conquered, and the land was delivered from the bonds which had hitherto prevented its development. The glorious era of David and Solo-

---

* The Egyptians, numbering about 6,000, were led by Ptolemy Lathyrus ("Chickpea"), whose antagonism toward Judaea derived solely from the hatred he felt toward his mother and comonarch, Cleopatra III, who, like her mother, Cleopatra II, followed a pro-Jewish policy.

mon seemed to have returned, foreign tribes were obliged to do homage to the ruler of Judaea. . . . The banks of the Jordan, the sea-coast, the caravan tracks that passed from Egypt through Syria, were all under the dominion of Judaea."

The Syrian threat to Jewish independence was dead. And Egypt posed no problems: besides being deeply involved in their own internal chaos, the Ptolemies considered it prudent not to antagonize the Roman Senate, which, as an ancillary to their recognition of Jewish independence, had made it known in no uncertain terms that the Ptolemies were no longer to stray beyond their frontiers. This was less to protect the Jews than to protect the Egyptians and, by extension, the Romans themselves. Should the Egyptians choose to disregard Rome's admonitions against further interference in Palestinian affairs, their overconfidence would have been no match for the military might of the Jewish nation. Rome, which depended more than ever on its North African client-kingdom for feeding its rapidly expanding domains, had no desire to go to war over that vassal if such a venture could be averted through diplomacy and threat.

The Senate accepted Hyrcanus's word that the brilliant campaigns he had undertaken were aimed solely at strengthening his border kingdom; and to Hyrcanus's credit, it must be conceded that he had no desire to aggrandize beyond Israel's hereditary limits. In truth, Rome would have preferred that Judaea be less militarily capable; she certainly did not want to see a new major power emerge in Asia Minor. With Syria rapidly destroying itself, and Egypt on a short leash, the ideal situation for the Romans would have been Judaea's remaining confined to the limits it enjoyed at the inception of the postexilic period. But involved as they were with the Jugurthine Wars, the Social War in Italy, and the putting down of the slave revolt led by Spartacus, in addition to solidifying their position in the West, the Romans could do little more than stand by somewhat apprehensively as John Hyrcanus led his people in creating what could well have become

Rome's major adversary in the eastern Mediterranean. Before long, however, this apprehension was laid to rest.

When Rome finally made her move into western Asia, it was not to put down the Jewish nation—but to pick up the pieces.

The fact that Judaea did not endure is attributable less to external factors than to internal ones. During the heyday of the Seleucid Empire, the Jews had their northern enemies to "blame" for the myriad and, at times, near-fatal threats to their nationalistic aspirations. With the Syrians now eliminating each other, the Jews could only "blame" the collapse of their nation on themselves. . . .

PART TWO

...And the Fall

13 John Hyrcanus— Beginning of the End

The Pharisees and the Sadducees, like the Hasmonaean Dynasty, were the result of evolution rather than original intent; and like the dynasty itself, by the time of John Hyrcanus, the evolution was complete.* The two sects—willing to settle for nothing less than exclusive leadership of the nation—stood opposed in all spheres: religious, social, political. Yet they shared a brace of common denominators: an acceptance that civilization had advanced light years since Mosaic times and an unbending intransigence. The acceptance hastened the concretion of their respective ideologies; the intransigence hastened the concretion of their respective dooms.[1]

Because the Jews were essentially a religion-oriented people, the basic conflict lay in the role religion was to play in the governing of the nation, now that it had achieved independence from the Syrians. The Sadducees—the merchants and aristocrats, the Temple hierarchy, the more wordly who had traveled abroad as soldiers and ambassadors—demanded a return to strict orthodoxy. Conversely, the Pharisees—an amalgam of Scribes, orthodox laity, and lesser civil and religious functionaries—demanded a more rationalistic approach to the old religion. However, the common simplistic notion that the Sadducees were the religious "conservatives" and the Pharisees the "progressives" is simply meaningless.

The Pharisees held the Mosaic Law to be a two-fold expression

* Neither sect is identified by name in any sources prior to the Hyrcanean period.

of Divine Will, manifested in the *Written* Law (that is, the Torah) and the *Oral* Law (the teachings of the Old Testament prophets commingled with unwritten traditions that had been transmitted "orally" down through the ages). (Thus, the "law and the prophets" Jesus claimed to have "come to fulfill"—added evidence that Jesus was of Pharisaic persuasion, anti-Pharisee attitudes ascribed to him to the contrary.) To these pietists the Law was thus "interpretable," and not, as their ideological foes argued, immutable. By resorting to hermeneutics, they were able to give new and acceptable meanings to those Torah traditions which conflicted with reason or conscience or which had become outdated with the passage of time and the evolution of societal concepts. (For example, the Sadducees interpreted literally the *lex talionis*—"an eye for an eye, a tooth for a tooth"—whereas the Pharisees interpreted this barbaric law, itself derived from the Code of Hammurabi, as referring to monetary compensation in lieu of physical retaliation.) If they were more "progressive" than the Sadducees, it was in their contention that the Torah fell under the purview of continual development.

For the Sadducees—to whom orthodoxy served as a means to an end—the Written Law was the only acceptable religious authority for the nation. Rigorously enforcing all that was stipulated in the Mosaic Law, they relegated to the realm of heresy and superstition the vast corpus of belief and practice that had arisen since the Torah's codification. Thus they were more secular in their thinking, their orthodoxy notwithstanding, since they permitted total freedom in those areas not touched upon by the Torah. And one of the many areas most definitely *not* touched upon was the concept of the Jewish nation as a temporal monarchy. Moses and the Lord would have dismissed as anathema the idea that a High Priest could pursue a policy of military and political aggrandizement during the off-hours he was not busy collecting *t'rumahs;* perhaps this would explain why Moses's brother Aaron served as High Priest, while the Lawgiver attended to temporal exigencies—according to biblical tradition.

Of the two parties, the theocratic Pharisees were the less realistic. Thanks to the new enlightenment which had long since permeated the Middle East, any nation constituted along ecclesiastical lines—the "modernity" of its ecclesiasticism notwithstanding—was doomed to failure, if only on geographical grounds: were Judaea situated on some Arctic tundra, as a theocracy it might have stood a chance. But while the Sadducees were more pragmatic in following a national-political policy, their pragmatism was vitiated by the patent hypocrisy that was of necessity a concomitant of that polity. They aimed primarily for a political ascendancy that would bring them material prosperity and greater power; their insistence that the Torah alone be supreme reflected their desire for a clearly delineated social order that was firmly in the hands of an established religious hierarchy over which they enjoyed total control. Similarly, their rejection of the Pharisaic notion that *all* aspects of national life should be governed according to religious precepts reflects the Sadducean unwillingness to permit religion to interfere with their secular goals. Their approach can be compared to that of those high-living Renaissance popes to whom the idea of having mistresses, whores, and bastards, practicing simony, and comporting themselves as petty temporal monarchs was not at all incompatible with their vows of chastity, austerity, and devotion to a higher, spiritual integrity.

Throughout the broad range of Mosaic injunctions, the Sadducees were far more harsh than the Pharisees who, though having gained a reputation for severity in the judicial realm, were nevertheless inclined to temper scriptural severity with reason and traditional usage (as in their interpretation of the *lex talionis*). But because the Pharisaic philosophy embraced a far wider range of action, they frequently appear to have been more stringent. Even so, Pharisaic principles, both harsh and lenient, found sympathy among the multitudes. After the traumatic proscriptions of their worship by Antiochus Epiphanes and the half-century of brutal warfare that followed, and in light of the realpolitik pursued by the Hasmonaeans and their Sadducee supporters, the masses were inclined to favor the more sincere and far-ranging pietistic policy. The Sadducees, on the other hand, alienated popular support with their haughty demeanor and legalistic severity. It was only the identity of interests between these aristocrats and the increasingly autocratic Hasmonaean monarchs that enabled the Sadducees to maintain a political predominance in the face of widespread opposition.

Pharisaic opposition to John Hyrcanus derived less from doctrinal conflict than from their suspicion that, in imposing on an essentially religious nation an autocratic monarchy, he was making a mockery of his Divine Office. By now Judaea was part and parcel of the Hellenistic world, and like all Hellenistic monarchs, Hyrcanus had many expensive habits to support: grandiose ancestral tombs, standing armies, powerful fortresses, and an extravagant life style that harked back to the days of Solomon—gaudy palaces and harems and all the vulgar trappings of an Oriental court. Instead of paying taxes to Seleucid overlords, the masses—who always found extrareligious taxation particularly odious—now were forced to pay taxes to their own Hasmonaean overlords, a condition they found doubly odious. Simply stated, their attitude was, to paraphase Charles Cotesworth Pinckney's rather melodramatic response to the French, "Millions for our Lord, sir, but not one shekel for our king!"

In the military sphere, Hyrcanus's numerous adventures further antagonized the Pharisees; though his territorial aggrandizement was in many respects a defensive measure, fixing the nation's borders, it ran counter to their notion of exclusivity. And Hyrcanus's apparent aim to Judaize all of Palestine through forcible conversion was hardly calculated to win him friends among a sect to whom proselytizing, especially of a compulsory nature, was anathema. (As Eban points out: "There is no other instance in all of history of Jews as the agents, rather than the victims, of forcible conversion.") When, around 108 B.C., five years before his death, Hyrcanus had the audacity to mint his own coins, the alienation was complete: minting coins bearing his own name—to the ancients, the imprimatur of temporal sovereignty—was something no Jewish monarch, not even Solomon, had done before.[2]

Were Hyrcanus aware that his nation had divided along ideological (and class) lines, three factors would have militated against his attempting to ameliorate the situation. First, the obvious: as the nation's religious and temporal leader, he needed the support of both parties. From the Pharisees, who recognized him only as High Priest, he drew the support of the teachers of the Law, judges, civil affairs, and lesser Temple functionaries—and the masses; from the ranks of the Sadducees, who recognized his dual authority, came his ambassadors, his generals, his Temple and governmental leaders—and his financial backing. Second, Hyrcanus devoted the opening two decades of his reign almost exclusively to securing his nation's independence: the Jews still had enemies with which to contend. Third—and most provocative—he may have considered conciliation to be a herculean task, well beyond the scope of mortal energy, in which event he may well have elected to believe, no doubt naively, that the problem would somehow resolve itself.

There is, of course, always the possibility that Hyrcanus was ignorant of the growing schism. No evidence has survived to indicate that the rival sects had confronted each other openly; rather, they seem to have spent those early decades of Hyrcanus's reign only *on the verge* of open enmity. It is more probable, however, that Hyrcanus was indeed aware of the dissensions plaguing his nation, and that he adhered to a policy best described as not rocking the ark; since he needed the support of both factions, he was not about to favor one over the other. Thus the claim of Graetz, voicing the opinion of most commentators, that "Hyrcanus personally favored the Pharisees, but as a prince he could not quarrel with the Sadducees" can be dismissed out of hand. Though they had the sympathy and loyalty of the majority of the people, the Pharisees held a decided minority in the ruling Council of Elders. This would more than suggest that they were not so much "personally favored" as merely tolerated by Hyrcanus.

This policy of toleration seems to have been followed by the Sadducees. But when, toward the end of his reign, Hyrcanus's policies led to loud murmurings from the Pharisaic community, the Sadducees suggested that perhaps it was time for the pietists to be eased out of the nation's power structure. Reasoned the aristocrats: with the dynasty now fixed and Judaea launched securely as an independent Hellenistic state, the masses would undoubtedly accept what amounted to an historical inevitability—provided their contumacious leaders were removed from any positions of influence. For by now the Pharisees had become quite vocal in their opposition: Hyrcanus had profaned the High Priesthood through political ambition and a thirst for secular power. He was, in deed if not in name, a king. As such he was unacceptable.

Our only source for the specific incident that turned Hyrcanus against the pietists—an incident that Graetz rightly characterizes as "trivial in comparison with its results"—is Josephus (*Ant.* XIII. X. 5). While most commentators believe the tale to be apocryphal, it bears repetition if only because it *could* have happened the way Josephus describes it.

As the story goes, on returning from a military victory over some rambunctious Arabs in the Transjordan, Hyrcanus commanded that a big feast be held to which were invited leaders of both parties. At the height of the banquet, after all present had eaten and toasted the prosperity of the nation, Hyrcanus embarked upon a lengthy theological discourse. After swearing total allegiance to the Torah, he "confessed" that he might have committed acts not entirely consonant with his august position as

Judaea's High Priest. He then politely invited his Pharisaic guests to correct him if he had "been in error."*

The Pharisees were outraged both by Hyrcanus's "interpretation" of his priestly obligations and his arcane rationale. But being in the minority, they felt helpless to do little more than join in the Sadducee-led paeans to Hyrcanean leadership—until one of their number gathered enough courage to rise and speak his piece: "Since thou desirest to know the truth, if thou wilt be righteous in earnest, lay down the high priesthood, and content thyself with the civil government of the people." (The allusion here, which is often overlooked by scholars, is that the Pharisees were willing to accept temporal monarchy—so long as one of their own was granted ultimate religious authority. Was Josephus, himself a man of Pharisaic persuasion, trying to tell us something?) Hyrcanus asked his accuser to get down to specifics. Instead of saying what was really on his mind, the elder fell back on a flimsy excuse that would be tantamount to the College of Cardinals demanding Paul VI's abdication because he rides in a custom-made sedan instead of astride a mule: "We have heard it from old men, that thy mother had been a captive under the reign of Antiochus Epiphanes." Which is to say, she had been taken prisoner during a Syrian raid on Modin (a claim that may or may not be fictitious but which was nevertheless handed down in rabbinic literature).

Hyrcanus dismissed the charge as beneath the dignity of a response: such grounds for removal from the Divine Office were without legal or traditional foundation. Then one of Hyrcanus's favorites, the Sadducee leader Jonathan, rose to declare that the elder's "reproach" was shared by all the Pharisees, a charge that "would be made manifest if [Hyrcanus] would but ask them the

---

* Here Graetz poses an intriguing thesis: "Was this apparent humility only a cunningly devised plan to discover the real disposition of the Pharisees toward him? Had the Sadducees inspired him with suspicion against the Pharisees, and advised him to find some way of proving the sincerity of their attachment?"

question, 'What punishment they thought the man deserved?'"
Asked by Hyrcanus how the elder should be punished for having
cast aspersions on his ancestry, the Pharisees replied that "he
deserved stripes and bonds, but it did not seem right to punish
reproaches with death." Though aware that the Pharisees rarely if
ever imposed the death sentence, the enormity of the crime notwithstanding, Hyrcanus interpreted the response to mean that
the elder had indeed spoken for all of them: "At this gentle
sentence [he] was very angry." Question asked, question answered.

Perhaps the true story of Hyrcanus's turning on the pietists can
be deduced from Josephus's aside: "It was this Jonathan who
chiefly irritated [that is, stirred up] him, and influenced him so
far, that he made him leave [that is, withdraw all support from]
the party of the Pharisees, and abolish the decrees they had
imposed on the people, and to punish those that observed them."
In the event, sometime in the last four or five years of Hyrcanus's
reign, the Pharisees were removed from the Council of Elders,
from the minor Temple posts they had managed to hold onto,
and from the courts of law. The Sadducees now enjoyed total
domination in Judaea. It was a high state they were to enjoy—
save for the nine-year reign of Hyrcanus's daughter-in-law,
Queen Alexandra Salome—until the dissolution of Judaea eighteen decades later.

Josephus ends his account of Hyrcanus's reign, the longest of
any Hasmonaean dynast, by informing us that once he "had put
an end to this sedition [!], he after that lived happily, and
administered the government in the best manner." The historian
does not qualify "the best manner." It may have been this rather
equivocal evaluation that moved Whiston—his definitive trans-
lator into the English language—to append the curiously amusing footnote: "Here ends the high priesthood, and the life of this
excellent person John Hyrcanus, and together with him the holy
theocracy, or Divine government of the Jewish nation [which

was to be followed by] the profane and tyrannical Jewish monarchy, first of the [Hasmonaeans], and then of Herod the Great, the Idumaean, till the coming of the Messiah." Were Josephus alive to have read proofs of this translation (1737), he surely would have demanded deletion of that last, throat-constricting dependent clause![3]

The sixty-year-old John Hyrcanus was the first Hasmonaean male dynast to die in his own bed, and from natural causes. He was also the last. With the accession of his eldest son, Aristobulus (*né* Jehuda), fratricide-regicide became as fixed in the royal line as did the unwritten (and usually unobserved) law of primogeniture.

14   Aristobulus I— The First King

Actually, Aristobulus's assuming the throne was not so much an accession as an outrageous theft. Josephus (*Ant.* XIII.) considers him to have been the first Hasmonaean king (he "put a diadem on his head"), and insinuates his acceptance of the regnal cognomen Philhellene ("Greek-lover"). *Was* he indeed the first? Coins dating from his reign bear only the legend "Jehuda, High Priest." This has led most commentators to believe he did not officially adopt the title but allowed himself to be represented as such to his Hellenistic neighbors, who thought infinitely more of him than did even his own subjects (or his own *family*). The contemporary Alexandrian Greek historian Timagenes, quoted by Strabo, cites Aristobulus as "naturally a man of candour, and of great modesty . . . and very serviceable to the Jews." While Josephus's low opinion of our hero could well have been influenced by his own Pharisaic prejudices, it must be conceded that any prince who would imprison his mother and three brothers and murder his favorite sibling is hardly a man with whom your average rabbi would deign to break bread. And while it is true that Aristobulus's military victories further secured his nation's borders (the "serviceability" to which Timagenes has alluded), such accomplishments must be weighed in the context of his moral shortcomings. Ghengis Khan was "very serviceable" to his Asiatic hordes, but one doubts most strenuously that his initiation into a proper gentlemen's club would have been digestible to the overall membership.

Because Aristobulus's brief reign (104–103 B.C.) marked the transition for the Palestinian Jews from an autocratic theocracy to an autocratic monarchy, and suspecting that perhaps some of the more revealing coins dating from his reign have yet to be unearthed, we tend to agree with Josephus. For with King Aristobulus I came the fixing in the Hasmonaean family of the one component the lack of which would cause any self-respecting Oriental dynasty to blush for want of validity: the court-intrigue syndrome—the surest sign that an autocracy has "arrived." If Aristobulus did not actually proclaim himself "King of the Jews," it is probably for the same reason that he has had to take second place to his brother and successor, Alexander Jannaeus, as one of Judaism's more spectacular human embarrassments: time was not in his favor.

In bequeathing to his people an economically healthy (and politically distressed) nation, John Hyrcanus fixed by testament the line of succession: Aristobulus, being the eldest son, was named High Priest; temporal powers were vested in the royal widow (whose name is lost to history), whom Hyrcanus named "mistress of the realm." Had Hyrcanus hoped to appease the Pharisees (which is doubtful) by dividing the temporal and sacerdotal leadership, this was hardly the way to do it. Though Hellenized, the nation was not yet ready to follow the Hellenistic custom of accepting a queen regnant. Aristobulus was as confident of this as he was of his own popularity, having acquitted himself admirably during the wars in Samaria against the sons of Cleopatra Thea. One can with little difficulty summon up a vision of Aristobulus sitting around his father's court fairly salivating in anticipation of the royal demise, for immediately following the obsequies for Hyrcanus he seized the temporal authority—which he found more to his liking than being simply a High Priest—by throwing the "mistress of the realm" into that realm's dungeon.[*]

---

[*] Josephus's claim that he proceeded "to kill her in prison with hunger" may be challenged if only on the grounds that Jewish mothers are usually accorded less filial disrespect, but since no evidence exists that she came

Then, lest his authority be challenged by his siblings—a common malaise among Oriental potentates—he imprisoned three of them: Jonathan, Absalom, and one whose name has gone unrecorded. The fourth, known to history as Antigonus I, he "seemed to have an affection for . . . and made him . . . a partner with him in the kingdom." It has never been established whether Aristobulus's affection for this next-younger brother was based on his conviction that Antigonus was totally loyal to him, thus posing no threat to his ambitions; whether their having been comrades-in-arms on the battlefield weighed in the decision; or whether, as is to be speculated upon, the two enjoyed what is euphemistically referred to as "the Greek disease"—a homosexual attachment, a custom that was but one of the numerous by-products of the Hellenization of the East. Perhaps the three theories—and the two brothers—walked hand in hand.

Within weeks of their rather unorthodox assumption of sovereignty, the royal siblings undertook a successful campaign in and north of the Galilee region; as had their father when he conquered the Samaritans and Idumaeans, they compelled those who chose not to flee to submit to forced conversion. (Timagenes, again quoted by Strabo, tells how the Hasmonaean boys "bound" these latest victims to Judaism "by the bond of the circumcision of their genitals." The Galileans were originally a predominantly Gentile race; since Jesus and his earliest Disciples are held to have been of this converted stock, it is interesting to muse on the sharp turn Western Civilization might *not* have taken had these Hasmonaean brothers remained at home.)

The Sadducees, knowing Aristobulus to be capable of winning their nation many highly placed friends in the neighboring Hellenistic monarchies, chose to see in his proselytizing program, as did those who had rationalized away John Hyrcanus's exploits

---

out of the dungeon, Aristobulus must stand before history as having at least precipitated her death. Perhaps she resorted to self-induced anorexia as a means of expressing her total displeasure with this particularly poisonous fruit of her womb.

in this vein, a manifestation of his being so ardent an upholder of the faith as to endanger his life in order that lost souls might see the light. This, despite the fact that such practices were specifically proscribed by the very Torah which they held to be the supreme authority for the nation's governing. Even the populace, by and large, admitted a guarded admiration for a brace of princes who brought glory—and more territory, hence greater prosperity—to their nation. The hard-core Pharisees, to whom proselytizing was morally as well as traditionally unsupportable, merely muttered in their beards and wondered when—and where—it would all end.

By continuing his conquest eastward toward Damascus, Aristobulus would have brought under Judaean control the vital caravan routes that led from the Euphrates southward to Egypt. But fate—or perhaps, as Graetz claims, Divine Providence— decreed otherwise: Aristobulus became suddenly ill and was compelled to hasten back to Jerusalem for a consultation with the Court physicians. His return coincided with the coming Festival of the Tabernacles, and he was reminded that it was incumbent upon him as High Priest to lead the nation in the celebratory rites. In light of his illness (which has gone undiagnosed but sounds suspiciously like a form of stomach cancer) Aristobulus recalled his beloved brother to deputize for him in the Temple. Antigonus had been pushing on toward the Plain of Damascus when he received the message to report home. Had he been blessed with prescience, he probably would have continued on to Damascus instead. He might have died at the hands of the Syrians—but such an ending would have had more meaning than dying at the hands of his own brother.

If we are to believe the available sources (which are disappointingly meager), a cabal at court had been trying to drive a wedge between the two brothers. The charge is a curious one. No evidence exists that Antigonus was even remotely associated with any plot to overthrow Aristobulus. Nor is there any evidence that the Pharisees—who were, of course, plotting against the king—

intended to put Antigonus on the throne. Nor, for that matter, does any evidence exist that Antigonus even *wanted* the throne; his great passion was war. And the suspicion that Aristobulus, who must have resented his brother's growing popularity with the people, engineered a plot that got out of control can be dismissed: had he wanted to kill off his favorite, he need not have taken so circuitous a route. It is more probable that the only thing the conspirators hoped to "drive" was Aristobulus—off his throne and out of his mind. Thanks to Antigonus, who unwittingly played into their hands, they succeeded on both counts. When poor Antigonus—who knew not from priestly decorum, and assumed the occasion called for a show of panoply—appeared in the Temple "most splendidly adorned, and with his soldiers about him in their armour," the calumnious courtiers convinced Aristobulus that his brother had taken the first step toward seizing the throne. Suffice to say, they failed to tell the ailing king that the loyal (and ingenuous) Antigonus had beseeched the congregation to pray for his brother's speedy and full recovery.

The cabal was led by Aristobulus's consort, Salome (not to be confused with the Salome of "seven veils" fame, a lineal descendant in the sixth generation). A subsequent chapter will be devoted to Salome, the only queen to reign over the Jewish people in her own right.* Nevertheless, a few remarks are in order here, since she would appear to have been two distinct entities: when we compare her style as queen consort with her style, twenty-seven years later, as queen regnant, we are confronted with an anomaly who, metaphorically speaking, entered history as Lady Macbeth and departed history as the Venerable Bede. The charge of regicide laid to Salome seems rather difficult to equate with her subsequent career as the only "good" Has-

---

* Technically, the first was Athaliah (c. 843-835 B.C.), but hers was a usurpation, and the throne she held was only that of the preexilic southern kingdom, Judah.

monaean. But it all seems so *logical*. And no other accounts have come down to refute the allegation.

That Salome was not of the aristocracy is indicated by the highly irrefutable historical suspicion that she was of a Pharisaic family; that is, if one is to accept the claim that Simon ben Shetach, leader of the Pharisees, was her brother. If this claim is rejected, then it would be fairly impossible to understand how she was able to inherit the throne of her second husband, much less hold on to it. Aristobulus had begun his reign where his father had left off, confirming the exclusion of the Pharisees from any positions of influence. Thus, in marrying an heiress of the enemy camp, he undoubtedly put passion before politics. Of course, the rather intriguing thought that the Pharisees somehow engineered the marriage in order to establish a voice at court is so outrageous as to appear logical, so wicked as to defy arbitrary dismissal. Salome was some years her husband's senior; was Aristobulus seeking a mother-substitute? She was also a great beauty; was it then a marriage of unilateral passion? Alas, we'll never know.

A few questions arise concerning the conspiracy. Was it aimed at putting Jonathan on the throne? Did Jonathan make any deal from the dungeon, such as promising to restore the Pharisees to positions of influence, should the plot succeed? Was Salome concerned solely with eliminating her husband? *Did* she in fact name his successor, or was she merely an amenable pawn in Judaean court politics? And—where were the Sadducees while all this was going on?

No evidence exists that Jonathan was aware he would ever emerge from incarceration. Nor have we evidence that as a precondition to release and enthronement he promised to be pro-Pharisaic. (Though it is quite possible Salome might have at least exacted such a promise before agreeing to marry him.) Logic would dictate that if Salome had not wished to divest herself of Aristobulus she would not have become involved. And regarding Josephus's extraordinary claim that Salome indeed "made Alex-

ander Jannaeus [Jonathan] king, who was superior in age" of the
surviving brothers-in-law, perhaps we should go along with
Graetz: "It is more probable that Alexander ascended the throne,
being the nearest heir to it [that is, the eldest], without the aid
of the widow." As for any question of possible Sadducean implication in the plot, it is quite probable they knew nothing of it; the
cabal was a classic court intrigue, a secret, intrafamilial she-
nanigan.

Traditionalists may cavil at the idea that the Jewish nation
would have tolerated, as they did, Jonathan's marrying Salome. It
was against Mosaic Law for a hereditary High Priest to marry his
brother's (or anyone else's) widow. But it should be realized that
the Pharisees had less difficulty than the Sadducees in contraven-
ing any Mosaic *dictum* when it suited their purpose, the validity
of that "purpose" notwithstanding. The fact that the Sadducees,
who were the purists, accepted this dynastic marriage suggests
that Salome won them over with an extraordinary charm that has
gone unrecorded; that Jonathan would accept as a wife only the
woman who had paved the way for his elevation; that Salome
was ipso facto popular with the masses, who saw in her a heroine
who had delivered them from the miserable Aristobulus, in
which case the Sadducees may have seen little to be gained (and
a lot to be lost) in raising their hackles over a legalistic point;
or—what is more probable—that the Sadducees did not give a
damn *whom* their new king married, so long as he hewed to their
ideological line.

Aristobulus refused to believe it when told of Antigonus's
flashy performance in the Temple. Conversely, he refused *not* to
believe it. He would ascertain the truth for himself. Toward that
end, a message was dispatched for Antigonus to appear before
him; it was "desired" that the prince "would come unarmed."
After sending off the message, the king ordered "his guards to lie
in a certain place that was under ground, and dark" in Strato's
Tower, with instructions to let the unsuspecting prince pass—

"but if armed, they should kill him." En route from the royal sickroom, the messenger was waylaid in the corridor by Salome who demanded to know the king's orders, and then countermanded them. The messenger was ordered to tell Antigonus "his brother had heard that he had made himself a fine suit of armour for war, and desired for him to come to him in that armour, that he might see how fine it was." Antigonus immediately bedecked himself in battle garb and went off to preen before his brother. Aristobulus's guards followed their orders.

On hearing of the murder of this brother whom he had loved and trusted, Aristobulus gave in to so monumental a spasm of grief that he started to hemorrhage violently: "he was disturbed in the mind, upon the guilt of such wickedness, inasmuch that his entrails were corrupted by his intolerable pain, and he vomited blood." In addition to being afflicted with mental grief and physical misery, Aristobulus was further afflicted with a clumsy valet. While the unnamed miscreant was carrying away a basin of blood the king had spewed forth, he inadvertently slipped in the puddle of blood that had oozed from the slain Antigonus. When Aristobulus learned that his and his brother's blood had thus become "mixed," he interpreted it as a sign of Divine Displeasure with recent events in the Holy City. Bellowing forth with "a deep groan" and conceding that he was not "to be concealed from God, in the impious and horrid crimes I have been guilty of," Aristobulus accepted that "a sudden punishment is coming upon me for shedding the blood of my relations." He then demanded to know of "thou most impudent body of mine, how long wilt thou retain a soul that ought to die, in order to appease the ghosts of my brother and my mother?" The answer was, in so many words: "Not too long now."

With Aristobulus eliminated, Salome ordered released from the royal dungeon her three brothers-in-law and married the eldest, Jonathan, who was seventeen years her junior. The Pharisees breathed a collective sigh of relief—a sigh that was decidedly premature. For, whereas Aristobulus had done in only his immediate relatives, Jonathan—who Grecized his name to Jannaeus and adopted the illustrious regnal name Alexander—did in just about everybody. Especially the Pharisees.

Any illusions the Pharisees had regarding the new king's being superior to his predecessor were quickly dispelled when Jannaeus began his reign by murdering one of his brothers, allegedly on the grounds that he had "affected [that is, desired] the kingdom," and exiling the other, toward whom he seems to have had some affection. If, as Russell theorizes, Salome "aided and abetted him in these plans," then Eban has been most courtly in apostrophizing her as being possessed of a "gentle spirit." At the risk of sounding overly romantic, the present writer would prefer to believe Salome was ignorant of this latest fratricide. He would also like to believe that Salome's forbearance of this Hasmonaean horror to share her bed (between mistresses and whores and military disasters) for twenty-seven years reflects a remarkable willingness to accept a tragic error with utmost stoicism (the error being that of a widowed consort raising the wrong brother-in-law to the throne).

As is always the case when a people accept as their leader a heinous wretch, whether through imposition or open election, the fact that Alexander Jannaeus was tolerated for close to three decades by the Jews of Palestine is less a comment on the man's achievements than on the nation's failings. Jannaeus could no more have flourished without the support of a strong element of the populace than could Hitler have built his crematoriums or Nixon traduced the concept of democracy single-handedly. Moralists would have us believe that horrible leaders are imposed by the Deity in order to punish recalcitrant nations. With all due respect, the present writer prefers to go along with the more rationalistic theory that, the human condition being what it is, nations invariably (and inevitably) maneuver themselves into the position where, for good or for bad, they end up with what they deserve. This is, of course, an extension of the Tolstoyan theory that leaders are the crea*tions* of their times, and not the crea*tors*. Not all the Judaeans "deserved" Jannaeus any more than did all Americans "deserve" Nixon. But since mankind has chosen to abide by the palpably logical thesis that the majority *must* rule in any given situation, then mankind has no choice but to abide by the admittedly illogical thesis that whenever a horror achieves political eminence, perhaps the wisest course for the disenchanted is to keep an eye on the calendar and hope for the best.

15 Alexander Jannaeus— "The Thracian"

For want of a better excuse, one may suspect that Jannaeus's warped personality was attributable to that most classic of adolescent traumas: parental rejection. The poor prince, so Josephus informs us, "happened to be hated by his father as soon as he was born, and could never come into his . . . sight" (*Ant.* XIII. XII. 1). According to family gossip, one night John Hyrcanus received a dream-vision visitation from the Lord, who had ventured down to Jerusalem to discuss the Hasmonaean succession. When Hyrcanus inquired which of his two sons, Aristobulus or Antigonus, would succeed him on the throne, the Lord came up with a shocker: it would be the latest addition to the royal nursery. Disappointed, because he loved Aristobulus and Antigonus, Hyrcanus ordered that the infant be banished from court, to be raised in the farthest hinterlands of the Galilee region. When he went to his grave, Hyrcanus was convinced he had finessed the Lord's will.

He hadn't.

Graetz's portrait of Jannaeus is a creditable one and bears repeating: He "was as warlike as the family from which he sprung, but he was wanting in the generalship and the judgment of his ancestors. He rushed madly into military undertakings, thus weakening the power of the people, and bringing the State more than once to the verge of destruction. The seven and twenty years of his reign were passed in foreign and civil wars. . . . His good luck, however, was greater than his ability, for it enabled him to extricate himself from many a critical position into which he had brought himself, and also, upon the whole, to enlarge the territory of Judaea."

Whereas his Maccabee antecedents had managed to translate adversity into triumph through shrewdly exploiting the ineptitudes of their Seleucid foes, Jannaeus's success in dealing with his foes must be attributed solely to the good fortune which invariably embraces those least deserving of it. His first act on coming to the throne was to issue coins confirming his sovereignty over the kingdom; his second act was to come within a coin's-breadth of losing that kingdom to Egypt.

After taking a hard look at the map of Palestine, he decided to redraw it. His first priority: the major Mediterranean coastal cities of Gaza and Ptolemais. Both had come within the orbit of Antiochus Grypus and Antiochus Cyzicenus, neither of whom was in a position to resist Jewish encroachment. In a two-pronged lightning attack, Jannaeus sent one army rushing toward Gaza while he personally led the attack on Ptolemais wherein resided a sizable Jewish population on whose assistance he hoped to bank. Unfortunately, a powerful local tyrant had beat him to Gaza and ousted the Seleucids; Jannaeus's army was thus forestalled. Jannaeus decided to concentrate on taking Ptolemais and then leading a concerted attack on the southwestern trading city. Again, misfortune stalked him: at Ptolemais he had stepped into a Ptolemaic imbroglio. Again, a mother and son were sharing the Macedonian throne of Egypt. Again, each hated the other's Macedonian guts.

Before long, all of Palestine was crawling with Egyptians.

When the horribly obese Ptolemy Physcon followed his sister-wife, Cleopatra II, to the grave in 116 B.C., he left Egypt by testament to his niece-widow, Cleopatra III, with the right to choose as consort either of their two sons. She chose the younger, her favorite, Ptolemy IX Alexander I, of whom we are told by Posidonus that "like his father, he was monstrously fat—unable to walk when sober, except with an attendant on each side to support him, though when drunk, he could display extraordinary ability in indecent dances." The army, however, insisted that Cleopatra choose her elder son, Ptolemy VIII Lathyrus ("Chickpea"). Ptolemy Alexander was dutifully trundled off to Cyprus.

Chickpea was at first subservient to his mother—who like all Cleopatras was congenitally domineering; subservience gradually turned to antipathy, and by maturity that antipathy had grown into open hatred.[1] Chickpea's arrival at maturity had coincided with John Hyrcanus's arrival at Syria to exploit the civil war between Antiochus Grypus and Antiochus Cyzicenus, and the Egyptian king had led a small army north to fight on the side of these Seleucid cousins (who also happened to be his brothers-in-law). His intention had been not so much to repulse the Jews as to earn Syrian assistance in deposing his mother-consort. When John Hyrcanus sent him reeling back to Egypt in 107 B.C., Chickpea went after Cleopatra. She framed him on a charge of attempted assassination, and Chickpea was forced by the Alexandrians to flee to Cyprus, whereupon fat Ptolemy Alexander was hauled back by his attendants to join his mother on the throne.

While raising an army of Cypriot mercenaries in hopes of returning to Alexandria, Chickpea was called upon by an embassy from Ptolemais soliciting his aid in breaking Jannaeus's siege. As an added attraction, the envoys allowed as how Gaza, Phoenicia, and all the other major Hellenistic cities of Coele-Syria would support his restoration. Chickpea, believing them, readied his armies to sail. Meanwhile, the people of Ptolemais had suffered a change of heart: realizing that Cleopatra would attempt to halt her son's ambitions on the Asia Minor mainland, they decided it might be better to submit to Jannaeus than to run the risk of being caught up in an Egyptian dynastic war. But Chickpea was not to be stopped. With 30,000 myrmidons he landed at Sycamine and began a march south on Ptolemais. As Chickpea advanced, Jannaeus withdrew. He had made a shambles of the city without being able to capture it; and his army at

Gaza stood in peril of total annihilation should the local tyrant there elect to ally himself with Chickpea.

Jannaeus decided upon what must be termed, for want of a better word, diplomacy. Claiming friendship against a common enemy—Cleopatra—Jannaeus sent word that he would put the forces of the Jewish nation at Chickpea's disposal in order to help him gain his "rightful inheritance." Chickpea found the offer tantalizing and entered into a pact with Jannaeus—who in the interim had secretly dispatched an embassy to Alexandria with the promise that he would help Cleopatra defeat her son.

Chickpea learned of the double-dealing and immediately resumed the war, leading his mercenaries on a bloody rampage through the Galilee, bent on destroying every last Jew.* Jannaeus was forced to retreat to Asophon on the banks of the Jordan, the vengeance-ridden Chickpea led his army down the opposite bank, and the two armies stood facing each other across a small expanse of water. Having demonstrated his talents as a diplomat, Jannaeus now demonstrated his prowess as a military tactician: he drew Chickpea and his army into crossing the river, hoping to ensnare them in a trap. When Chickpea crossed, the trap snapped shut—on Jannaeus. The Jewish army was embarrassingly routed; Tigranes claims 50,000 were slain, and "as for the rest, they were part of them taken captive, and the other part [the Cilician and Pisidian mercenaries] ran away to their own country."

The Judaeans were frightened at this latest turn of events; Cleopatra was downright hysterical. Should—as now seemed imminent—Palestine fall to Chickpea, could Egypt be far behind? Quickly marshaling her forces, Cleopatra set out to confront her disobedient (and detested) son. As she personally led

---

* He "abode in certain villages of Judaea, which when he found full of women and children, he commanded his soldiers to strangle them, and to cut them to pieces, and then to cast them into boiling cauldrons, and then to devour their limbs as sacrifices" (*Ant.* XIII. XII. 6).

her armies north, he marched his armies south into Egypt; mother and son literally passed each other en route to their respective targets!

Meanwhile back at Jerusalem, Jannaeus was being roundly condemned by even the Sadducees for having initiated the whole mess by trying to take Ptolemais and Gaza in the first place; had he not been so greedy, they argued, their country would not now be overrun with Egyptians. Having failed at diplomacy and tactical strategy, Jannaeus was now forced to try his hand at abject humility. Catching up with Cleopatra at Ptolemais where she was personally supervising the siege of that city, Jannaeus threw himself and his nation on her mercy. He "gave her presents, and such marks of respect as were but proper" (*Ant.* XIII. 2)—and reminded her of his promise to assist in destroying her son (but tactfully ignored advising her of the counterdeal he had entered into with Chickpea). Cleopatra had by now sent part of her army racing back to Egypt, while Chickpea and his mercenaries had been forced back north into Palestine where he took refuge at Gaza and prayed for a miraculous deliverance from his furious mother.

Also praying for deliverance were the Judaeans. If ever a whopping dollop of pure luck was needed to avert their again coming under Egyptian suzerainty, that moment was upon them: after thanking Jannaeus for his presents, Cleopatra decided to heed the advice of her counselors to seize Jannaeus and simply declare all of Palestine Ptolemaic appanage. The Jews had been lucky before. Would history repeat itself?

It would.

Cleopatra's leading general was Ananias, son of the aforementioned exiled priest Onias IV whom the queen's mother had befriended. Ananias argued that any attempt to annex Palestine would antagonize the powerful Jewish community at Alexandria. Cleopatra saw the wisdom of this argument; she also realized that any attempt to hold on to Palestine would undoubtedly be a severe drain on her military strength. As the Jewish nation indulged in an orgy of prayers of deliverance, Cleopatra and Jannaeus "made a league of mutual assistance." Though the fine points of this "league" were either never published or are lost to history, it is safe to assume they involved little more than a mutual promise to stay out of one another's way. Cleopatra withdrew to Egypt,* leaving Jannaeus free to make war on his Palestinian neighbors—and on his own people.

Had the Judaeans suspected where their monarch's seemingly unquenchable thirst for fighting would eventually lead them, they might have accepted Egyptian hegemony. And had they elected to do so, they probably would have been better off. Cleopatra was a foreigner, but at least she was well-disposed toward the Children of Abraham—which, especially regarding the Pharisees, proved to be more than could be said for their own High Priest-King.

Now free of any threat from Chickpea—who wisely withdrew to Cyprus—Jannaeus proceeded to reorganize his army. Then he proceeded to reorganize Palestine.

The collapse of the Seleucid Empire had contributed not only to the independence of the Jews but to that of the Nabataeans as well. These Arabs had evolved into a powerful kingdom from a group of brigand tribes that had been allies of the Maccabees during the period of Judah and Jonathan. Occupying the lands that today comprise the Kingdom of Jordan, they became wealthy from the caravan traffic that moved across their region between the Persian Gulf and the Mediterranean. While Jannaeus had been stumbling round western Palestine, the Nabataeans had been quietly moving into eastern Syria. It was not the Nabataean intention to conquer all of Coele-Syria, which would

---

* She died a year later (Fall, 101 B.C.), aged sixty—according to Greek tradition, at the hands of her favorite son and consort, the so-called Dancing Ptolemy, who reigned alone until 89 B.C. when he was expelled by the Alexandrians. He died a year later while leading an unsuccessful attack against Cyprus, whereupon Chickpea was invited back to claim the vacant Alexandrian throne.

have been both impractical and impossible; in truth, they had not so much "conquered" eastern Syria as marched in to take possession of a region that had left itself open to conquest. The Nabataeans wanted only two things from Jannaeus: recognition of their right of eminent domain over those trade routes, and recognition of their sovereignty in the Transjordan. But Jannaeus chose to see in the Nabataeans a threat to his eastern-northeastern borders.

Had Jannaeus chosen to negotiate a détente with these Arabs, he might not have turned a containable neighbor into an uncontainable enemy. But Jannaeus did not believe in negotiation. He launched upon a series of swift and bloody rampages that saw the Nabataeans pushed back across the Jordan; in so doing, he succeeded in antagonizing irrevocably these Arabs—a "success" that was to haunt the Jewish nation in the next generation. Then, assuming (erroneously) he had secured his eastern flank for all time, Jannaeus headed west to Gaza; within a year he managed to reduce the population considerably and all but level the city, simply because they had threatened to side with Chickpea. Now having demonstrated what he could do to any Gentiles who crossed his path, it was time for Jannaeus to demonstrate what he could do to any Jews who took that same route.

Jannaeus returned to Jerusalem in 96 B.C. to find his popularity decidedly waning. The Pharisees, who must surely have regretted helping him from the dungeon to the throne, considered his militarism and the attendant hardships visited upon the nation only slightly less a total abomination than the open contempt he exhibited toward his High Priestly office. The Sadducee priests were beginning to question his inattention to his Divine obligations. And the Sadducee generals, comparing their leader's record with those of his antecedents, had by now concluded that as a strategist Jannaeus left much to be desired. The aristocrats and merchants, however, were pleased with the added prosperity that was accruing to the nation; and the military was brought to rationalize that, fortuitous as Jannaeus's victories on the battlefield had been, they were victories nonetheless. Therefore it was still safe for Jannaeus to walk the streets of Jerusalem—though it is unlikely that he spent much time in this particular endeavor, preferring, as he did, to devote his hours to drinking and wenching. (There is no record that Salome made any attempt to exert a salubrious influence on her husband; the poor queen probably decided to retreat into the background and hope for better days.)

Though there was nothing the king could (or would) do to answer the charges of his critics that he was a reckless militarist, he was willing to concede—at the urging of the Sadducee priests—that his subjects were not entirely wrong in condemning his absence from the Temple. When the Festival of the Tabernacles came around, he agreed to lead the nation in the appropriate festivities. What started as a celebration of one of the oldest of the Mosaic holidays became the opening battle in the civil war that eventually wrecked the Jewish nation.

Sources fail to agree as to who fired the first salvo. Secular historians, including Josephus, claim that as Jannaeus stood before the High Altar preparing to make the required sacrifices, he was suddenly pelted with a barrage of citrons carried by the people for use in the rites. Rabbinic legend, perhaps in order to vindicate their Pharisee forebears, has it that Jannaeus precipitated the outburst by contemptuously pouring over his feet the libation which Law required be poured over the Altar. In the event, after flinging their citrons, the people flung their insults. These ranged from casting aspersions on his ancestry (that old Pharisaic saw about his grandmother having once been a Syrian captive) to declaring him morally as well as Aaronically unfit to hold the Divine Office. The infuriated Jannaeus turned loose his Sadducee-financed mercenaries on the rebellious crowd, and upwards of 6,000 Pharisees and their sympathizers were cut down. Assuming the incipient revolt had been nipped in the bud, Jannaeus now felt free to resume his expansionist policies. As the

Pharisees returned to their communal prayers, Jannaeus returned to war, scoring a spectacular success against the Nabataeans in the Transjordan. But this time, instead of retreating, the Nabataeans swarmed down into eastern Palestine. In the battle that ensued at Gadara a few miles southeast of the Sea of Galilee, those of Jannaeus's troops who were not slaughtered were easily routed; Jannaeus himself, after falling into an ambush, barely managed to escape with his life.

Surprisingly, the Nabataeans did not press the attack, concerned as they were only with securing their western borders and assuming that Jannaeus had gotten the message to stay west of the Jordan. Jannaeus may not have gotten the message, but the Pharisees certainly did: they saw in the Arab defeat of their nemesis a sign from Heaven that the moment had come to rise up. By the time the bedraggled Jannaeus made his way back to Jerusalem with the sorry remnants of his army (90 B.C.), the Pharisees were in open revolt.

It took Jannaeus two years—and the hiring of more Sadducee-financed mercenaries—to put down the insurrection that is said to have claimed upward of 50,000 lives. Now aware that he had to negotiate a settlement to the conflict that was tearing his nation apart—and, not incidentally, leaving Judaea open to possible foreign conquest—Jannaeus approached the Pharisees with olive branch in hand. What, he wanted to know, did they demand of him in order to maintain the peace? They made only one demand: not his abdication from the High Priestly office, nor his renunciation of the throne, but simply—his death. And to demonstrate how sincere they were in this demand, the Pharisees decided to follow the example set by their ideological foes and enlist outside aid.

The logical move would have been to hire foreign mercenaries. But the Pharisees were impecunious—and slightly illogical. They enlisted the aid of the Syrians! So frantic were they to bring down the royal house, they were prepared to bring down the nation into the bargain. Before long they would regret their stupidity, but by then it would be too late: Jannaeus was hardly the type to forgive and forget. War they wanted, war he would give them!

Sitting (actually, tottering) on the Seleucid throne was Cleopatra Thea's grandson Demetrius III Eucaerus ("the Fortunate"). He was not so much the king of Syria as the strongest of a veritable plethora of "Antiochan" and "Demetrian" warlords, each of whom controlled a small portion of what remained of a once-mighty empire. When the Pharisees sent him word to bring his army south into Palestine on their behalf, Eucaerus saw this as a true stroke of fortune. He would achieve the (now laughably chimerical) goal of reestablishing suzerainty over Palestine; this, he reasoned, could only strengthen his position against his various brothers, half brothers, stepbrothers, and cousins. Why, he would even be in a position to oust his Ptolemaic uncle and conquer Egypt! Or so he thought. . . .

The battle was fought at Shechem—ironically, the city where the Lord had promised the land of Canaan to the patriarch Abraham and his "seed" in perpetuity. A rather large number of that "seed" joined Demetrius, whose overall strength totaled 43,000. Jannaeus arrived on the scene with little more than half that number: 20,000 pro-Sadducee militiamen and 6,200 hired Greek mercenaries. Before the fighting got underway, Demetrius tried to lure away Jannaeus's Greeks, while Jannaeus tried to bribe the Pharisees into returning to the fold. Both leaders were spectacularly unsuccessful in this endeavor, the battle was joined, and Demetrius scored a quick and resounding victory. With his brigades disastrously routed, Jannaeus was forced to flee into the mountains. As Demetrius hastily regrouped his forces for a march on Jerusalem—which would have fallen easily to the Seleucid—Jannaeus suffered another stroke of good fortune: 6,000 of the Pharisees suddenly realized—as if they could help *but* realize—that their nation was once again on the verge of becoming a tributary of their traditional enemies. They tracked down Jannaeus in the mountains where he was hiding and extended their *mea culpas*. Jannaeus accepted their switch of allegiance and quickly made plans to purchase more mercenaries. Meanwhile, on learning that the Jews who had called him into Palestine had now defected—and either overestimating Jannaeus's strength or underestimating his own—Demetrius executed a hasty (and unnecessary) retreat out of Palestine and into the footnotes of history.

As was to be expected of an irrational, besotted, quite probably syphilitic, and thoroughly indignant autocrat, Jannaeus chose not to take the one path that might have brought a peace of sorts to his disturbed realm. True, he had accepted the apologies of the Pharisees; but then he had needed them. Now he no longer did. Thanks to the Sadducees, whose funds seemed limitless, Jannaeus rebuilt another army and proceeded to beat the bushes of Judaea in search of every Pharisee he could find. After destroying one fortress where a large number of repenters had taken refuge, and slaughtering most of them, he dragged a battalion of pietists back to Jerusalem in order to set an example. As Josephus informs us, the autocrat "did one of the most barbarous actions in the world . . . for as he was feasting with his concubines, in the sight of all the city, he ordered about eight hundred of them to be crucified; and while they were [still] living, he ordered the throats of their children and wives to be cut before their eyes . . . and these executions he saw as he was drinking and lying down with his concubines. Upon which so deep a surprise seized the people, that eight thousand of his opposers fled away the very next night, out of all Judaea, whose flight was only terminated by Alexander's death."[2] Having set the example he desired, Jannaeus set off on another expedition.

Demetrius the Fortunate's younger brother, Antiochus XII, had by now carved out a slice of the Seleucid pie, establishing himself as a powerful warlord in Damascus. So detested by the Damascenes was Antiochus that no resistance was offered when the Nabataeans again came marching in. Again Jannaeus set out to push the Arabs back beyond the Jordan; again he suffered a humiliating defeat; and again, instead of following up their victory with a successful march on Jerusalem, the Nabataeans chose to remain beyond their own borders. Josephus's claim (*Wars* I. IV. 8) that Aretas III, the Nabataean king, "retired by mutual consent" indicates that he and Jannaeus must have arrived at a rapprochement. (Was there to be no limit to Jannaeus's luck?) In all probability, Aretas's intentions had been merely to win Judaean recognition of his authority in the Transjordan and eastern Syria; he was wise enough to realize that overrunning Palestine was one thing, but establishing hegemony was another matter. If Aretas accepted Jannaeus's promise not to wage further war on the Nabataeans, it was an acceptance the Arab would soon regret.

Jannaeus may have been unarguably a horror, but at least he was a persevering horror, if we are to believe Josephus (*Ant.* XIII. XV. 5): "Although he fell ill from hard drinking, and was troubled with a quartan ague for three years, yet he would not leave off going out with his army." (That "quartan ague" may have been cirrhosis of the liver, although advanced syphilis should not be ruled out; in addition to being the most bellicose of the Hasmonaeans, Jannaeus was the most fun-loving.) It would seem that he returned to Jerusalem periodically only to replenish his war machine. After tapping his Sadducee bankers for more mercenaries, Jannaeus "went out with his army" into the Transjordan once again. This time he met with better success. Aretas had overstepped his bounds by involving himself with the Syrians, and was now powerless to prevent Jannaeus from taking a twelve-city buffer area. Jannaeus took no more. His time was running out. After returning home to hire more mercenaries, sample the season's vintage, and pass judgment on the latest crop of Jerusalem doxies, Jannaeus prepared to conclude his reign by capturing a number of independent Greek cities which had somehow taken root in northern Palestine while no one had been looking.

It was 76 B.C., time for the forty-nine-year-old Jannaeus to bid farewell to this vale of tears—a vale which *he* certainly had not helped to make any less tearful. To the nation at large, he was a great hero who had fixed Judaea's borders coexistent with those carved out by King David. The Sadducees had succeeded in weaning away from the Pharisees a large segment of the populace by pointing to the prosperity that had come upon their land through the king's successes on the battlefield. That these "successes" derived less from military brilliance than outrageous luck was of little import: so far as the average Judaean was concerned, his king's achievements more than compensated for the many crimes he had committed at the expense of his ideological foes. But while he was a hero to the people, Jannaeus was still total anathema to the Pharisees, who attached to him the most shameful epithet they could come up with: "The Thracian." (This would be analogous to Sadat of Egypt being called "The Zionist" by his detractors.) The demoralized Pharisees had no way of knowing it, but just as the Thracian's time had come, so was their time coming.

Just before his death, while besieging one of those surreptitious little Greek cities, Jannaeus bequeathed the kingdom to his wife, Salome—which was probably only fair play, inasmuch as she had in a way given him the kingdom in the first place. That he did so when he already had two grown heirs would suggest a premonition on Jannaeus's part that the boys would come to no good; if so, the premonition was a shrewd one: Aristobulus II and Hyrcanus II were definitely no bargains. Perhaps Jannaeus felt confident that their mother could keep them in check. If so, it was a well-placed confidence. She was indeed able to control them for the nine years she reigned over Judaea in her own right.

That the Pharisees were willing to accept a female dynast should be apparent: she was one of their own. That the Sadducees were amenable would suggest a willingness, albeit a begrudging one, to make peace with their ideological opponents. That the people as a whole accepted a woman on their throne reflects the influence of the neighboring Hellenistic dynasties in which powerful roles were played by dominant women, most notably in Egypt with that legion of Cleopatras.

In addition to bequeathing her a powerful realm, Jannaeus bequeathed Salome a sage bit of advice—Make peace with the Pharisees!

(As if Salome *needed* such advice.)

When Queen Alexandra (as Salome now chose to call herself) returned to Jerusalem with the body of her fallen husband, the populace mourned the passing of a brave soldier, the Sadducees lamented the death of a great champion, and the Pharisees rewrote the calendar. After proclaiming that the anniversary of Jannaeus's death was to be celebrated as a day of great rejoicing throughout Israel, the pietists settled down to the more immediate business at hand: seizing control of the nation.

16 Alexandra Salome— Strained Interlude

Like Victoria, she gave her name to an era: "The Golden Age of Queen Alexandra Salome." Unlike Victoria, about whom biographies abound, she remains a stranger. And an enigma. Yet all the ingredients are there for a first-rate historical brew. She burst on the scene full-blown, like Pallas Athena from the cranium of Zeus. A congenital beauty, she aroused history's attention by collaborating in the regicide of her first spouse; endured, with presumed passivity, twenty-seven years as the wife of a militaristic voluptuary young enough to be her son; suffered the classic maternal grief of seeing the fruit of her womb go to rot; and departed this life as a religiously sincere yet politically myopic earth mother figure whom the rabbis venerate while the historians question. She placed, above all considerations, the power of the royal house into which she had married, while siding wholeheartedly with that house's most pronounced antagonists. By nature born to rule, by inclination she chose only to reign, thus leaving the administration of the country, in Josephus's understated words, "destitute of a proper support." She was concerned less with the future of her realm than with its present, though logic would demand she must have been aware of the inherent fallacy in such an approach. The nation was "ripe" for religious reform—and therein lay Alexandra's fatal flaw: her inability (dare we say, unwillingness?) to appreciate the fine line that separates religious reform from religious persecution. Her reign marked the pinnacle of untroubled independence in Judaea, "the only tranquil period during eighty years of Has-

196

monaean strife," as Eban has characterized it. In short, she kept the peace for nine years. But at what a price!

Externally, there were few problems with which to be concerned. The Syrians to the north and the Egyptians to the south posed no threat (save, possibly, to themselves); to the east, the Nabataeans, aware of the "big brotherly" eye Rome was casting over western Asia, were quite content to remain beyond their borders. The only major threat to the realm came toward the close of the Golden Age when Tigranes, king of Armenia, overran Syria and tried to follow suit in Palestine. This Alexandra was able to forestall by paying a munificent bribe—and enjoying a bit of luck: Tigranes had to rush home to face a Roman invasion that eventually saw his hastily assembled empire wind up as an insignificant Roman province.

Why, then, did Alexandra's reign begin on so peaceful a note and end on so bloody a one?

To answer this question would be to answer one of history's more perplexing—and unanswerable—conundrums: Why does religious zeal inevitably lead to religious excess? The Crusades were organized by the Church to "rescue" the Holy City of Jerusalem from the Infidels—a "rescue" that saw a religious mission become transmogrified into a religious blood bath. The Inquisition was undertaken in order to show mankind that one must endure the fiendish tortures of hell in order to realize "salvation." The Protestant Reformation and the ensuing Counter Reformation turned the continent of Europe into a centuries-long charnel house of wholesale slaughter. While it is still an unprovable axiom that hell hath no "fury like a woman scorned," it is a provable truism—as history enjoys demonstrating—that hell hath no fury like a caste which believes it and it alone holds the keys that unlock the doors to the Kingdom of Heaven.

The Pharisees did not set out to exact revenge on the Sadducees. First, they would bring the Judaeans back to the ways of the Lord. *Then* they would exact that revenge. That the Sadducees soon saw themselves losing favor with the masses was a situation with which they could live. Their daily pursuits were in no way interfered with; they were, after all, the queen's generals, ambassadors, merchants. That they were removed from the Sanhedrin (as the Council of Elders was now known) and the Temple hierarchy they found as acceptable as they found dismissible the entire Pharisaic Reformation as a temporary aberration.

Acting on the advice of the Pharisees, the queen invited Judah ben Tabbai, a celebrated scholar in the Alexandrian Jewish community, to come to Jerusalem and assist her brother, Simon ben Shetach, in the religious revival. "Neglected customs were renewed with all pomp and solemnity," writes Graetz; among these was

> the ceremony of pouring a libation of water upon the altar during the Feast of Tabernacles, which had been mockingly ridiculed by Alexander [Jannaeus]. . . . Upon these occasions . . . all the people would . . . crowd to the holy mount [the Temple] to witness or take part in the proceedings. At times these bore a lively character, such as torch-light processions and dancing; at other times they took the more solemn form of musical services of songs of praise. This jubilee would last the whole night. At break of day the priests announced with a blast of their trumpets that the march was about to commence. At every halting-place the trumpets gathered the people together, until a huge multitude stood assembled. . . . Then the water was drawn into a golden ewer. In solemn procession it was carried back to the Temple, where the libation was performed. The water streamed over the altar, and the notes of the flute, heard only upon the most joyful occasions, mingled with the rapturous strains of melody that burst from countless instruments.

But there was more to the religious reformation than cacophonous torchlight parades and water brigades. A program of mass education was initiated (though it must be reported that the schools in which the curriculum was confined to the study of the

Law were open only to males who had passed the age of sixteen).
Many of the Sadducean legalisms, such as the literal interpretation of the *lex talionis,* were abolished. And the Penal Code was
imbued with some of the more rationalistic aspects of the Oral
Law. One rather interesting reform was rooted in the Pharisee-
sponsored program to reduce the high rate of divorce. Any man
who repudiated his wife was obliged to surrender "a certain sum
of money, by which she could support herself." But "as there was
but little current coin amongst a people whose wealth consisted
principally in the fruits of the soil or in the cattle, the husband
would often pause before allowing a momentary fit of passion or
excitement to influence his actions." In hoping to reduce the
divorce rate, the Pharisees unwittingly gave civilization the custom of alimony!

There may have been "little coin amongst the people," but
there was a great deal among the priests. The Sadducees had
ruled that the daily offerings, as well as the funds to support the
priests and other Temple minions, should not be paid out of the
national treasury, but with individual—and voluntary—contributions. The Pharisees carried this one step further: every citizen
over the age of twenty was compelled to surrender an annual
minimum of a half-shekel to the Temple's upkeep. "Every citizen"
included those in the Diaspora, from which group, advises
Graetz, the collections "were the richest, the Judaeans who dwelt
outside Palestine being very generous as well as very wealthy."[1]

The nation was now restored by the Pharisees to its hereditary
posture of exclusivity and total piety. The sons of Abraham and
Isaac and Jacob had been promised by the Lord that He would
always champion His Chosen People if only they would honor
Him, obey Him, trust in Him. Regrettably (and embarrassingly),
they had strayed. But all that was now ended. For all time. There
would be no more backsliding. No more deviation from the ways
of the Lord. The Pharisees had transported Holy Israel back to
the bosom of the Lord, and He had settled upon them the moral,

social, emotional (and financial) sovereignty over those who inhabited His Promised Land. What need had Israel now of generals, ambassadors, merchants? Would not the Lord fight Israel's battles? convince the nations of the world that the Children of Abraham were above intercourse with the heathens? cause the vines to sprout with the tenderest grapes, the land to fairly flow with milk and honey? The Lord was their Shepherd; they would not want—except to savor the sweet smell of revenge. . . .

Reneging on their insistence that the *lex talionis* be interpreted symbolically (had not the Lawgiver Moses decreed otherwise?), the Pharisees ordered the execution without trial of all those Sadducee leaders who had either advised, authorized, or condoned Jannaeus in the blood bath that followed the nation's near-disaster with Demetrius the Fortunate. The aristocrats were now in dire need of a champion at court. And what better, indeed more *logical*, champion than the ineffectual Hyrcanus's younger brother, Aristobulus II?

It was common gossip around Jerusalem that Aristobulus positively loathed the High Priest—less because of the office he held than the office he would inherit. Like his noxious namesake of a previous generation, young Aristobulus probably could not have cared less whether the Pharisees *or* the Sadducees were the dominant party; theological and philosophical arguments were matters with which Aristobulus was eminently unconcerned. All that concerned him was that he might succeed his mother on the throne—if need be, over the dead body of his inept brother, the rightful heir. The Sadducees had no particular love for young Aristobulus. (Nor did many others, his mother included, if the truth be known.) But personality was not the issue here. Aristobulus had the makings of a first-rate autocrat.

In a scene worthy of Sophocles, Aristobulus led into his mother's chambers a delegation of Sadducee leaders come to protest the Pharisee persecutions, and to remind the queen of the services their party had rendered to the nation. Poor Alexandra was torn. She had brooked no objections to the Pharisee purges; yet she dared not alienate the good will of those being purged. As the queen equivocated, she was advised most tactfully by her visitors that if something were not done to protect them from Pharisaic wrath they might be compelled to offer their services to the Nabataeans or even—*in extremis*—the Syrians. Aristobulus was cognizant of the quandary in which he had helped to place his aging and essentially religious mother. After the Sadducees had spoken their piece, he stepped forth to denounce her bitterly for siding with men of the cloth who would resort to such base endeavors as open persecution of those who did not share their religious convictions. The queen was frantic. She saw her nation on the verge of another civil war. Was there no way out of this dilemma, she pleaded? No compromise? Aristobulus made the queen realize that the Pharisees would not—*could* not—be stopped. Then what, cried the anguished queen, was to be done?

Aristobulus had the answer: Grant the Sadducees permission to leave Jerusalem—for their own safety—and to "inhabit" a number of fortresses throughout the land.

Alexandra eagerly seized upon this as an equitable solution. With the exception of three major strongholds—Alexandrium, Machaerus, and Hyrcania—all fortresses outside Jerusalem were ordered transferred to Sadducee control. The Sadducees were eminently satisfied, the crisis was ended: with the Sadducees removed from Jerusalem, the persecutions would cease. And cease they did. So far as the Pharisees were concerned, the Sadducees intended only to "inhabit" those fortresses—not garrison them. Also, the Pharisees felt secure: they had exacted their revenge. They had gotten the country back on the path of righteousness. Let the Sadducees go! The sooner the better!

Obviously, the Pharisee hierarchs had not taken a full measure of Aristobulus. Their preoccupation lay in reconstructing the nation as a theocracy within the context of a monarchy—surely an anomaly here, if not a contradiction in political terms. They had no time to consider mundane problems; mundane problems fell within the purview of the Lord. That the Lord failed to inform His pious friends at Jerusalem that Aristobulus was shrewdly laying the groundwork for a usurpation of authority would suggest that either Aristobulus maneuvered in total secrecy or the Lord was stone blind. In any event, Aristobulus realized that any precipitate action by him or on his behalf would be doomed in a realm that was content to be guided by so pious a queen as his mother, operating through the medium of the pietists. Keeping his followers under a tight rein, Aristobulus covertly strengthened his "habitations" and smuggled in droves of mercenaries. He would bide his time and await the natural death of his mother before undertaking what would appear to be, on the surface, an easily soluble religious conflict but which was, to all intents and purposes, shaping up as a dynastic war along class lines.

Shortly after the invasion by Tigranes of Armenia had been repulsed, Queen Alexandra took to her bed, presumably from the afflictions of old age (she was seventy-three, a truly advanced age for the times). Aristobulus began to move. After being assured by the court physicians that his mother's days were numbered, he displayed a profound show of filial grief, offered up the proper sacrifices in the Temple for his august mother's recovery—and then "stole away secretly by night with only one of his servants, and went to the fortresses, wherein his friends . . . were settled" (*Ant.* XIII. XVI. 5).

When Aristobulus's activities—and intention—became common knowledge, the Pharisees panicked in the realization that it would not be long before he "would be able to settle himself firmly in the government [and] that he would inflict punishment upon them for the mad treatment his house had had from them." Within a fortnight, Aristobulus had gained control of twenty-two "strong places," whereupon a delegation of Jerusalem elders led Hyrcanus into his moribund mother's chambers "and desired that she would give them her sentiments about the present posture of affairs."

The languishing monarch gave them her "sentiments." She hoped that Hyrcanus would be a wise ruler and would lead the nation in following the policies of his Uncle Simon and the elders. As Hyrcanus promised to do so, Uncle Simon allowed as how these were indeed wise sentiments—but not exactly what the frantic pietists wished to hear at this unsentimental time. They wanted to know her thoughts for dealing with Aristobulus and his Sadducees. The queen reminded them of the obvious: "they had many circumstances in their favour still remaining, a nation in good heart, an army, and money in their several treasuries" (*Ant.* XIII. XVI. 5). As the Pharisees rushed out to prepare for war, the sorrowing queen expressed the further "sentiment" that the two brothers—and the two sects—should become friends, kissed her imbecilic son farewell and, with a gasp and a shudder and a hollow groan of maternal and queenly sorrow, turned her head to the wall and gave up the ghost.

She was the last independent ruler of the Jewish nation.

17 Civil War— Enter Antipater

By the time rigor mortis had overtaken Alexandra Salome, Aristobulus had overtaken the kingdom. When the message came that his mother had finally expired, Aristobulus raced his Sadducees hellbent for Jerusalem. The Pharisees, anxious to avoid bloodshed in the Holy City, set out to intercept them; as he was nominal High Priest, so Hyrcanus II was nominal commander of the defending army. The pious ones were confident that victory was to be theirs: they were fighting a just cause; the Lord was on their side.

Their cause might have been just, but the Lord had apparently decided to sit this one out. Battle was joined at Jericho; it was the briefest military confrontation engaged in by any Hasmonaean. The professional soldiers loyal to Hyrcanus immediately deserted to Aristobulus, and Hyrcanus was forced to beat a hasty retreat back to Jerusalem with those still loyal to him—for the most part Pharisees who had abandoned religious scruples against bearing arms. They took refuge in the Temple, which Aristobulus soon had under siege. Encouraged less by the power of the invaders than by the pious shrieks of the faithful who feared that the Temple would be reduced to a shambles, Hyrcanus agreed to surrender. Thus ended the opening engagement of the Hasmonaean Civil War.

Three concerns militated against Aristobulus killing his brother outright: his awareness that the pathetic Hyrcanus had never really wanted to be king in the first place; a desire not to alienate further the Pharisees—and thus, by extension, the majority of the citizenry; and the foresight the Pharisees had had in seizing Aristobulus's wife and children as hostages. Therefore the victor suggested a compromise: were Hyrcanus to relinquish his offices, he would be permitted to retain the estates which were his by appanage—provided he agree to retire completely into private life.

Hyrcanus agreed; happy to get away with his life and his fortune intact, he was not too dense to suspect that basically he was hardly the stuff of which kings are made. And when Aristobulus promised that there would be no persecutions, the Pharisees—barring the intransigent handful—were prepared to accept him as King and High Priest. Aristobulus kept his word. There were no further religious persecutions—for which Aristobulus could be blamed. As Graetz has noted, the Pharisees and Sadducees "might have become extinct as parties, had it not been for the advent of a man whose measureless ambition and personal interest brought him to the fore, and who, together with his family, became the vampire of the nation, sucking its noblest blood away."

To seal the agreement, Aristobulus's son Alexander was married to Hyrcanus's daughter Alexandra. "On these terms," advises Josephus, the two brothers "were reconciled in the Temple, and surrounded by the people they warmly embraced each other." At the conclusion of the festivities of reconciliation, and assuming he had left all wordly worries behind, Hyrcanus walked out of the Temple . . .

. . . and into the arms of one of the sleaziest entrepreneurs that history, ancient as well as modern, has ever known. This was Antipater (Graetz's "vampire"), an audaciously scheming Idumaean whose determination to found a dynasty on the rubble of the Hasmonaeans was exceeded only by his success. He was the father of Herod the Great.

It is well within the realm of speculation that had Hyrcanus been able to foresee the consequences for Judaea and for himself of his sordid mésalliance with Antipater, he might have rushed back to Aristobulus, rescinded the terms of the fraternal compromise, and asked—nay, pleaded—to be put to death on the spot.

One rather wishes he had.

Antipater (sometimes referred to as Antipas) was a scion of one of the wealthier Idumaean families forcibly proselytized by John Hyrcanus; his father (also named Antipater) had served as *strategos* of Idumaea during the reigns of Jannaeus and Alexandra Salome. Thus the man whose machinations were to help topple the Hasmonaean Dynasty cannot be said to have simply appeared one day as if from under a rock.[1]

More than a supreme opportunist, Antipater was a master manipulator. His talent for switching allegiances at the right moment throughout the series of contentions that marked the emergence of Roman imperialism in the East made no less an eminent fence-straddler than Jonathan Maccabee pale in comparison. Realizing that it was only a matter of time before the Romans would be coming into Palestine, Antipater had begun his scheme to arrive at an accommodation whereby the militarily and economically powerful Jewish nation would become a Roman satellite, with his own heirs ruling Palestine as Rome's client-kings. Even while Queen Alexandra was still alive, he had, through dissimulation and well-placed bribes, purchased the affections of his own Idumaeans as well as the revivified independent trading cities of Gaza and Ascalon. The time had now come to go after the prize plum: Judaea itself.

Seeing in the weak Hyrcanus an eminently suitable pawn, Antipater set about rekindling the embers of Sadducee-Pharisee hatred (not that *they* took too much rekindling). With the immense wealth his father had accumulated (through graft) as governor of Idumaea, Antipater "convinced" the Pharisees that their position was extremely exiguous as long as the Sadducee-sponsored Aristobulus retained the royal dignity. Also, he dropped a few choice hints in certain quarters that the Pharisees would not for long accept the loss of their hold on the nation's sovereignty. And then he cornered Hyrcanus with the thesis that Aristobulus had no intention of allowing him to live out his life tending his estates as promised; rather, Aristobulus would *have* to eliminate him, on the theory that a living legitimate pretender posed a challenge to his position—especially a pretender who still commanded a following among the majority of the people.

Hyrcanus refused to believe his own brother would do such a thing; *he* posed no threat to Aristobulus; he did not even *want* any part of public life. Besides: what kind of support could *he* possibly have? Hadn't the majority all accepted Aristobulus as their rightful King and High Priest? Wrong, came the somewhat patronizingly murmured response from Antipater, who added that Hyrcanus *owed* it to the faithful to resume the offices that were his by inheritance; indeed, the Lord—not to mention the spirit of his dead mother—would never rest until he had steered his nation from the paths of militarism and Sadduceeism as embodied in Aristobulus, back to the ways ordained by Moses, may his name shine like a beacon for all eternity.

Hyrcanus lent an ear.

But there was one problem: he might command the respect of the people, as Antipater guaranteed, but Aristobulus commanded the support of the Establishment. Wrong, Antipater again demurred, with an avuncular pat on the back. He had "convinced" many of the Sadducee leaders that their best interests lay in accepting the inevitability of Roman hegemony. Were the Romans coming? Hyrcanus asked. Eventually, Antipater replied, adding that he had arrived at an "arrangement" with Aretas, king of the Nabataeans, whose armies would be placed at Hyrcanus's disposal.

Hyrcanus lent the other ear.

Antipater allowed as how Aretas had personally requested him to bring Hyrcanus to Petra to discuss matters. Allowing Antipater to take him by the hand, Hyrcanus crossed the Jordan to the Nabataean capital where Aretas—who had been bought off by Antipater—gave his solemn oath: if, after regaining his sovereignty, Hyrcanus would agree to return the twelve cities in the Transjordan his father, Jannaeus, had taken as a buffer area, Aretas and his Arabs would restore that sovereignty. As Antipater stood to one side nodding benignly, Hyrcanus and Aretas sealed the bargain. With an army of 50,000 Arabs, Hyrcanus returned to claim his patrimony.

Aristobulus led his troops out of the Holy City to confront the invading army—and was dealt a humiliating defeat as well as a resounding rebuff: large numbers of his militiamen transferred their allegiance to Hyrcanus, as did the nation as a whole—either from fear of being completely annihilated by Hyrcanus's Transjordanian friends or from fear of Divine Retribution for having abandoned their legitimate High Priest in the first place. Hastily withdrawing from the scene of battle, Aristobulus and those few whose loyalty he still commanded beat a hasty retreat back to Jerusalem, there to take refuge in the Temple Mount area. Aretas and Hyrcanus were welcomed to the Holy City as saviors: with the air ringing to the cheers of the Pharisee-oriented citizenry, in marched the Arabs. The claim of Josephus that in all Jerusalem "none but the priests" continued to support Aristobulus and his handful of die-hards would suggest that any fear the Levites might have entertained concerning the desecration of the Temple through the medium of Arab siege-engines was more than offset by Aristobulus's propensity for greasing the proper pietistic palms. The Temple Mount was well walled and well fortified. Aristobulus could withstand a long siege.

He did.

Josephus records two rather curiously charming incidents (*Ant.* XIV. II. 1–2) that allegedly occurred during that long siege of 64–63 B.C. which are probably apocryphal but which nevertheless reflect the piety of the Judaeans during these thoroughly impious times. The first concerns an extraordinary *homme religieux* named Onias whose reputation had been secured when his prayers to the Rainmaker to alleviate a drought resulted in the near-inundation of the Promised Land. Now anxious to end the siege and reclaim his throne—an anxiety fueled by his omnipresent Idumaean *éminence grise*—Hyrcanus ordered that Onias immediately go into another of his celebrated fits of Divine Petition and call down the curse of the Lord upon Aristobulus and his loyalists. Onias refused to employ his extraordinary talents for what he considered to be so base a purpose. When Hyrcanus insisted that he do as commanded, Onias raised eyes and palms heavenward and cried aloud, "O God, the king of the whole world, since those that stand not with me are thy people, and those that are besieged are also thy priests, I beseech thee, that thou wilt neither harken to the prayers of those against thee, [nor] bring to effect what these pray against those." Onias was rewarded for his spirit of brotherly love by being stoned to death at Hyrcanus's command.

The second quaint episode, Josephus would have us believe, stemmed directly from the Lord's desire to punish Hyrcanus for Onias's murder. If this was indeed the Lord's plan, He certainly followed a curiously circuitous route. It chanced that the Festival of Passover* was upon the nation, and the priests hiding in the Temple were most anxious to fulfill the duties incumbent upon them by offering the sacrifices germane to the occasion. Unfortunately, they had no animals with which to make these sacrifices; fortunately, they had the money—the Temple treasury—with which to purchase a herd. Sending out word to the besiegers that they would pay any price for the needed victims, the priests were informed that cattle were available—but only at the appallingly inflated price of a thousand drachmas per head. The priests, along with Aristobulus whose predicament was such that he was anxious to solicit a little Divine assistance, hoped that by observing the Passover properly they would be restored to a state of grace—and a state of release. Accordingly, they put the money in a bag and passed it through a hastily made aperture in the wall.

---

* The annual seven-day celebration both of the Exodus and of the miracles the Lord allegedly worked to secure the Israelites their freedom from Pharaoh's servitude.

Hyrcanus took the money—but refused to turn over the cattle. When the priests found they had been cheated, they prayed that the Lord would avenge them on their countrymen. Whether the Lord truly avenged the fleeced priests or had merely set up the situation whereby He would be justified in avenging the murder of poor old Onias is best left to theologians to debate. Suffice it to say, He "sent a strong and vehement storm of wind, that destroyed the fruits of the whole country."*

The siege continued, with the eyes of all Judaea turned toward what was happening in the area of the Temple Mount. So preoccupied were the Jews with their immediate problem, they were oblivious to an even larger problem that was about to overtake them.

The Roman armies had finally landed in western Asia.

Their commander, Gnaeus Pompeius Magnus—Pompey the Great—was at the moment tied down in Armenia where the aforementioned Tigranes was making a last-ditch effort to retain his creaking throne. Pompey was one of those commanders whose brilliance was matched only by his sluggishness; he never seems to have been in any hurry to don the mantle of success which the fates were eager to drape across his shoulders. While waiting for Tigranes to capitulate, Pompey sent his envoy Scaurus over into Syria to pave the way for Roman conquest. On arriving at Damascus, Scaurus quickly realized that the meager forces at his disposal were insufficient to contend with the many vultures into whose possession the carrion that was Syria had fallen. Scaurus was about to report back to Pompey when he learned that the Jewish nation to the south was torn asunder by dynastic strife. He took it upon himself to ascertain how this strife could best be turned to Rome's advantage.

Scaurus rode into Jerusalem, apprised himself of the situation,

* Josephus's charming tale can, of course, be interpreted to reflect that a violent thunderstorm just happened to level the nation's crops that year. Like so many religion-oriented authors—most notably the chroniclers of the Bible—Josephus was not above passing off natural phenomena as theophanies in order to score a point or two.

and ordered the Nabataeans to vacate the premises forthwith. When Aretas refused, Scaurus gently advised him that he was speaking in the name of Pompey. Aretas thought the matter over and then issued the order that his Arabs were to pack up their siege-engines and withdraw from Jerusalem with all possible dispatch.

Pompey's reputation had long preceded his arrival in the East.

18 The Song Is Over . . .

History has shown that superpowers rarely create exploitable situations; they rarely have to since the situations are more often than not created for them. Such was the case with Rome. With one or two exceptions, most notably Carthage which took more than a century to be put down, Rome was able to construct her mighty empire with maximal speed and minimal fuss because the nations she conquered had already laid themselves bare to conquest. This is not to imply that, had those once mighty nations not created their own chaos, Rome would not have prevailed. She would have simply had rougher going. For Rome was one of those inexorable forces to which history treats us from time to time. As had the Neo-Babylonians, the Romans came to occupy the Jewish state in Palestine, not to destroy it. Also like their predecessors, the Romans were goaded by the Jews into violating their original intent. Provocation of Nebuchadnezzar resulted in the scattering of Abraham's seed for fifty years; provoking Rome beyond measure precipitated a scattering that was to last two thousand years. When Santayana wrote: "Those who cannot remember the past are condemned to repeat it," he was undoubtedly speaking less as a brilliant philosopher than as an astute observer of the human condition.

Rome's absorption of Judaea was a foregone conclusion, as was her absorption of the entire Mediterranean world. Thus the question arises: Why, of all the nations she conquered, did Judaea come to so much grief at Rome's hands? The Egyptians were not thrown out of Egypt, the Syrians retained their homeland; so with the Parthians, the Greeks. Indeed, of all the peoples Rome conquered, it was only the Jews who lost their national integrity. Why? The Romans—like the Persians and the Macedonians—did not hold their religion against them. Anti-Semitism (more correctly, anti-Judaism) was never an instrument of state policy among the Romans; had they been "anti-Jewish," they would hardly have accepted so openly those flourishing communities of Abraham's "seed" that peppered their dominions. Was it then, as deists would have us believe, that the Jews lost their homeland because it was the will of God that they be dispersed among the nations of the world? Hardly. Attributing one's misfortunes to the whims of the Deity can be comforting in many ways, but as evidence, it is totally inadmissible before the bar of history. Having cooperated, however unseemingly, in allowing Rome to conquer them, the Jews refused to cooperate in accepting that conquest. Having failed to remember their own past— specifically, the Neo-Babylonian conquest of the early sixth century B.C.—they were condemned to repeat it. Unlike their neighbors in all directions, who managed to live with their Roman overlords without surrendering their territorial integrity, the Jews were not able to live with their Roman overlords for one appallingly simple reason: the Jews were not able to live with themselves.

Pompey had risen to eminence as the military champion of Sulla, the patrician who, under the guise of republicanism, had established a dictatorship aimed at curbing the power of the corrupt, oligarchic Senate—and had inadvertently set the stage for the generation of civil wars that was to culminate in the birth of the Roman Empire. While still in his late thirties, and by then the most important man in Rome, Pompey suddenly retired from public office after sharing the consulship, the state's highest annual office, for the year 70 B.C. That was also the year in which Julius Caesar—who had incurred Sulla's wrath and wisely opted to absent himself for a decade—returned to Rome to begin his rapid, methodical rise to political high estate. These two, Caesar and Pompey, whose monumental conflict was to hasten the end of republican government for Rome and embroil all of western Asia in Roman geopolitics, were at this time outwardly the best of friends. Of the two, it can be said that, whereas Caesar actively sought greatness, Pompey allowed greatness to be thrust upon him.

In 67 B.C., while the Hasmonaean brothers were burying their mother (and preparing to bury each other), Pompey was implored by the Senate to come out of retirement to deal with the widespread piracy in the Mediterranean that was threatening to cut off Rome's food supplies. His commission called for completion of the task within three years; he completed the task within three months—a feat which singled him out as the logical successor to Lucullus whose campaigns against Rome's major Asian foe, Pontus, after meeting with initial success, had become stalled. Given overall command of the Roman armies, Pompey headed east and drove Mithridates of Pontus from his throne and then moved on leisurely to conquer Armenia. It was at this point that he sent Scaurus on the reconnoitering mission that led to the latter's arrival at Jerusalem.

After ordering the Nabataeans out of Judaea, Scaurus agreed to adjudicate the dispute between Hyrcanus and Aristobulus. Obviously, for the factions which each represented, everything now depended upon winning the support of Rome. The ideal situation would have been for the brothers simply to divide leadership of the Jews: Hyrcanus to be High Priest, Aristobulus to be King, and for Hyrcanus to send his Idumaean Metternich packing. But the climate created by the Hasmonaeans and the people as a whole was hardly conducive to settling situations ideally. Antipater quietly murmured to Hyrcanus that a handsome bribe might not offend Scaurus's sense of moral outrage. He was correct; Scaurus was not easily offended. Aristobulus im-

mediately entered the auction with a larger bribe, whereupon
Antipater nodded for Hyrcanus to raise the ante.

Aristobulus was unable to match the latest bribe. But to
Scaurus (who probably kept all the bribe monies anyway),
Aristobulus seemed the more capable of the two brothers, better
able to maintain the peace until Pompey arrived with his legions.
As Scaurus returned to report back to Pompey, Aristobulus
proceeded to humiliate the retreating Nabataeans. More than
exacting vengeance, he was eager to have Pompey believe that, in
saving him the trouble of undertaking such a campaign, Aristobulus was the logical Hasmonaean to sit on the Jewish throne.
He was a born militarist like his father, more at home on the
battlefield than in the Temple. He undertook a series of campaigns throughout Palestine, and went so far as to organize a
fleet. His successes won him laurels at home; he was a hero to his
nation. Even the hierarchs who had accepted Antipater's bribes
and Antipater's logic were again prepared to see in Aristobulus a
real winner.

Antipater became slightly perturbed. Aristobulus was obviously envisioning Judaea, vis-à-vis Rome, as an independent
kingdom instead of a client-kingdom. Did these Jews actually
believe they could stand up to Rome? Why was Pompey daw-
dling in Armenia? While Antipater was only slightly perturbed,
Hyrcanus was hopelessly confused: from helping him besiege
Aristobulus, the nation had turned to supporting Aristobulus.
When Hyrcanus inquired of his mentor what they should do
now, Antipater suggested they maintain a low profile and await
Pompey's arrival. Meanwhile, a few sacrifices in the Temple
would do no harm.

Pompey finally arrived. After sweeping up the detritus of the
Seleucid Empire and incorporating Syria as a province of Rome,
he allowed himself to be briefed by Scaurus on the Judaean situation. Scaurus had been bribed further by Antipater to win

Pompey's favor for Hyrcanus and to present to Pompey the following thesis: the Jewish nation was actually unified behind Hyrcanus, who was, after all, their legitimate High Priest; were Pompey to recognize Hyrcanus in that office, the Jews would accept en masse Roman hegemony, and Aristobulus and his few loyalists would be easily eliminated. Pompey was pleased. In the Roman scheme of things, unified nations were, more often than not, less bothersome to digest than divided ones, provided unity was predicated on popular acceptance of Roman conquest.

As Pompey prepared to grant his recognition to Hyrcanus, brother Aristobulus—who obviously did not believe in dealing through middle-men—sent Pompey a magnificent vine wrought in gold and valued at upward of 500 talents (more than a quarter of a million dollars in present-day purchasing power). The vine, bearing a cluster of golden grapes and golden leaves, had been designed as an adornment for the Temple (Aristobulus felt that it would look better adorning Pompey). Along with the gift, Aristobulus sent an ambassador, one Nicodemus, to plead his cause: that the nation had *not* united behind Hyracanus, that Antipater was not to be trusted, and that Pompey's *only* hope for subduing Judaea without overextending himself militarily and financially was to accept Aristobulus as the rightful king.

Pompey was pleased with the gift but displeased with the donor, who had become too militarily active of late. Provided Aristobulus truly had the support of his people, what guarantee had Pompey that Aristobulus would be willing to accept client-king status? He had already overrun much of Palestine. And what about that navy he had been building? What did the Jews need a navy for? They were practically landlocked! Was Aristobulus contemplating an invasion of Rome? And, for that matter, did Aristobulus indeed command the loyalty of the nation as a whole? Had Scaurus lied or simply been misinformed by that wily Idumaean regarding Hyrcanus's strength? How could Pompey know for sure *which* of the two brothers truly had the s̄upport of the Jews? (He probably could not know; the Jews did not know themselves which of the two brothers to support!)

Antipater learned of Aristobulus's golden gift and rushed to Pompey's headquarters in Syria in the self-appointed role of Hyrcanus's ambassador. He openly accused Aristobulus, through his ambassador, Nicodemus, of having resorted to bribery in order to curry Pompey's favor (and merely shrugged off Nicodemus's charge that Antipater had himself made even larger bribes in the past). Then, treading cautiously (Antipater was soon aware that he had antagonized the Roman with his haughty, patronizing airs), Hyrcanus's friend suggested that unless Pompey ruled in his favor, the Roman conquest of Judaea would be a costly one. But should he decide for Hyrcanus, the Jewish nation was his for the taking. After hearing out the two ambassadors, Pompey deferred his decision until the following year (63 B.C.) at which time, he commanded, the two brothers were to appear before him personally, without ambassadors, at Damascus. Antipater returned to Jerusalem to spread a few more bribes and a few more dollops of Antipatrian logic, while Hyrcanus indulged himself in an orgy of prayers and sacrifices.

Hyrcanus was accompanied to the Damascus conference by "no fewer than a thousand Jews, of the best reputation," all of whom had "been suborned" by Antipater to back up the inept priest. Aristobulus, on the other hand, chose to bring along "some persons who were both young and insolent; whose purple garments, fine heads of hair, and other ornaments, made them objectionable, for they appeared not as though they were to plead their cause in a court of justice, but as if they formed part of a triumphal procession" (*Ant.* XIV. III. 2). This show of panache was a calculated risk on Aristobulus's part: surely, he reasoned, the military-minded Pompey could not but be more impressed by a suite of well-dressed warriors than by a delegation of decorous civil servants.

Pompey invited Hyrcanus to speak first. Having been well rehearsed by Antipater, he complained that it was all simply a case of an elder brother being deprived of his birthright by a sibling, who had, into the bargain, seized control of the government by force. Furthermore, Hyrcanus averred, all the raids that had been made by the Jews on their Palestinian neighbors were manifestations of Aristobulus's unconscionable avarice (which was true) and that the Jewish nation "would not have revolted, had not Aristobulus been a man given to violence and disorder" (which was only a half-truth at best). He then turned to his delegation, who claimed to represent the feelings of the overall majority of the Judaeans; bobbing and babbling like a flock of antediluvian geese, they swore most vociferously that Hyrcanus was incapable of uttering a falsehood. Was he not their High Priest, ordained by God? Imagining himself in the presence of the Croaking Chorus from Aristophanes's *Frogs,* Pompey raised an imperious hand for silence and then turned to hear out Aristobulus.

The latter's argument was terse and to the point: "it was Hyrcanus's own nature, which was inactive, and so contemptible, that had caused [me] to be deprived of the government." When Pompey demanded an explanation of his latest military escapades, Aristobulus averred, straight-faced, that his sole purpose had been to make easier Rome's conquest of Palestine.

Pompey eyed first the arrogantly confident Aristobulus and then the shivering wreck that was Hyrcanus, and without committing himself, he turned to a third, uninvited party that had also appeared at Pompey's headquarters (rather, at Pompey's feet): a deputation of Jerusalem elders—priests of both Pharisaic and Sadducean persuasion—who had come to cast their collective pox on both Hasmonaeans. Claiming that only *they* represented the overall consensus of Judaean thought, the elders declared that neither of the brothers was worth a talent. What then, inquired Pompey, had they to offer as an alternative? Their alternative: abolish the monarchy altogether and restore Judaea to its postexilic status as a temple-state. The priests promised they would remain tranquil and faithful tributary subjects of Rome—as their antecedents had been tranquil and faithful tributary subjects of the Persians *and* the Ptolemies *and* the Seleucids, until those damned Hasmonaean ancestors, the Maccabees, had upset the sacerdotal apple cart. Pompey then turned to Hyrcanus: Could he, in his position as legitimate High Priest, support the elders in their contention? Poor Hyrcanus was terrified. Antipater had not prepared him for this one.

Pompey had assumed that ordering the contending parties to appear before him would have forced the brothers to settle their differences; now he was presented with a new development—and at a time when he was concerned with the next item on his military agenda: conquering the Nabataeans (extending Roman authority to the Red Sea could only enhance immeasurably his prestige back at Rome). Therefore, not willing to become further bogged down in Jewish politics at this particular time—and aware that Judaea was his for the taking whenever he found it convenient to do so—Pompey delivered his decision.

The three delegations were all to return to Jerusalem and attempt to work out a peace among themselves. Now that their approaching status as a Roman tributary was a *fait accompli*, it behooved them—warned Pompey—to make the transition as peaceful as possible for all concerned. *But*, he warned, if on his return from the Nabataean campaign, a solution had not been arrived at, he would announce one of his own. (In truth, Pompey did not *have* a solution; as events were to prove, he did not *need* one.) Then, expressing the profound hope that the decision would be made for him, Pompey dismissed the three deputations.

Hyrcanus returned home in a mild panic, but was assured by Antipater that the forces of history were on their side; they should trust their luck to Aristobulus.

The priests returned home, confident that Pompey would realize the *only* solution lay in abolishing the monarchy and handing the nation back to them.

Aristobulus did not return home. He had good reason to suspect that Pompey had seen in the weak-minded Hyrcanus a better ward of Rome, but had feared that by declaring in favor of Hyrcanus he would be leaving himself vulnerable to a drawn-out battle with the stronger Aristobulus. His only hope now lay in cannily flattering Pompey, thereby convincing the Great One that it was in Rome's best interest to support him. Toward that end, Aristobulus graciously offered his assistance in the conquest of the Nabataeans. Pompey accepted the offer—less because he needed any Jewish assistance than because he wanted to keep a close eye on Aristobulus, whom he distrusted.

By the time the two led their armies into the Transjordan, Aristobulus was convinced he had won the game. The conviction was shattered when Pompey casually suggested that, lest Aristobulus's strength be diminished, perhaps it might be wise to surrender to the Roman legions the fortified positions his followers still held in Palestine. Aristobulus agreed to the suggestion and crossed back into Palestine—to prepare for war. Besides the troops loyal to him, Aristobulus was banking heavily on the assumption that the nation as a whole, presented with a Hobson's choice of living again under an autocratic monarchy whose scions had brought territory and prosperity, a weak monarchy whose strings were manipulated by—of all things—an Idumaean, or an autocratic and already outdated theocracy not averse to bleeding them dry quite lawfully, would put aside animosities and support his cause.

The infuriated Pompey did a hasty turnabout and gave chase; as Aristobulus sounded the clarion from Alexandrium, where he had chosen to make his stand, Pompey's legions arrived to begin the siege. When his surrender was demanded, Aristobulus agreed to negotiate provided a truce were called. Pompey ordered his siege-engineers to halt and prepared to enter into negotiations.

Aristobulus and his loyalists broke out of the fortress and headed for Jerusalem. He assumed that by sounding the alarm "The Romans are coming, the Romans are coming!" the people, priests, Pharisees, and Sadducees would help him defend their Holy City. But the alarm had just the opposite effect: the nation as a whole was not prepared to stand up to Pompey's legions.

Hyrcanus received an all-knowing wink from Antipater. The game plan was proceeding according to schedule.

Pompey moved his army south and encamped in the Jericho plains preparatory to an assault on Jerusalem. However, before he could get to Aristobulus whom he was determined to destroy for having made a fool of him, Aristobulus came to Pompey. It was not a Sabbatical Year, which mitigated the possibility of a food shortage; and the rather sturdy city walls could well have withstood a prolonged siege. But the fear, on the part of the masses, of Pompeian wrath, and the fact that Antipater had placed the proper amount of shekels in the right hierarchical hands, combined to convince Aristobulus that for him the battle was lost before it had even begun. Making his way to Pompey's camp with a wagonload of gifts, Aristobulus gave his solemn word that the city would surrender if Pompey suspended hostilities. Satisfied with the message, but doubting the sincerity of the messenger, Pompey retained Aristobulus as a hostage and then sent an envoy to take possession of Jerusalem.

Aristobulus *had* been sincere. But in the interim the Jerusalemites had entertained second thoughts about surrendering without a fight. When the envoy arrived at the city walls, the people shut the gates in his face. Pompey was livid when the envoy returned. Ordering Aristobulus clapped in chains, he set out with his army to capture the city and end all this Judaean nonsense—once and for all time.

Having had second thoughts, a number of Jerusalemites now had third thoughts. In short, the inhabitants were divided between those loyal to Aristobulus, who were resolved to die before surrendering, and those, especially the aristocrats and priests, who were persuaded by Antipater (speaking through Hyrcanus) that to fight would be futile, that Pompey was truly the only man who could unite the Jewish nation through an imposed resolution of differences.

Antipater was highly persuasive. When Pompey arrived to surround the city, the gates were immediately thrown open to him. The die-hards retreated to the Temple Mount. The siege began. The tenacity with which the royalists defended their position was exceeded only by the defensibility of the Temple Mount, the most militarily viable area in all of Jerusalem. Despite the numerous siege-engines at his command, it took Pompey's legions three months to breach the wall. In the massacre that ensued, 12,000 Jews were slaughtered (including a number of priests who were in the midst of making propitiatory sacrifices at the High Altar when the Roman legions broke into the Temple; these were probably not followers of Aristobulus but simply Temple minions who had been caught at their devotions when the siege began and who, unable to run the gauntlet, had remained at their divine stations to the bitter end).

Pompey was not only victorious, he was absolutely furious. He had come to conquer the city, not to destroy it. He resented having had to waste three months, and the lives of some of his best legionnaires, in vying for a prize that should have been handed over to him. Who *needed* this carnage? How *dare* these Jews think they could insult the power of Rome by even submitting to a siege? Who ever *heard* of such unmitigated gall? Pompey stomped about in a petulant fury.

Unfortunately, he stomped about in the Temple's sanctum sanctorum, the boards of which only the High Priest was permitted to tread—and then, only once a year on the Day of Atonement. To his credit, Pompey did not plunder the Temple of its riches; he even went so far as to order the cleansing of the edifice and the resumption of Judaic ritual without interference. But in committing that sacrilege of sacrileges, entering the Holy of Holies, he unwittingly incurred the undying hatred of many of the religious faithful who had been prepared to abandon their support of Aristobulus and accept Roman suzerainty. These now slipped out of the city in the general confusion that followed Pompey's blood bath and Pompey's pique. . . .

His irritation expended, Pompey called the hierarchs together and announced that Judaea was now a tributary of Rome—not a particularly startling piece of news. As for boundaries, those Mediterranean coastal cities captured by John Hyrcanus and Alexander Jannaeus were to be removed from Jewish authority, as was the province of Samaria. However, a number of territories acquired by the Hasmonaeans in previous generations were to remain part of the Jewish province—most notably Idumaea to the south, the Galilee region in the north, and Peraea, a stretch of land east of the Jordan, areas in which the populations were predominantly Jewish. Judaea was to resume its postexilic status as a tributary temple-state, with no proscriptions on its religion. Hyrcanus II was recognized as High Priest and given the temporal honorific of Ethnarch, but the monarchy was abolished. Having spoken in the name of Rome, Pompey departed for home; in his caravan were included, in chains and in humiliation, Aristobulus, his two sons Alexander and Antigonus, and a number of Judaean prisoners (who were to form the nucleus of Rome's Jewish community, in time one of the most prosperous in Europe).[1]

As Hyrcanus II assumed control of the devastated and truncated Jewish nation, Antipater tightened his hold on Hyrcanus. The Jews began to repair the damage done by the departing Roman legions, and to adjust to the loss of their independence. It was not a difficult adjustment. Pompey's decision had placated the majority. Though the Jews had lost their political independence, they could take a measure of comfort in having lost it to a foreign power that respected their religiosity (which pleased the Pharisees) and their autonomy (which pleased the Sadducees). Now under the umbrella of Roman protection, they need not fear incursions from any of their neighbors, all of whom had already come under that same umbrella.

But Antipater was most unhappy. Having envisioned Judaea as a client-kingdom of Rome, he had intended to kill off the monarch, not the monarchy. How could he hope to make his sons kings when there was no throne upon which to place them? So far as Antipater was concerned, this temple-state status was totally unacceptable. He would have to re-create a Jewish kingdom.

The question: How?

The answer: by stirring up the Pharisees and Sadducees once again—trusting to the apparent eagerness of the Jews to turn on each other—and making sure that he was in the position to support whomever might be Rome's man in the East at any given time.

Militating in Antipater's favor was his ability to flourish behind Judaea's nominal leader, the abominably weak Hyrcanus. As Antipater flourished, an ever-growing number of that nominal leader's unwilling subjects kept their eyes peeled beyond the horizon, ever on the outlook for the surviving Hasmonaean heirs. . . .

19 ...But the Melody Lingers On

By the time of Pompey's return (61 B.C.), Julius Caesar—largely through the bribery that was endemic in the state's political life—had safely launched himself on the road that was to culminate in his becoming dictator of Rome.[1] In a masterpiece of diplomacy, he persuaded Pompey (popular with the military) and M. Licinius Crassus (the wealthiest man in Rome and Caesar's financial backer) to forget their many political differences and join him in a troika that would far outweigh the power of the oligarchic Senate. Caesar's conduct of this First Triumvirate serves to illuminate but one facet of his multifaceted genius: the ability to identify his own interests with the common interest and to gain his own political ends while putting his opponents clearly in the wrong. It was just such a talent that allowed Caesar to avoid prosecution on charges involving certain constitutional irregularities by having himself appointed a provincial governor for a five-year term.* With Caesar away from Rome, the oligarchs sought to detach Pompey from the alliance, an attempt

---

* He had brought before his oligarchic opponents a bill that would provide Pompey's veterans—who had virtually doubled Rome's territorial holdings—with the promised land grants that were customarily made to Roman troops upon their discharge from active service, but which had been held up by the Senate. So deserving were the veterans of the grants, and so justly framed was the bill, that the Senate, forced to reject it only because passage would signify a political victory for Caesar, wound up alienating the military establishment while at the same time making Caesar a hero in the eyes of the veterans and their families. He then had the bill passed by a plebiscite—which passage involved the alluded-to constitutional irregularities.

Caesar forestalled by giving Pompey his daughter Julia in marriage.

By 54 B.C., however, with the death of Crassus and then of Julia, open conflict between the two titans of the Roman state had become inevitable. Sides were taken by the restless natives, and the Senate wooed Pompey by making him sole consul of Rome with the avowed task of restoring civil order. Over the next two years, Pompey, still popular with the military, gravitated toward an oligarchic-inspired alliance designed at destroying Caesar—who had, in the interim, gone on to enhance further his personal prestige by conquering Gaul (modern-day France). On January 10/11, 49 B.C., Caesar led a small force of loyalists across the Rubicon River and invaded Italy. Caesar had two decided advantages: his characteristic speed in action, which he knew would have a devastating effect on Pompey's proclivity for vacillation; and his known policy of clemency, which contrasted sharply with Pompey's tendency to treat even neutrals as enemies of the state.

Within less than two months, Caesar had forced Pompey's armies to flee Italy into Greece, after which he turned his attention to the rich province of Spain, where Pompey's loyalists were in firm control; by the end of the year, Caesar had subdued the entire Iberian Peninsula. On August 9, 48 B.C., his armies routed those of Pompey at Pharsalus. Caesar was master of Rome. With his erstwhile cotriumvir in hot pursuit, Pompey fled to Egypt where he was captured and beheaded by the agents of the twelve-year-old Ptolemy XII—brother-consort of the powerful Cleopatra VII (*the* Cleopatra).

At that point Caesar made a move that was to alter drastically the course of Jewish history. Instead of returning to Rome to receive the triumph awarded all military victors, Caesar moved on to Alexandria in order to resolve the dispute between Cleopatra and her second brother-husband, Ptolemy XIII. The Queen of the Nile was overwhelmed by Caesar's maturity and charm; he, in turn, was besieged by Ptolemy XIII's partisans. The siege was to be lifted only through the assistance of a Jewish army sent by Antipater, who had been following the convulsions in the Roman world most assiduously. . . .

Antipater's position during the decade-long conflict between Caesar and Pompey had been far from tenuous. Though Hyrcanus was merely tolerated by the majority of the people, the office he held accorded him enough official respect so that Antipater was in the extraordinary position of being able to wield immeasurable influence over the nation simply by controlling one inept individual. So secure was Antipater—and so insecure was Hyrcanus—that the Idumaean did not even have to operate covertly. With Jewish funds, readily supplied by the Sadducees who were anxious to be on the "winning" side, he courted the favor of Rome in the person of Pompey. Pompey was still the most powerful figure in the Roman world during this period, and his lieutenants served as proconsuls of Syria, of which province Judaea was merely a component.* The Sadducees were riding high, the Pharisees were spouting platitudes ("Love thy handicraft and shun governing; estrange thyself from worldly power"). Caught in the middle were the masses, who indeed "shunned" political affairs and went to Temple regularly.

Those who had been anxiously awaiting a Hasmonaean champion were soon rewarded. Aristobulus's younger son, Alexander II, had managed to escape while en route to Rome and made his way back to Palestine; by 57 B.C. he had amassed an army of more than 11,000 heavily armed and highly motivated partisans, and had gained control of the powerful Hasmonaean fortresses of Alexandrium, Hyrcania, and Machaerus.[2] When word of Alexander's successes reached Jerusalem, a ground swell began to grow in support of the prince. Even the republicans saw a

* The campaign against the Nabataeans, which Pompey had broken off in order to pursue Aristobulus back to Jerusalem, was left to Scaurus, who did little more than harass Aretas's Arabs before withdrawing on receipt of a handsome blackmail paid by Antipater—with Sadducean shekels. Antipater obviously believed in touching all bases.

Hasmonaean restoration as an acceptable alternative to Hyrcanus and Antipater; when Alexander invaded the capital city at the head of a guerrilla army, the two were forced to flee. So confident was Alexander, he had coins struck commemorating his reign ("King Alexander and High Priest Jonathan"). The Sadducees cautiously treaded water, prepared to support a restoration, provided success of such a venture proved attainable; the Pharisees continued spouting platitudes. We can never know if "King Alexander" intended to secede from Roman suzerainty or petition Rome for client-kingdom status; his reign did not last long enough for him to arrive at any fixed determination. Antipater rushed the appropriate bribes to Gabinius, who had only recently relieved Scaurus as Roman proconsul in Syria, and a Roman army was sent to put down the "king."*

The battle, which took place on the outskirts of Jerusalem, was a lopsided affair, with Alexander forced to withdraw hastily to the stronghold at Alexandrium. At the urging of Hyrcanus, and suitably compensated by Antipater and the Sadducees who now saw in Alexander a "loser," Gabinius deigned to travel down from his headquarters at Damascus in order to supervise personally the siege of Alexandrium. The siege was almost as brief as the battle that had precipitated it. Alexander agreed to surrender the fortress provided his followers were not harmed and he himself was permitted to go free.

If Antipater was upset when he learned of the leniency shown by Gabinius, he was downright livid when Hyrcanus—perhaps hoping, in his bumbling way, to end the schism dividing the Jewish people—permitted Alexander to marry at last his daughter Alexandra, to whom the prince had been engaged for several years. (It was their daughter Mariamme who was to become the most beautiful—and ill-fated—of Antipater's numerous daugh-

* Commanding the army was a brilliant young general who was subsequently to abandon Pompey's cause and throw in his lot with Caesar; he became known to history as Marc Antony.

ters-in-law, and their son Jonathan who was to be the last High Priest of Israel.)

The Idumaean's anger was assuaged somewhat when Alexander—having concluded that the time was not yet ripe for a Jewish insurrection—simply laid down his arms, metaphorically speaking, and went off with his bride on an extended honeymoon. Hyrcanus beamed at what he considered a masterful diplomatic stroke; he was sure the marital alliance had unified the nation. Antipater had his doubts—doubts that quickly became convictions when, some months later, Aristobulus and his elder son, the future Antigonus II, escaped from Roman captivity and made their way back to the Promised Land.

Again, the standard of revolt was raised. Again, Hyrcanus panicked. Again, Antipater apprised Gabinius of this latest turn of affairs. Again, a detachment of Roman legions converged on the fortress of Machaerus where father and son were waiting with their partisans. Again, the uprising was short-lived. And again, Antipater and Hyrcanus relaxed when, following a prolonged siege, Aristobulus was forced to surrender and was—again—shipped off to Rome in chains.

But that relaxation quickly became transformed into mild panic when Gabinius, honoring a promise he had made to Aristobulus's wife in return for the surrender of the fortress, allowed young Antigonus to go free. Unlike his brother, Alexander, Antigonus did not go off on any honeymoon. Rather, he went off to build up a guerrilla army. . . .

Three disparate parties—one predictable, two very unlikely—contributed to the next attempt at a Hasmonaean restoration.

Defying the will of the Roman Senate, the proconsul Gabinius decided to go to the aid of Ptolemy XI Auletes, who was attempting to reclaim the Egyptian throne from which he had been deposed and to which he was not even entitled in the first place. As Gabinius headed his legions south toward Alexandria, Hyrcanus's nephew/son-in-law, Alexander, returned from his honeymoon and "made many of the Jews revolt to him; and so he marched over the country with a great army, and slew all the Romans he could light on" (*Ant.* XIV. VI. 2).

The strength of Alexander's support impressed the Sadducees; even the less irrational Pharisees stopped platitudinizing long enough to realize that their nation had been granted what amounted to yet another last-minute reprieve. (There were to be others.)

The restoration might well have succeeded. Given the situation at Rome, and granting (perhaps naively) that Alexander would have been willing to accept the status of a client-king, the Judaeans were in a good position to ride out the Roman tidal wave that was soon to engulf the eastern Mediterranean world. Alexander's father was managing to ingratiate himself with Caesar who, as was to be demonstrated, was kindly disposed toward the Jewish people. Add to this the awareness that all the Jews needed was to buy time, and one is compelled to agonize over Alexander's failure to "light on" Hyrcanus and Antipater. For it was only Antipater's shrewd maneuvering of Hyrcanus into openly supporting Gabinius that saw the restoration fail and the nation fall. There was to be, it is true, one more restoration—under Alexander's brother, Antigonus—and the Jews of Palestine were to enjoy a period of independence. But by then they had missed the boat completely: Antigonus's reign was to be less a harbinger of future success than a reiteration of past failure.

It will be remembered that Ptolemy VII Lathyrus (Chickpea) had managed to reclaim the throne of his dead mother following the expulsion from Egypt of his brother, Ptolemy Alexander (the obscene dancer). After enjoying a rather calm (for Ptolemies) second reign, Chickpea died in 80 B.C. and was succeeded by the deposed dancer's son, also named Ptolemy Alexander (X and II, respectively). Young Ptolemy Alexander had spent the years of his uncle's reign in exile at Rome as a protégé of the dictator Sulla. Because Chickpea left no legitimate heir, the Romans decided to send the boy home to take the throne, under the tutelage of his quite elderly (and quite ugly) aunt and step-mother, Berenice III.[3] Within a week of his return, young Ptolemy infuriated the Alexandrian mobs by murdering his popular consort. (For some mysterious reason, Ptolemaic women, though prohibited from reigning without a consort, were invariably more popular than their male counterparts.) A few weeks later the young king was himself murdered by Berenice's partisans. In addition to enjoying the briefest reign of all Ptolemies (nineteen days), this latest regicide enjoyed the further, and somewhat dubious, distinction of being the last legitimate male in the Ptolemaic line.

Chickpea had sired a brood of progeny by an unknown concubine; it was the eldest of these love children whom the Alexandrians declared king—by default: they preferred a bastard to a vacant throne. Taking the regnal name Ptolemy XI Neos Dionysios, his dilettantish penchant for playing the pipes earned him the cognomen "Auletes."*

Rome did not take kindly to this latest turn of affairs. Ptolemy Alexander, perhaps because he was young and childless, and quite possibly out of some premonition that he would not last long enough to sire an heir, had bequeathed Egypt to Rome. The will was disputed by the Egyptians, who, although they had by now settled quite comfortably into the Roman orbit, nevertheless resented having been willed away to their overlords like so many cattle. Thus Auletes had been compelled to spend most of his reign in an attempt to secure Roman recognition of his kingship. In 59 B.C., by which time Caesar's star was in the ascendancy, Auletes bribed him with a gift of 6,000 talents and was permitted to return to Alexandria. In the following year his unpopularity with the Alexandrian canaille led to his expulsion. Auletes had

---

* Properly interpreted "flute player," though many historians deficient in musicology persist in translating *auletes* as "oboe player.'" Invention of the oboe was centuries in the future.

also contributed 8,000 armed cavalrymen (and almost half of the Egyptian treasury) to aid Pompey in the latter's conquest of Syria and Palestine; unable to determine which of the two, Caesar or Pompey, would emerge as the master of Rome, Auletes had purchased the good will of both, But during this period, purchasing the favor of both titans also carried with it the danger of freely earning the disfavor of both. Thus when Gabinius, a pro-Pompey man, invaded Egypt and restored Auletes to the throne, it was against the express wishes of the Caesarean-controlled Senate which, maintaining the validity of Ptolemy Alexander's will, preferred *no* king at Alexandria.

Antipater and Hyrcanus were, of course, still pro-Pompey; Caesar had yet to establish his influence in the East. For that reason, they had no objections to Gabinius's campaign; they just wanted him to hurry and return to Palestine. In order to hurry Gabinius along, Antipater suggested that Hyrcanus support the Roman's Egyptian sortie with money, weapons, corn, and even auxiliaries of pro-Hyrcanian Jewish mercenaries. (Antipater did his share by bribing the Jewish frontier guards at the Pelusium Approaches to let Gabinius pass unmolested on his march down to Alexandria.)

Hyrcanus and Antipater panicked when, after restoring Auletes, Gabinius decided to undertake a campaign against the Parthians, now Rome's only major antagonists in western Asia. The Hasmonaean Alexander was meeting with success, more and more Jews were coming over to his side—and Antipater's dreams were going up in smoke. He quickly dispatched a messenger to remind Gabinius of the past services rendered by Hyrcanus, and to point out that a Hasmonaean restoration was not in the best interests of Rome (for "Rome" one can read here "Antipater"). Gabinius hurried back north. Meanwhile Antipater and Hyrcanus called on the Sadducees to furnish the funds whereby those loyal to Alexander were to be "convinced" they were supporting a losing cause. Many accepted the bribes and defected, although 30,000 Judaeans remained loyal to the young prince.

In the battle that ensued in the vicinity of Mount Tabor where Deborah and Barak had fared better a millennium before against the Canaanites, a third of Alexander's loyalists were killed by Gabinius's legions (augmented by pro-Hyrcanian Jewish mercenaries), and the rest scattered to the winds. Young Alexander managed to escape. While Hyrcanus again panicked at the thought of his son-in-law still being at large, Antipater urged Gabinius to "settle the affairs" of the nation "as was agreeable to Antipater's inclinations" (*Ant.* XIV. VI. 4). Gabinius settled.

Judaea was broken up into five districts, each of which was directly subservient to Gabinius—through Antipater. Hyrcanus was stripped of his temporal authority (Ethnarchy) and restricted solely to his priestly authority. As Gabinius then went on to defeat the Nabataeans once and for all, the Jews of Palestine awakened to a nightmare: their nation was, to all intents and purposes, in the firm control of an Idumaean! Compounding that Idumaean's problem—trying to placate a rebellious populace—the wealthy triumvir Crassus, on replacing Gabinius as proconsul of Syria, looted the Temple preparatory to his campaign against the Parthians. Such an infamous act was one that even the most openly pro-Roman Sadducees found difficult to countenance.

Antipater and Hyrcanus had to placate a grumbling populace who demanded to know *why* their High Priest should support a nation whose proconsuls periodically invaded the sanctity of their Temple and carted off its treasures. Fortunately, Crassus was killed by the Parthians; Hyrcanus, at the suggestion of Antipater, was able to convince the outraged priests that the man who had defiled their Temple had been properly punished by God. It was a rather specious bit of reasoning, but it did serve to deflate an incipient rebellion against Hyrcanean "leadership" (for want of better terminology). What grumbling remained was all but dissipated when Antipater managed to ingratiate himself with Crassus's successor, Gaius Cassius Longinus. By 51 B.C. the followers of Aristobulus had found a new champion in one Peitholaus who had begun an anti-Hyrcanean uprising in Galilee and was marching south on Jerusalem. At the purchased insistence of Antipater, Cassius and his legions put down the uprising. Peitholaus was killed, and those of *his* 30,000 loyalists who managed to survive were sold off, along with their families, into slavery.

Meanwhile, back in Rome Aristobulus was frantically petitioning the now powerful Caesar to be allowed to return to Judaea and reclaim his throne. At the beginning of 49 B.C., with Pompey and his supporters in the Senate now in flight, Caesar acceded to the request. With the pro-Pompey forces still in control in Palestine, the idea of their being bogged down by a Jewish insurrection was a pleasing one to Caesar. Aristobulus was released from prison, decked out in battle garb, and given two powerful Roman legions to escort him back to Jerusalem. When he heard that his father was returning, bearing Caesar's blessing, Alexander came out of hiding and quickly rallied about him those who had escaped Crassus's prior blood bath. Tragic to relate, some of Pompey's loyalists still at Rome learned of the Caesarean enterprise, and Aristobulus was murdered. Concurrently, Alexander, who had declared openly (and rather prematurely) in behalf of Caesar, was captured and beheaded by Cassius's successor as proconsul of Syria (and Pompey's current father-in-law).

Antipater and Hyrcanus, along with the Sadducees *and* Pharisees who by now had decided to support irrevocably *any* Roman, relaxed, now that Aristobulus and Alexander were dead—

—until they were reminded of a small piece of news they seemed to have overlooked in their avidity to control Judaea as vassals of Pompey.

Alexander's brother, Antigonus II, was still alive. . . .

20 The Mésalliance

On learning that Caesar had triumphed over Pompey at Pharsalus, Hyrcanus inquired of Antipater whether the time had not come for the Jewish nation to switch its allegiance. It had. And it did.

In transferring their loyalty to Caesar, the two gained the support of even the rabid anti-Hyrcaneans, who had never forgiven Pompey and his lieutenants for their periodic transgressions of the Temple's sacred portals. Reasoned they: Caesar must be marvelous if only because he had won out over Pompey. Hyrcanus then inquired of Antipater whether they should not now commit some grandiose gesture on Caesar's behalf. Antipater agreed. Should the Jews go to war against the pro-Pompey faction still in Palestine? inquired the High Priest. No, no, cautioned Antipater. Then what *should* the Jews do? asked Hyrcanus. Replied Antipater: they should simply wait for an opportunity to present itself which they would then exploit to their advantage.

The opportunity presented itself—thanks, again, to the Ptolemies.

In deciding to settle the sibling dispute among the three children of the now-silenced Ptolemy Auletes, Caesar had sided with Cleopatra and her current brother-husband, Ptolemy XIII. While Caesar dallied with his mistress, as Cleopatra had quickly become, in the boudoir of her Alexandria palace, the partisans of the rejected sibling, Ptolemy XII, put the palace under siege. Compounding Caesar's carelessness, the Parthians were tying down the Roman armies to the north. A cry went out from

Caesar throughout the Levant for mercenaries to come to his aid. Antipater heard the cry. When Syrian mercenaries en route to Caesar's assistance arrived at Ascalon, they found their passage into Egypt blocked by troops loyal to Ptolemy XII. Antipater and Hyrcanus personally led a force of 3,000 Jewish mercenaries that broke the bottleneck and allowed the relief columns to move rapidly toward Alexandria. Also at the suggestion of Antipater, Hyrcanus supplied much-needed refreshments for the entire mercenary force during the week-long journey down the Sinai Desert.

Unlike most of her namesakes, Cleopatra had never been too popular with the Alexandrian Jews, who now comprised upward of two-fifths of the capital city's population. When, however, they saw a task force of their coreligionists march into the city, led by no less an eminence than the High Priest of Israel (a shrewd gambit here on Antipater's part), the Alexandrian Jews were immediately won over to the queen's "cause": the overthrow of Ptolemy XII and the reenthronement of the more malleable Ptolemy XIII. The siege was lifted, Caesar prevailed, Cleopatra's brother was brought back to share the throne with her—and Antipater took great pains to point out how the day had been saved by his dear friend Hyrcanus's troops and funds.

Kissing his pregnant mistress goodbye,[1] Caesar departed Egypt in the summer of 47 B.C., returning home by way of Syria. He wished to ascertain that all the pro-Pompey elements had been excised (they had), and to reward handsomely those who had come to his rescue (he did).

Singled out for honors was Antipater, upon whom Caesar bestowed "the privileges and citizenship of Rome, and freedom from taxes everywhere." At Antipater's suggestion Hyrcanus was reconfirmed as High Priest of the Jewish province.

Caesar was about to move on when Antigonus unexpectedly appeared on the scene and made an impassioned bid that Caesar pass over his uncle and his uncle's scheming adviser and recognize him as the rightful king. Hoping to play on Caesar's sympathy if not his sense of what Antigonus considered fair play, the prince reminded Caesar of how his father, Aristobulus, had died out of loyalty to him, as had his elder brother, Alexander, and "desired that [Caesar] would take pity on him, as he had been ejected from his dominions." When that gambit failed, Antigonus openly accused Hyrcanus and Antipater of "governing the [Jewish] nation by violence, and acting lawlessly."

Caesar demanded that Hyrcanus reply to the charges. Hyrcanus broke out in a cold sweat. Quickly jumping into the breach, Antipater "showed that Antigonus and his party were given to innovation, and were rebellious persons," and he "reminded Caesar of the labours he had undergone when he assisted him in [the Alexandrian War], relating what [Caesar] had witnessed himself." And he added "that Aristobulus was justly carried away to Rome, as one who was an enemy to the Romans, and could never be brought to be friendly to them"; that Alexander's beheading at the behest of Pompey was "only his deserts" for having been "caught in the act of committing robberies." So convincing was Antipater, both in thesis and presentation, that Caesar gave the Idumaean "what position he himself should choose, and left the determination to himself" (*Ant.* XIV. VIII. 4–5). Antipater modestly "chose" to become Procurator of Judaea—answerable directly, and only, to Caesar.*

Caesar sailed away to Rome, Antigonus rode off to consult with the Parthians, Antipater led Hyrcanus back to Jerusalem— and the Jews of Palestine, save for the royalists lying low in the hinterlands, resigned themselves to having been delivered over to the complete authority of a family of non-Israelites whose ancestors had been forced to surrender their foreskins to the feeble-

* Caesar granted many privileges to the Jews throughout the Roman world, even going to the extraordinary length of granting periodic remissions from all taxation. It is interesting to note that the Jews have often fared well at the hands of history's more fascinating despots. As they mourned the death of Caesar with justification, so would they mourn the deaths of Napoleon Bonaparte and Oliver Cromwell, both of whose empathy for, and consideration of, the Israelites is often overlooked in the litany of their baser accomplishments.

minded Hyrcanus's grandfather and namesake—and never quite got over the experience.

Because of the position he held as Caesar's favorite Jew and because "Hyrcanus was of a slow and slothful temper" (*Ant.* XIV. IX. 1), Antipater was able to dispense with the formalities of seeking his priestly puppet's acquiescence in naming his eldest son, Phaesel, as governor of Jerusalem and Peraea, and his younger son, the twenty-six-year-old Herod, as governor of the Galilee region.* Of the two heirs, attention must be directed to Herod—one of the most remarkable and colorful figures of antiquity—a man who followed a political philosophy that blended farsightedness with expediency, wisdom with ruthlessness. These qualities soon became apparent to the Judaeans—as did the horrible realization that Antipater & Sons had, with the assistance of the Sadducees (actively) *and* Pharisees (passively), begun a systematic program of draining the nation (or to use Graetz's more colorful metaphor, "sucking its noblest blood away"). It all began with a *condottiere* named Hezekiah.

At the head of a band of adventurers, Hezekiah had overrun the Galilee region. Herod, hoping to reduce any possible Jewish turbulence, put down the robbers and executed their brigand chief. The Sanhedrin—by now a veritable potpourri of Pharisees and Sadducees—were beside themselves with fury when they learned Antipater's son had taken matters into his own hands; in this tribunal alone rested the authority to impose a death sentence. (Though they had betrayed their nation, the elders remained sticklers when it came to the finer points of the Law.) "In fear, because they saw that Herod was a violent and bold man, and very desirous to play the tyrant," they openly wondered how long their High Priest, toward whom even the most hidebound traditionalists had become "ill disposed," was going to tolerate so intolerable a situation (*Ant.* XIV. IX. 3).

* Caesar had, at the suggestion of Antipater, returned Peraea and Galilee to the Jews; he also rescinded the Gabinian partition of Judaea into five districts.

 Notes

2. THE EXILE

1. The story of Nebuchadnezzar in the Book of Daniel is as lacking in historical validity as the book itself. Written, according to tradition, by the "prophet Daniel" during the period under discussion, it is actually a piece of apocalyptic fiction composed anonymously during the Maccabee period. The grass-eating lunatic identified as "Nebuchadnezzar" in that rather curious canonical tome is most probably an unflattering portrait of Nabonidus, the penultimate Neo-Babylonian king.

3. THE RETURN

1. Jeremiah was hardly the first of the Israelite prophets to express disenchantment with sacerdotal hypocrisy. Amos, earliest of the so-called Writing Prophets (nominal authors of the Old Testament prophecy books), had sounded the clarion centuries before (cf. especially Amos 5:21 ff.), and Micah had already given to the world what is unarguably the sanest, most rational definition of religion: "What doth the Lord require of thee, but to do justly, and to love mercy, and to walk humbly with thy God?" (Micah 6:8, in the King James translation). Jeremiah, however, was the first to give his people an *alternative* to priestly hypocrisy, an alternative that was reinforced by the writings of Ezekiel, the only prophet of the Exile period. It was these two giants—truly men for all seasons—who planted the seeds of "portability" without which Judaism would have undoubtedly succumbed.

2. The Samaritans eventually seceded from the Jerusalem cult and reorganized their own hierarchy in the north, with its cultus devolving

272   *Notes*

upon the temple they built atop Mount Gerizim (eventually destroyed
by John Hyrcanus). Accepting only the Torah as their Holy Scripture,
thus denying recognition to the historical and prophetic books of the
Jewish Bible (the "Old Testament") which by then had undergone
their final recensions and gained wide currency, the Samaritans also
came to reject the concept of Resurrection that through Pharisaic
teachings became popular during the New Testament period, though
they did continue to believe in the advent of the Messiah (an on-
going concept among all Jews, who do not accept Jesus as the fulfillment of messianic expectation). Approximately one hundred Samaritans survive to this day in Israel—ironically, the sole remnant of world
Jewry to have lived continuously in the Holy Land.

3. Interestingly, each and every word of these books (plus the two
remaining Mosaic books, Genesis and Exodus) is read once a year in
all synagogues, a custom begun by Ezra the Scribe. The present
writer recalls the occasion of his *Bar Mitzvah* when the "portion" read
at that day's services was Chapter 13 of Leviticus, which describes in
detail how a priest is to deal with a leprous congregant. When asked
whether he would follow the Mosaic "prescription," the Rabbi replied:
"Wouldn't *you*, as a good Jewish boy, follow the injunctions of our
Great Lawgiver?" To this, the writer replied: "*Ein shuldig mir, Rebbe*
—but if *I* met a leper, I'd send him to a doctor." The Rabbi became
indignant, which served only to precipitate great indignation on the
writer's part, and a major theological confrontation was avoided only
when the writer's grandfather stepped forward and resolved the issue,
albeit inconclusively, with the pronunciamento: "No need to argue, no
need to argue—we don't grow lepers in New Jersey."

4. THE HELLENIZERS

1. A rabbinic legend, derived from Josephus, tells of an alleged
visit by Alexander to Jerusalem during this campaign. The reigning
High Priest defied the Macedonian out of loyalty to the moribund
Persian Empire. The account concludes with a miraculous deliverance
from Alexandrine wrath through divine intervention: Alexander is
alleged to have ended his visit by making an offering to the One God
in the Temple. It is quite a charming legend, but a totally fictitious
one. In describing the visit (*Ant.* XI. VIII. 4), Josephus claims it

followed Alexander's conquest of Gaza. But according to reliable historical sources, Alexander marched down the Mediterranean coast from Gaza to Egypt in seven days. In addition to his not having had the time to pass through Judaea, much less the inclination, there is no source outside of Josephus that even alludes to such a visit.

2. It was also at Alexandria that the Septuagint, the first translation of Hebrew Scripture, was undertaken. According to the legendary account, Ptolemy II was eager to add a copy of the Torah to his great museum (one of the wonders of the ancient world, actually a library). Toward that end, he sent a letter to Eliezar, the High Priest at Jerusalem. Eliezar sent seventy scholars to Alexandria where, after seventy days in a house on the Island of Pharos, they produced a complete translation (thus, *Septuagint*—"seventy"). This fanciful tale acquired some variations. From Philo, as well as such later Church Fathers and exegetes as Iranaeus and Clement of Alexandria, came the tale that the translators, seventy-*two* in number, worked independently, and when each had completed his task their work was found to be identical word for word. In any event, it is probable that the translation was undertaken for the simple reason that the Greek-speaking Alexandrian Jews were no longer able to read the Hebrew language. (Though the Septuagint was originally confined to the five Mosaic books, the term subsequently came to apply to the rest of the Old Testament translated into Greek. Indeed, most of the Apocrypha and all of the New Testament were written originally in Greek; Hebrew was at that time a dying language.)

6. MATTATHIAS—THE BEGINNING

1. The canonical genealogy goes back to Mattathias's grandfather, Simeon (in the King James Version) or Symeon (in the New English Bible), who was supposedly of the "Joarib" line of priests. Josephus (*Ant.* XII. VI. 1) takes it one step further, naming one Asamoneus as Mattathias's great-grandfather; it was from this assumedly mythical Asamoneus that the family's patronymic was derived. Some present-day scholars, including the highly respected John Bright (*A History of Israel*, p. 410, fn), see a possible correlation between "Joarib" and Joiarib, one of the Levites who returned from the Captivity (cf. Nehemiah 12:6, 19). If the claim, both in I Maccabees and Josephus's

Antiquities holds true that the Hasmonaeans were indeed of the sacerdotal tribe of Levi—a piece of knowledge of which Simon Maccabee made sure his people were aware (cf. I Macc. 14:29, in the KJV)—then the popular selection of the Hasmonaeans as High Priests in quasi-perpetuity should not have so antagonized the Pharisees, as proved to be the case during the reign of Simon's son John Hyrcanus. There is, of course, always the possibility that this ancestry was manufactured—by the chronicler of I Maccabees to strengthen the Hasmonaean legitimacy; by Josephus because he himself is said to have been a descendant of the Maccabees and may well have drawn on the biblical account (this despite the fact that he was also Pharisee-oriented, if not a practicing member of the sect!).

2. The ritual of circumcision, the origins of which are lost in prehistory, has long been practiced among the preliterate tribal peoples of Africa. It may have entered the Middle East via Egypt in ancient times, for it has been traced there as far back as 4000 B.C., close to twenty-five centuries prior to the Israelite Exodus. For the Hebrew people then, the ritual signified—as it does to this day—the Covenant entered into between Abraham and God, as recorded in Genesis (17:10–27). It is still practiced by the Arab peoples—who are, both traditionally and anthropologically, brothers of the Jews.

3. A process that led to the production of much of the so-called Wisdom Literature written during the Intertestamental period, and of the Talmud, which is still a vital part of orthodox Jewish legalism. The Wisdom Literature (e.g., Proverbs, Job, Ecclesiastes, and Song of Solomon in the Old Testament, I Esdras, Tobit, Baruch in the Apocrypha) reflects the Scribes' attempts to plumb the depths of the Law and extract the more general principles of conduct applicable to every individual. The Talmud, conversely, represents a more detailed approach: since the Law was an unsystematic collection of Mosaic decrees that were occasionally contradictory, the Scribes wished to organize and expand it so as to cover every possible contingency with precepts that were at least *derived* from Mosaic Law, if not specifically treated therein.

4. Though postbiblical rabbinic tradition has identified Ezra as the first of a century-long succession of scribal leaders known as the Men of the Great Synagogue (of which body Simon the Just is held to have been the last surviving member), present-day scholars tend to

see in this tradition an artificially imposed scheme while accepting the tradition in its broad outline. The cognomen "The Scribe" was probably applied to Ezra not because he belonged to this class but because he had been appointed by the Persian overlords to serve as royal secretary—or scribe—for Jewish religious affairs.

7. JUDAH MACCABEE—THE RELIGIOUS WAR

1. Framed as an answer to the anti-Semitic tract of Apion, an Alexandrian scholar who was a contemporary of Josephus, *Contra* [Against] *Apion* defends the Jewish people against attacks that were current in the Greek-speaking world of the first century A.D., and reviews the customs and beliefs that were prevalent among the Diaspora Jews of this period. *Contra Apion* seems to epitomize the essential irony that underlay Josephus's life. While the entire period of his literary career was spent in producing works ostensibly aimed at a Greco-Roman audience (*Antiquities of the Jews* and *The Jewish Wars*), all his work was in reality designed to answer the charges of renegade or traitor that were frequently hurled at him by his countrymen—charges which continue to be hurled to this day by many, other than recondite Jews.

2. Emmaus was to figure somewhat extraordinarily in subsequent history as the site where, according to the New Testament (Luke 24:13), Jesus made his first post-Crucifixion appearance before mortal eyes.

3. This became the first holy day in the Hebrew catalog that had not been ordained by Moses—which the more orthodox Jews of the period were to hold against Judah Maccabee (though their counterparts today have no qualms about celebrating this non-Mosaic festival).

4. In a rather amusing passage in his *Antiquities* (XII. IX. 1), Josephus writes: "Whence one may wonder at [the historian] Polybius of Megalopolis, who, though otherwise a good man, yet saith that 'Antiochus died because he had a purpose to plunder the temple of Diana in Persia [Elam]'; for the purposing to do a thing, but not actually doing it, is not worthy of punishment." Obviously reflecting his Pharisaic bias, Josephus claims "it is much more probable that this king died on account of his sacrilegious plundering of the temple at

Jerusalem." However, Josephus most magnanimously chooses not to "contend about this matter with those who may think that the cause assigned by . . . Polybius . . . is nearer the truth than that assigned by us." Here Josephus appears to be following the "line" set down in the earlier Apocrypha accounts (I Macc. 8:16; II Macc. 9:9–12), which attributes Epiphanes's death to a fatal spasm of "bitter grief" over his having "made an unjustified attempt to wipe out the inhabitants of Judaea."

8. JUDAH MACCABEE—THE POLITICAL WAR

1. Josephus adds Nicanor was one of the king's companions who had lived, and escaped, with him from Rome. But since Nicanor had been a general under Antiochus Epiphanes, Josephus—who may have been (mis)quoting Polybius—has obviously erred here.

2. The day upon which the battle took place; it corresponds to early March in the Gregorian calendar. The practice of celebrating this holiday has long since been abandoned (not that it was ever celebrated much).

9. JONATHAN—HIGH PRIEST

1. The "kingdom" of Pergamum was in fact a city-state in what is today the Turkish province of Izmir. Imaginative town planning and a tradition of cultural patronage combined to make it the most spectacular Hellenistic city in Asia Minor. Its period of glory came under the pro-Roman Attalid Dynasty which was founded by Attalus I in 241 B.C., and whose last monarch, Attalus III, bequeathed Pergamum to Rome upon his death in 133 B.C.

10. JONATHAN—"FIRST FRIEND"

1. An opinion concurred in by Edwyn Bevan, perhaps the foremost authority on the Seleucids and Ptolemies (*see* A Note on the Bibliography).

2. For the record, the boy-king, who unknowingly was merely the pawn in Tryphon's ultimate objective, the usurpation of all the Seleucid domains, was named Antiochus VI Theos Epiphanes Dionysios—perhaps the only monarch in history whose cognomen was to be longer than his "reign."

3. It was through this sordid union that all future Ptolemies descended.

11. SIMON—HIGH PRIEST AND ETHNARCH

1. These "fortresses" included the strategically vital cities of Gazara, Bethsura, Azotus, and the seaport of Joppa (present-day Jaffa).

2. Cf. *Antiquities* (XII. XI. 7); see also footnote 1, Chapter 6.

3. Sources are undecided as to exactly when Tryphon killed the infant king. If he had already done so, then he had kept it a secret. Both Cleopatras assumed he was still alive (although they could not have cared less one way or the other, save for political considerations).

4. The "former condition" was, of course, that of the greatness enjoyed by the empire under the earliest Seleucids. The "condition" to which Sidetes, the last of the powerful Seleucid kings, succeeded in "restoring it" was to a state of truncation. By the time his successors were finished with the once powerful empire, all that remained was Antioch, a head without a body, which was mercifully put out of its misery when the Romans delivered the *coup de grace* in the early 60s B.C.

5. The "brethren" is unexplainable, unless reference here is to two or more younger brothers taken by Ptolemeus when he captured his mother-in-law. All sources are unclear as to just how many sons Simon had. Still another brother was eventually turned over by Hyrcanus to Sidetes as a hostage.

12. JOHN HYRCANUS—END OF THE BEGINNING

1. The lack of sibling (not to mention marital) affection Cleopatra II and Physcon entertained toward each other is perhaps best exemplified by Physcon's first act upon reaching Cyprus. He hacked to death the infant he had sired by his sister and sent her the pieces as a birthday present. (One source claims that Cleopatra II sent the pieces back to Physcon on *his* birthday!)

13. JOHN HYRCANUS—BEGINNING OF THE END

1. Responsible commentators deny the traditional claim that the Sadducees (Heb., *Tsedukkim*) took their name from Zadok, the High

Priest who anointed King Solomon. Graetz, drawing on the tradition handed down by the postbiblical rabbis, cites one "Zadok" as the sect's leader during its early phase; he may well have been their eponym. "Pharisees" is a corruption of the Hebrew *Perushim,* "Separatists" or "Separated Ones."

Philosophical divergence between the two sects produced sharp disagreement on three major doctrinal points. The Sadducees repudiated the idea of personal immortality (the concepts of afterlife. resurrection, and Divine retribution that figure prominently in Pharisaic lore), denied the existence of angels and demons which played so paramount a role in Pharisaic cosmogony (and in that of Christianity), and, most significantly, rejected the Pharisaic spirit of religious determinism and fatalism, asserting instead that men were endowed by God with free will with success or failure depending on natural consequence as opposed to Divine interposition. Following a somewhat existentialist line, the Sadducees believed that God does not concern Himself with human affairs on an individual basis but gives His protection to people *as a group,* provided they fulfill His commands, and punishing them for violating these commands. Conversely the Pharisees held that, with God taking cognizance of all human endeavors, there could be no virtue in doing good if man did not have the power to exercise the option between good and evil. It was this belief in man's responsibility to the Deity for his conduct, combined with a belief that man enjoyed free will in addition to Divine providence and prescience that led, in turn, to the Pharisaic belief in Divine retribution. In holding that there would be Divine justice for any injustices suffered on earth by those who remained faithful to God, the Pharisees were able to offer what amounts to a refutation to the Sadducees' rather pseudo-Sartreian existentialism.

Because the word "pharisee" has come down to us as a synonym for religious sham, it would be well to put this into proper perspective. Although by the New Testament period they numbered no more than 6,000, the Pharisees enjoyed the largest following among Palestinian Jews; their interpretation of the Torah not only dominated Judaism but became almost synonymous with it. In the synoptic Gospels they are vigorously attacked by Jesus and his Disciples (e.g., Mark 7:1–23; Matt. 23:1 ff.; Luke 11:37–54; cf. Matt. 3:7; 5:20; 9:11–12; 12:1–3, etc.). These attacks are questioned by responsible commentators (and less emotional observers), who suggest that Jesus and the Pharisees were not as mutually antagonistic as the attacks would imply and who suspect that many of the references to the Pharisees (the present writer would amplify that "many") were, through errors in transcription (for want of a better excuse), really references to the Sadducees. By then the aristocratic Sadducees, having based their doctrines more on opportunism than on religious conviction, had turned full circle from their initial goals of political independence and, under direct Roman rule, had become the chief supporters and administrators for the provincial government. (When the Jewish nation in Palestine was ended, both sects were swept from the historical stage, although the Pharisees managed to "survive" in the rabbinical schools that comprised the Patriarchate which assumed "leaderhip" of the dispersed Jewish nation during and following the Roman Empire period.)

The Gospels appeared long after the lifetime of Jesus (for whose existence, it should be noted, we have no historical evidence). The first, Mark, was written approximately forty years after the assumed Crucifixion, and was the basis for the other synoptics, Matthew and Luke. This would support the contention of responsible scholars that the attacks against the Pharisees *ascribed* to Jesus were, rather, a reflection by the Gospel writers of the conflict between Jews and Christians toward the close of the first century A.D. (And here it should be borne in mind that Jesus was only the *eponym* of Christianity, which religion was "started" by Paul—himself a practicing Pharisee, as well as an extraordinarily neurotic shill, who turned on his own people with an irrational vengeance.) Not only did Jesus *not* reject the Torah, he adhered to the Pharisaic notion of the Torah as a twofold expression of Divine Will ("think not that I am come to destroy the law [the Written Law] or the prophets [the Oral Law]: I am not come to destroy but fulfill," Matt. 5:17). It was Jesus's Gentile followers, a century later, who were to reject the Torah and Judaism as a dead law and a dead religion.

2. On the obverse side was the legend "John the High Priest, and the Community of the Jews," and on the reverse side a "double horn of abundance with a poppy head inside, ancient Greek symbols of plenty and fertility, indicating no doubt the prosperity of his reign" (D. S. Russell, *see* A Note on the Bibliography).

3. Two passages in *Antiquities* (XVIII. III. 3 and XX. IX. 1)

referring to the ministry of Jesus, known as the *Testimonium Flavianum*, have long been hailed by Christians as irrefutable non-Christian (i.e., extra-Gospel) evidence for the historical existence of Jesus. Christian scholars have now accepted that these passages were interpolated into the text by an early Christian editor. It has been established that the third-century A.D. Christian apologist Origen acknowledged that Josephus did not believe Jesus was the Messiah, while the fourth-century Church historian Eusebius quotes the passages substantially as they have come down to us; thus it is assumed that the spurious passages were interpolated sometime in the second half of the third century A.D., that is, between the periods in which Origen and Eusebius wrote.

15. ALEXANDER JANNAEUS—"THE THRACIAN"

1. Concurrent with his elevation to the throne, Chickpea was forced by his mother to divorce his favorite sister, Cleopatra IV, and take to wife in her stead a younger sister, Cleopatra V Selene. Cleopatra IV fled to Cyprus in the hope of enlisting her obese brother Ptolemy Alexander's support in dethroning their mother, but he backed down. She next went on to Syria and married her cousin Antiochus Cyzicenus, whose half brother and mortal enemy, Antiochus Grypus, was the husband of her sister Cleopatra Tryphaenia ("delicate"). When Grypus captured Antioch and Cleopatra IV was taken prisoner along with Cyzicenus, her sister Cleopatra Tryphaenia— in an act that belied her cognomen—delicately ordered her hacked to pieces. In the following year, Cyzicenus ousted Grypus from Antioch but retained custody of Tryphaenia whom he sacrificed to her murdered sister's ghost.

When Cleopatra III forced Chickpea from the throne, she ordered him to divorce Selene, who was sent north to marry either of the two contesting Seleucids, Grypus or Cyzicenus, as part of a plan (never realized) to reestablish Ptolemaic influence in Syria. Selene married both of them. After their deaths, she married her stepson Antiochus X Eusebes Philopator, by whom she became the mother of Antiochus XIII Asiaticus—the last Seleucid king.

2. (*Ant.* XIII. XIV. 2; cf. *Wars* I. IV. 6.) It may have been some of these fleeing Pharisees who settled at Qumran in the area of the Dead Sea and began the aesthetic community known as the Essenes,

though many scholars suspect they were simply joining a community already in existence. The Essene Library (the so-called Dead Sea Scrolls), unearthed in 1947 and the greatest archaeological discovery of the twentieth century, has already altered profoundly many long-held traditional attitudes regarding the origins and conceptualizations of Christianity (which would explain why the Vatican tried frantically to buy up and suppress the Scrolls). The passage in the Scroll *Commentary on the Book of Nahum,* "He hanged living men on wood . . . which was not formerly done in Israel," in all probability refers to Jannaeus's slaughter of the Pharisee leaders.

Recommended without reservation for the reader is Edmund Wilson's *The Dead Sea Scrolls, 1947–1969,* unarguably the clearest, sanest, most informative, and most readable study to date on this unique archaeological treasure.

16. ALEXANDRA SALOME—STRAINED INTERLUDE

1. One of the more elevated attributes of the Jewish people—who may well have "invented" the concept of charity—has been the eagerness, down through the ages, of the uprooted Jews to contribute to the support of their brethren living in the ancestral homeland. A case in point would be the recent Yom Kippur War of 1973 when millions of dollars were raised by American Jewry alone within *hours* of the Arab attack on Israel. The billions of dollars that have flowed into Israel from Diaspora Jews (in the United States alone) since its founding as a state in 1948 would more than suggest the strong ties of affinity that have always united world Jewry. (Radical Zionists, who maintain that *all* Jews should live in Israel, have yet to suggest an acceptable answer to: How could Israel possibily survive without the Diaspora?)

17. CIVIL WAR—ENTER ANTIPATER

1. Nicholas of Damascus, the first-century B.C. Greek historian, claimed Antipater "was of the stock of the principal Jews who came out of Babylon into Judaea" following the Captivity. The historian was a close friend of Herod the Great, and Josephus rightly dismisses this ridiculous claim with the logical argument that Nicholas's "assertion was to gratify Herod" (*Ant.* XIV. I. 3).

18. THE SONG IS OVER . . .

1. By a curious coincidence that has received scant notice from most historians, Pompey's siege of Jerusalem was the turning point in his career; the unbroken series of military triumphs in Asia came to an end, to be followed by a succession of public humiliations at home. Pompey had been schooled on the battlefield; politically inexperienced, he proved no match for the all-powerful Senatorial oligarchs. For the remainder of his life, he was the unwitting tool of political factions of which he had little true comprehension.

19. . . . BUT THE MELODY LINGERS ON

1. "Caesar" means hirsute; ironically, Caesar was totally bald at maturity. The patronym, which was adopted by subsequent Roman emperors, came to signify a paramount ruler, and has survived as *Kaiser* in the Germanic tongues, *Tsar* or *Czar* in the Slavonic languages, and *Qaysar* throughout the Islamic world.

It should be apparent that any attempt to reduce the history of this extraordinary Roman to a few background paragraphs would be ludicrous; to treat his career, however superficially, other than in the context of his influence on the Jewish nation, is decidedly beyond the scope of this book. (*See* A Note on the Bibliography.)

2. Situated east of the Dead Sea, Machaerus, like the other two impregnable fortresses, had been built by Alexander Jannaeus. Later demolished, it was subsequently rebuilt by Herod the Great and became a major Jewish stronghold during the Revolt of A.D. 66–70. Josephus claims Machaerus was the site where John the Baptist was imprisoned and beheaded, but this has been discounted on the grounds that no mention is made of Machaerus in the New Testament account of the Baptist's life and ministry.

3. Berenice was also (to keep the genealogy straight) Ptolemy X's first cousin once removed, having been the eldest child of Chickpea by his first sister-wife, Cleopatra IV. Chickpea also sired two sons by his younger sister, Cleopatra V Selene, but since all sources claim Chickpea died without legitimate issue, it is probably that the two boys predeceased him.

20. THE MÉSALLIANCE

1. The son Cleopatra bore Caesar was, at the age of two years, named consort to his ambitious mother; she murdered Ptolemy XIII to make way for the child, who was given the regnal name Ptolemy XIV Caesarion ("son of Caesar"). When Cleopatra committed suicide following her and Marc Antony's defeat by Octavian at Actium (31 B.C.), the child was sent for safety to the Red Sea coastal city of Berenice; he was overtaken by Octavian's messengers and put to death in the following year—thus marking the official end of the three-hundred-year-old Macedonian Dynasty of Egypt.

21. ANTIGONUS II—THE LAST HASMONAEAN KING

1. A naturally defensible mesa rising some 1,300 feet above the western shore of the Dead Sea. Originally fortified by either Jonathan Maccabee or Alexander Jannaeus [the sources are unclear since both had the same Hebrew name), Masada was subsequently rebuilt as a great palace-fortress by Herod the Great. It was here that the mass killings and suicides of the Zealots ended the anti-Rome Jewish Revolt in A.D. 73. Today a national shrine, its ruins are the site where recruits for Israel's armored corps take their oath of allegiance with the words "Masada shall not fall again!"

22. THE LAST HASMONAEANS

1. The so-called Massacre (or Slaughter) of the Innocents attributed to Herod—an attribution which helped to "substantiate" the hideous and totally fallacious charge of deicide against the Jewish people—has been dismissed by all responsible scholars as a complete fabrication. As recorded in only one of the three synoptic Gospels (Matthew 2:16), Herod is said to have commanded the murder of all male children in Bethlehem two years old and under, after the Wise Men had failed to inform him of the whereabouts of the infant Jesus. Although Herod was in fact capable of such barbarity, no mention is made of the "Massacre" in any of the contemporary accounts, and it hardly fits in with the more credible chronology of events in Jesus's life as recorded in the Luke Gospel. Indeed, no conclusive proof exists that

Jesus was born during Herod's lifetime—although most commentators who accept the historicity of Jesus, date his birth to the year of Herod's death, 4 B.C. In dismissing the Massacre as a fabrication, biblical exegetes note the rather interesting parallel in the incidents surrounding Jesus's birth and that of Moses; this could well account for the inclusion of the "incident" in the Matthew Gospel—often referred to facetiously by biblical scholars of all denominations as "the Jewish gospel."

2. The pious aims, if not the bloody tactics, of the Zealots apparently won the approbation of Jesus, who chose one of their number, Simon Zelotes, as one of his initial Disciples. Indeed, Jesus may have had an even closer tie with the Zealots, as is contended by the many responsible commentators who believe that the insurrection for which Barabbas was arrested as well as Jesus's cleansing of the Temple (which was, incidentally, controlled by the Sadducees, and *not*, as the New Testament would have us believe, the Pharisees) were part of a Zealot plot to take control of Jerusalem. For a totally fascinating study of this assertion, the reader's attention is directed to Professor S. F. G. Brandon's superb *Jesus and the Zealots*.

3. Agrippa II had been given by the emperor Claudius the minor kingdom of Chalcis, a tiny realm in the Ante-Lebanon Mountains. Agrippa was one of the most orthodox of all Hasmonaean-Herodians; he even went so far as to demand that the husband submit to circumcision before Agrippa allowed any of his sisters to enter into the dynastic marriages he arranged. The most notable (and interesting) of Agrippa's sisters was Berenice, with whom he is believed to have had a notoriously incestuous affair—his allegiance to the Mosaic Code notwithstanding—and who ended her days as mistress of, successively, the father-and-son emperors, Vespasian and Titus. When the Jewish Revolt broke out, Agrippa supported Rome, pragmatically, and attached himself to Vespasian when the latter become emperor in A.D. 69. In his later years Agrippa became a friend (and, in the opinion of many scholars, the editor) of Josephus. He died in A.D. 100—the last monarch of Jewish blood, albeit diluted.

A Note on the Bibliography

Of the numerous volumes read in preparing this book, most were written for the professional scholar and historian, and are, with few exceptions, tedious, albeit informative. But for the reader who might wish to pursue specific areas in more detail, a number of extremely well-written and authoritative books are currently available, and are recommended without reservation.

For a detailed, comprehensive, and lucid work dealing with the Hellenistic period, one could do no better than *The Harvest of Hellenism* by F. E. Peters, which carries with it the added dividend of being a joy to read. D. S. Russell's *The Jews from Alexander to Herod* is especially recommended for the clarity with which this renowned British scholar covers the origins of the major Jewish sects during the Hasmonaean period. John Bright's *A History of Israel* is, in my opinion, the definitive survey of biblical history; and for the reader wondering how the Jewish nation survived two thousand years of Diaspora, and unable to comprehend that nation's *mystique*, Cecil Roth's *A History of Israel*, Abba Eban's *My People, The Story of the Jews,* and Amos Elon's superb *The Israelis, Founders and Sons* should provide the answers.

Robert Payne's *Ancient Rome* is an immensely readable as well as informative survey of the overall saga of the Romans from the Etruscan period until the collapse of the empire a millennium later; it is currently available in a paperback edition.

The Seleucids and Ptolemies were probably no better served by any scholar than Edwyn R. Bevan, whose writings on these extraordinary families are a treasure trove of detail as well as proof that reading history can be a source of genuine pleasure. Fortunately, *The House of Ptolemy* is still in print, as are his witty articles in Volumes VIII and IX of the *Cambridge Ancient History*. (Unfortunately, *The House of Seleucus* [1902] and *Jerusalem Under the High Priests* [1904] are no longer in print; however, they are to be found in many first-rate research libraries, and well worth tracking down.)

Michael Grant's superbly written (and beautifully illustrated) biographies, *Julius Caesar, Herod the Great,* and *Cleopatra,* I consider the best treatises available on these three historical personages (one hopes Grant will get around to doing a similar study on Pompey). Also, a reading of Samuel Sandmel's *Herod* will prove delightful as well as informative, most notably those chapters dealing with Herod the Great vis-à-vis his Hasmonaean in-laws and descendants.

S. G. F. Brandon's *Jesus and the Zealots* is especially recommended for those readers who, like myself, may be having some difficulty in equating the lack of historical evidence for the existence of Jesus with the conviction that surely Jesus must have lived. Of all the material in print (much of it dismal) dealing with the Qumran Community and the more credible account of the origins of Christianity, none, in my opinion, can approach Edmund Wilson's superlative *The Dead Sea Scrolls, 1947–1969*.

The complete works of Flavius Josephus are, of course, available, although the average reader, like myself, may find the William Whiston translation (1848) tedious at times. For those who may wish to confine their readings of Josephus to the period covered in this book, Nahum N. Glatzer's *The Second Commonwealth* is highly recommended; this is a one-volume condensation (available in paperback) of the *Antiquities* (Books XII and IV–XX) in the Shilleto revision of the Whiston translation, and Professor Glatzer's footnotes help bring the text into bold relief.

Heinrich Graetz's six-volume *History of the Jews*, though published in 1893, is still in print. Another, and more up-to-date set is *The Family Bible Encyclopedia;* especially recommended are the entries by Victor Jules Grossfeld on the major personalities of the Second Commonwealth period.

Assigning dates is always a problem when writing on the First and Second Temple periods; in this, I have followed William L. Langer's *An Encyclopedia of World History,* a one-volume ready-reference work that belongs in the home of anyone even remotely interested in any aspect of history from the dawn of civilization to our own time.

Also recommended: *From the Stone Age to Christianity* by W. F. Albright; *From Ezra to the Last of the Maccabees* by Elias Bickerman; *Maccabees, Zealots and Josephus* by William Reuben Farmer; *The Jews and Judaism During the Greek Period* by W. O. E. Oesterly; D. S. Russell's *Between the Testaments,* and Nahum N. Glatzer's recent one-volume abridgment (in paperback) of Emil Schürer's classic five-volume *A History of the Jewish People in the Time of Jesus* (originally published 1892–1901).

Index

74 75 76 77 10 9 8 7 6 5 4 3 2 1